CANADIAN Culinary Math

Principles and Applications

AMERICAN TECHNICAL PUBLISHERS
Orland Park, Illinois

Michael J. McGreal
Linda J. Padilla

Cover Photo Credit:
Rolandas Grigaitis/Shutterstock.com

American Technical Publishers Editorial Staff

Editor in Chief:
Peter A. Zurlis
Director of Product Development:
Cathy A. Scruggs
Assistant Production Manager:
Nicole D. Burian
Technical Editor:
Sara M. Marconi
Supervising Copy Editor:
Catherine A. Mini
Copy Editor:
James R. Hein
Editorial Assistant:
Lauren D. Bedillion
Art Manager:
Sarah E. Kaducak
Cover Design:
Bethany J. Fisher
Illustration/Layout:
Bethany J. Fisher
Darrell E. Dwyer
Melanie G. Doornbos
Digital Media Manager:
Adam T. Schuldt
Digital Resources:
Cory S. Butler
James V. Cashman
Tim A. Miller

1 2 3 4 5 6 7 8 9 – 22 – 9 8 7 6 5 4 3 2 1

Printed in the United States of America

ISBN 978-0-8269-4280-7
eISBN 978-0-8269-9623-7

This book is printed on recycled paper.

Acknowledgments

About the Authors

Michael J. McGreal, M.Ed., CEC, CCE, CHE, FMP, CHA, MCFE, is the Culinary Arts Department Chair at Joliet Junior College. He has received many honors over his 38 years of foodservice experience, including the American Culinary Federation Presidential Medallion. Chef McGreal is also the author of *Culinary Arts Principles and Applications* and *50 Effective Knife Techniques.*

Linda J. Padilla taught mathematics at Joliet Junior College for over 30 years. She holds degrees in mathematics, education, and counseling. Linda has extensive experience collaborating with other disciplines and has developed curriculum strategies and applications for math in the culinary arts. Her work on math applications in the culinary field has also been featured at national conferences.

Technical Reviewers

The authors and publisher are grateful for the technical reviews provided by the following culinary arts professionals:

Harriette Schumacher-Cain
Culinary Arts Instructor
Nova Scotia Community College

Kyle A. Mitchell
Culinary Arts Instructor
Kalamazoo Valley Community College, Michigan

Rebecca Norwood
Director of Education
New Orleans Culinary & Hospitality Institute

Sean Kettley, CCC, RSE
Culinary Arts & Cook Apprenticeship Instructor
Nova Scotia Community College

Gilbert Noussitou, CSE, CCC, PID
Culinary Arts Instructor
Camosun College, British Columbia

Samuel Glass, M.Ed, CEC, CCE, AAC
Culinary Arts Professor
Centennial College, Ontario

Acknowledgments (continued)

The authors and publisher are grateful for the images provided by the following companies, organizations, and individuals:

- All-Clad Metalcrafters
- American Egg Board
- Browne Foodservice
- Calculated Industries
- Carlisle FoodService Products
- Charlie Trotter's
- Chef's Choice® by EdgeCraft Corporation
- Classic Party Rentals
- Cooper-Atkins Corporation
- Daniel NYC
- Detecto, A Division of Cardinal Scale Manufacturing Co.
- Edlund Co.
- Florida Department of Citrus
- Fluke Corporation
- Idaho Potato Commission
- Lavu, Inc.
- Perdue Foodservice, Perdue Farms Incorporated
- Vita-Mix® Corporation
- Vulcan-Hart, a division of the ITW Food Equipment Group LLC

Contents

Contents (continued)

Contents (continued)

Online Learner Resources

Canadian Culinary Math Principles and Applications includes access to online learner resources that reinforce text/workbook content and enhance learning.

- Quick Quizzes®
- Flash Cards
- Formulas and Tables
- Media Library
- Internet Resources

Book Features

Canadian Culinary Math Principles and Applications is a full-color text/workbook that shows and explains how and why foodservice workers use metric, imperial, and customary measurement systems in the professional kitchen. Its step-by-step illustrations and real-world culinary math problems will both engage and benefit learners who are enrolled in high school, college, or apprenticeship programs as well as those choosing to study independently.

The path to excellence in the Cook trade requires both a strong culinary background as well as a solid understanding of math. This practical text/workbook will help learners better prepare for provincial and Red Seal trade credentialing exams.

Features of this edition include the following:

- Each chapter is divided into sections to allow maximum teaching and learning flexibility.
- Each section ends with a checkpoint consisting of short-answer review questions.
- Color-coded figures and problem-solving steps highlight the similarities and differences between the metric, imperial, and customary systems in foodservice settings.
- Each chapter concludes with 50 math exercises for a total of 350 contextual math problems.
- Leaf icons identify 70 sustainability-focused contextual math problems.
- The appendix contains all of the culinary math formulas used in the text/workbook plus key reference tables and forms.

Detailed Illustrations provide visual clarity and context for math principles and applications.

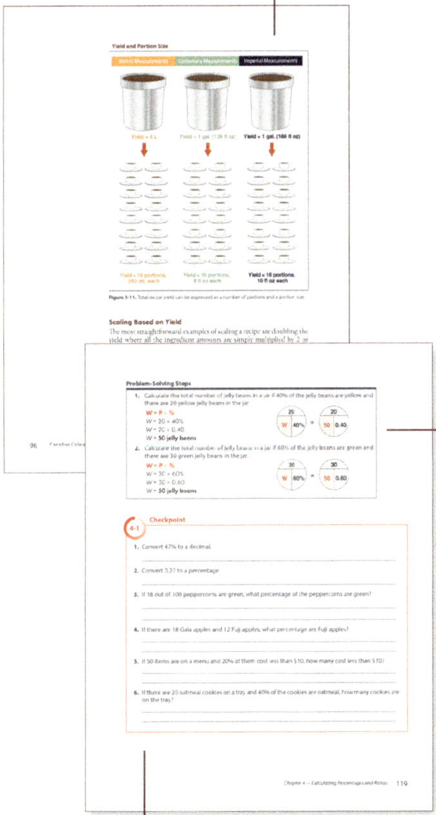

Chapter Objectives identify the main concepts addressed in each section of the chapter.

Key Terms are listed on each chapter opener. All vocabulary terms are italicized and defined at first use.

Problem-Solving Steps present key math applications in a clear, step-by-step format.

Leaf Icons indicate a contextual math problem with a sustainability focus.

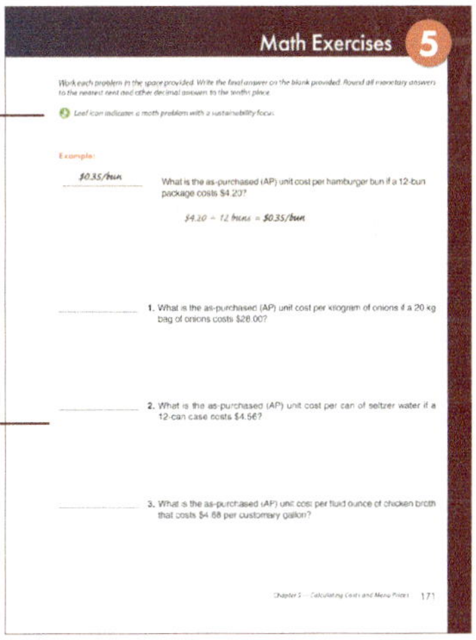

Math Exercises give learners the opportunity to apply the math skills covered in the chapter.

Checkpoints at the end of each section ask learners to review and apply the concepts covered to reinforce learning. Checkpoint answers are provided at the end of the text/workbook.

Online Resources

Canadian Culinary Math Principles and Applications includes access to online learner resources that reinforce content and enhance learning. These interactive resources can be accessed using either of the following methods:

- Key **atplearningresources.com** into a web browser and then enter access code **267628**.
- Use a Quick Response (QR) reader app on a mobile device to scan the QR code located on the opening page of each chapter.

Learner Resources

Canadian Culinary Math Principles and Applications includes access to online learner resources that reinforce text/workbook content and enhance learning. The learner resources include the following:

- **Quick Quizzes®** provide learners with multiple choice questions for each chapter, with each question linking to the referenced content from the text/workbook and to the glossary.
- **Flash Cards** offer learners a simple method for reviewing the terms, definitions, symbols, abbreviations, and tools used in the text/workbook.
- **Formulas and Tables** include a listing of all the math formulas used in the book, reference tables from the appendix, and a pricing form and daily sales record.
- The **Media Library** consists of high-quality videos and animations that reinforce the content covered in the text/workbook.
- **Internet Resources** link to organizations, associations, and companies related to the trade.

Instructor Resources

Instructor resources are available for *Canadian Culinary Math Principles and Applications* that provide the tools needed to implement a comprehensive instructional program.

- The **eTextbook**™ provides access to the same content as the printed text/workbook using any internet-connected device.
- The **Instructional Guide** explains how to make use of various instructional tools and includes detailed instructional plans for each chapter and section of the text/workbook.
- **Premium PowerPoint® Presentations** include objectives, content excerpts, checkpoint questions, math exercises, and instructor notes for each chapter and section of the text/workbook.
- **Assessments** include test banks for each chapter of the text/workbook as well as a pretest and posttest.
- The **Answer Key** provides answers to the text/workbook math exercises.
- The **Learner Resources** are included with the instructor resources for ease of use.

To obtain information on other related training materials, visit **atplearning.com.**

The Publisher

Using Math in Food Service

A career in food service can be exciting and rewarding. However, many people believe that working in food service is simply fun and entertaining due to the glamour associated with celebrity chefs. Cooking shows may be entertaining, but they rarely focus on the less glamorous side of the industry, especially the physically demanding nature of the work and the business skills necessary for success. The path to success in food service requires both a strong culinary background and the most fundamental business skill—a solid understanding of basic math.

A foodservice operation cannot succeed unless employees, managers, and owners have solid math skills. Math is used in virtually all areas of the operation, including the following:

- **Pricing menu items** – Math skills are required when determining the price of menu items. A foodservice operation only earns money if the operation charges more money for the items that it sells than the amount of money it spends to produce those items. Pricing menu items appropriately and selling enough of them are primary factors in the success of a foodservice operation. The math used in pricing a menu item starts with adding the cost of the ingredients in the recipe. Other factors such as labor costs are also used to determine menu item prices.

- **Ordering food and supplies** – Before food and supplies are ordered, the prices charged for similar products from different suppliers are evaluated to keep expenses to a minimum. Making these evaluations is not always as simple as comparing one supplier's price to another. Often, adjustments must be made to account for packaging differences so that prices can be accurately compared.

- **Measuring recipe ingredients** – Math is used every day in the professional kitchen to adjust quantities of recipe ingredients. A cook must know how to convert the quantities of each ingredient in the recipe to account for the adjustment in servings. It is also sometimes necessary to convert units of measure when a recipe is increased or decreased. Math skills are often required to know the measurement equivalents and conversion factors required to convert units of measure.

- **Preparing food** – Food items often need to be used in more than one menu item. The food item may also need to be processed (cut up, broken down, or trimmed) before a recipe is prepared. The amount required to prepare all menu items as well as the amount of processing required must be calculated before computing how much of that food item to order.

- **Serving food** – Math is used in foodservice operations to determine how much food should be served for an event, such as a banquet. Using math skills to calculate the amount of food to prepare is essential. Guessing usually results in costly errors.

Photo Credit: Browne Foodservice

- **Storing food and supplies** – Foodservice operations often store enough food and supplies to prepare the menu items needed to serve customers. Before additional food and supplies are ordered, the amount of items already in storage should be counted. Most foodservice operations use an inventory checklist that details the amount of each item that should be in storage. After counting each item in storage, an employee can compare those amounts to the amounts provided on the checklist to determine what needs to be ordered.

- **Processing money** – Math skills are used to process money at all levels of a foodservice operation. Money comes into a foodservice operation when customers pay their bills, and money goes out of a foodservice operation to pay expenses such as food, payroll, and taxes. To be successful, the amount of money coming in must exceed the amount of money going out. This flow of money is closely monitored by the managers and owners of an operation.

- **Scheduling and payroll** – Managers determine how many employees are needed for each shift or day of operation. Calculating the appropriate number of employees is based on factors such as the time of year, predicted sales volume, number of reservations, and employees scheduled to take vacation. Managers are also responsible for processing payroll to ensure employees receive accurate paychecks in a timely manner. This involves adding the hours worked by each employee and multiplying the hours worked by the appropriate hourly wage. If an employee works overtime, the manager must make adjustments so the employee is paid correctly.

- **Tracking income and expenses** – Most foodservice operations use computerized systems to track income and expenses. Financial reports show how a foodservice operation is doing at a given point in time. Math skills are necessary to make sure that items are entered into the system properly. Math skills are also necessary for spotting errors and determining whether any action needs to be taken. If financial information is not monitored routinely, a foodservice operation can quickly fail.

1

Measuring in the Professional Kitchen

Foodservice operations must be able to produce food that is consistent day after day in order to be successful. The accurate measurement of the ingredients used in recipes is key to maintaining that consistency. Cooks must understand the standards used for measurement and be able to use the wide variety of measurement tools found in the professional kitchen. Math skills are required to perform these important measurements.

Section 1-1: MEASUREMENT SYSTEMS USED IN CANADIAN FOOD SERVICE

- Explain how standardized measures contribute to the success of foodservice operations.
- Identify the basic units of measure used in the metric, customary, and imperial systems of measurement.

Section 1-2: MEASUREMENT TYPES

- Explain how count, weight, and volume are used to measure ingredients and serve portions.
- Explain how weight and volume measuring tools are used in professional kitchens.
- Compare weight and volume.
- Identify how time, temperature, and distance are used in food service.

Section 1-3: MEASUREMENT EQUIVALENTS

- Describe measurement equivalents.
- Calculate measurement equivalents.

Key Terms

- unit of measure
- count
- whole number
- weight
- digital scale
- tare
- balance scale
- volume
- measuring spoon
- dry measuring cup
- liquid measuring cup
- ladle
- portion-controlled scoop
- ounce
- fluid ounce
- density
- measurement equivalent

Learner Resources
atplearningresources.com
access code 267628

All-Clad Metalcrafters

Section 1-1 MEASUREMENT SYSTEMS USED IN CANADIAN FOOD SERVICE

A significant challenge for any foodservice operation is to produce food that is consistent. Consistency is important because customers expect food from a particular foodservice operation to look and taste the same every time it is ordered. Since the same cook does not always prepare the same items each day, cooks for foodservice operations use standard units of measure to promote consistency.

A *unit of measure* is a fixed quantity that is widely accepted as a standard of measurement. Units of measure can express weight, volume, time, temperature, and distance (or size). Foodservice operations commonly use the metric, customary (or US customary), and imperial measurement systems. The customary and imperial systems are closely related, while the metric system differs from the other two. Success in the professional kitchen requires a working knowledge of all three systems of measurement. For example, some recipes are written only in metric or customary measurements. Also, many liquid products manufactured in Canada show imperial measurements. As a result, some recipes may use imperial measurements for liquids.

The Metric System

Measurement systems have basic units of measure for weight (mass), volume, temperature, and distance. The metric system uses grams (g) to measure weight and liters (L) to measure volume. This system also uses hours (hr) and minutes (min) to measure time; degrees Celsius (°C) to measure temperature; and meters (m) to measure distance. **See Figure 1-1.**

Metric Units of Measure		
Measurement Type	**Unit**	**Abbreviation**
Weight (mass)	gram	g
Volume	liter	L
Temperature	degrees Celsius	°C
Distance	meter	m

Figure 1-1. The metric measurement system uses grams to measure weight, liters to measure volume, degrees Celsius to measure temperature, and meters to measure distance.

With the exception of temperature, the basic metric units are often accompanied by metric-unit prefixes. Each prefix carries a specific meaning that converts the basic metric units into larger or smaller units of measure. **See Figure 1-2.** For example, when the prefix "kilo-", meaning 1000, is added to the root word "gram," it forms the word "kilogram," which means 1000 grams. The most commonly used prefixes in foodservice are "kilo-" and "milli-".

Metric Prefixes		
Prefix	**Abbreviation**	**Meaning**
kilo-	k	1000
hecto-	h	100
deca-	da	10
deci-	d	1/10 or 0.1
centi-	c	1/100 or 0.01
milli-	m	1/1000 or 0.001

Figure 1-2. The basic metric units are often accompanied by metric-unit prefixes. Each prefix carries a specific meaning that converts the basic metric units into larger or smaller units of measure.

The Customary and Imperial Systems

The customary and imperial systems use pounds (lb) and ounces (oz) to measure weight as well as gallons (gal.), quarts (qt), pints (pt), cups (c), gills, fluid ounces (fl oz), tablespoons (tbsp), and teaspoons (tsp) to measure volume. Cups are most commonly used in the customary system, and gills are only used in the imperial system. Both systems use hours (hr) and minutes (min) to measure time; degrees Fahrenheit (°F) to measure temperature; and feet (ft) and inches (in.) to measure distance. **See Figure 1-3.**

Customary and Imperial Units of Measure		
Measurement Type	**Unit**	**Abbreviation**
Weight	pound	lb or #
	ounce	oz
Volume	gallon	gal.
	quart	qt
	pint	pt
	cup	c
	gill (imperial)	—
	fluid ounce	fl oz
	tablespoon	tbsp
	teaspoon	tsp
Temperature	degrees Fahrenheit	°F
Distance	foot	ft
	inch	in.

Figure 1-3. The customary and imperial measurement systems use pounds and ounces to measure weight, a variety of units for volume, degrees Fahrenheit to measure temperature, and feet and inches to measure distance.

Checkpoint 1-1

1. Explain why cooks use standard units of measure.

___

___

2. Identify the basic units of measure in the metric system.

___

___

3. Identify the basic units of measure in the customary and imperial systems.

___

___

Section 1-2 MEASUREMENT TYPES

The three types of measurements used in food service to measure ingredients are count, weight, and volume. **See Figure 1-4.** For example, a recipe may call for 2 large eggs (count), 250 g of flour (weight), or 100 mL of milk (volume). Count, weight, and volume are also used to serve portions. For example, a guest might be served a meal consisting of a half dozen (6) oysters (count), an 8-oz steak (weight), and 250 mL of soup (volume). Other measurements used in food service are time, temperature, and distance measurements. Time and temperature measurements are used to ensure that food is prepared properly. Distance measurements are commonly used to determine table or room configurations and cookware or serving platter sizes.

Count

Count is a total obtained by counting. A measurement based on count typically involves whole numbers. A *whole number* is a number used for counting, such as 0, 1, 20, or 100. Count is used when precise measurements are not needed in a recipe and there is a general understanding about the size of the ingredient being used. For example, a recipe may call for 1 clove of garlic or the juice from 1 lime. However, count is most commonly used with eggs because they are graded to specific sizes. Unless otherwise stated, most recipes call for large eggs. Count is also used in recipes if the final product is countable. For example, a recipe may yield 6 loaves of bread or 24 cookies.

Ingredient Measurement Types

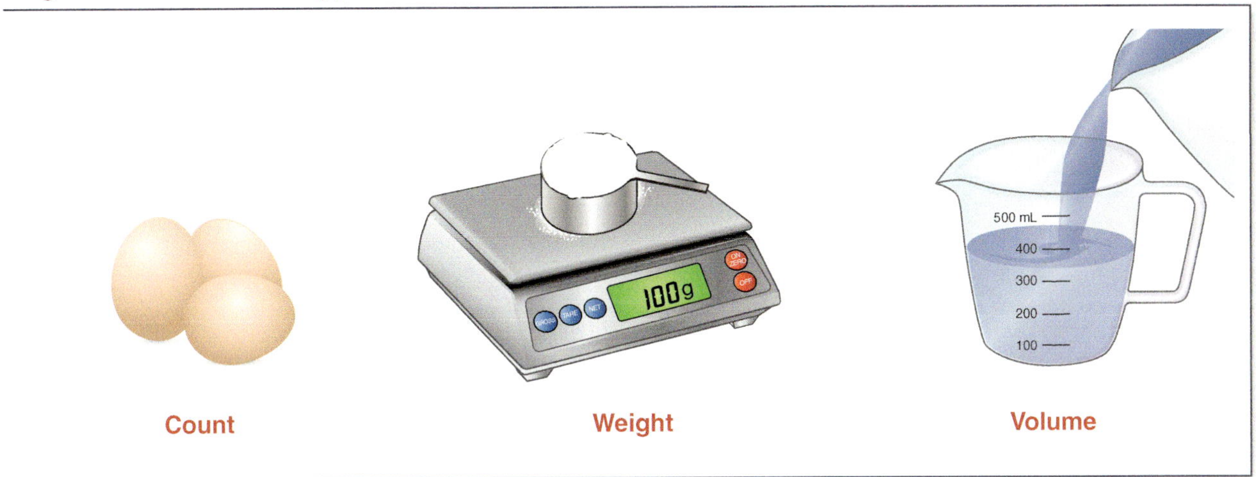

Figure 1-4. The three types of measurements used to measure ingredients are count, weight, and volume.

Weight

Weight is a measurement of the heaviness of a substance. The most common units for measuring weight used in the professional kitchen are the gram (g), the kilogram (kg), the ounce (oz), and the pound (lb or #). Examples of items commonly measured by weight include grams of salt, kilograms of potatoes, and pounds of beef.

The tools used for measuring weight are called scales. The two types of scales used in the professional kitchen are digital scales and balance scales. **See Figure 1-5.** Regardless of type, all scales must be set to zero after a container is placed on them and prior to adding any ingredients into the container. This is because the weight of the container must be considered before an accurate measurement of the ingredient can be made. The procedure for setting a scale to zero depends on the type of scale being used.

Scales for Measuring Weight

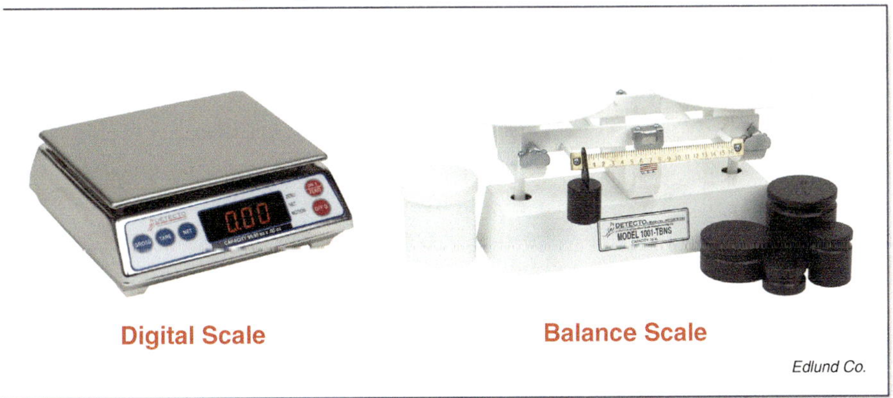

Figure 1-5. The two types of scales used in the professional kitchen are digital scales and balance scales.

Digital Scales. A *digital scale* is an electronic scale with a sensor that measures weight and displays the result electronically. Digital scales are often used for weighing consistent portions of food as well as measuring recipe ingredients. Digital scales measure weight in grams, kilograms, ounces, or pounds. Most digital scales have a switch to select whether the weight is displayed in metric or customary/imperial units.

To use a digital scale, an empty container is first placed on the scale platform. Then the scale is set to zero by pressing a button typically labeled "tare." *Tare* is another term for setting a scale to zero. Ingredients are then added to the container. Ingredients are no longer added once the scale shows the desired measurement amount has been reached.

Balance Scales. A *balance scale,* or baker's scale, is a scale with two platforms that uses a counterbalance system to measure weight. To use a balance scale, an empty container is first placed on one platform of the scale. The scale is then set to zero by adding counterbalance weights to the other platform until the scale is balanced. The ingredient to be weighed is added to the container, and counterbalance weights are placed on the other platform. The beam between the two platforms holds a smaller counterbalance weight that is used for fine adjustments of the scale. The scale is balanced when the weight on the two platforms is equal. **See Figure 1-6.**

For example, to measure 2 kg of flour, a 2-kg counterbalance weight is placed on the platform opposite the empty container after the scale has been tared. Flour is then added to the container until the scale balances, indicating that 2 kg of flour have been added. The smallest amount that can be weighed using a balance scale is based on the increments indicated on the beam between the two platforms. The maximum capacity of a balance scale is limited by the amount of counterbalance weight available.

Volume

Volume is a measurement of the physical space a substance occupies. In the professional kitchen, the most common volume units of measure are the milliliter (mL), teaspoon (tsp), tablespoon (tbsp), fluid ounce (fl oz), cup (c), pint (pt), quart (qt), liter (L), and gallon (gal.). Examples of items commonly measured by volume include liters of water and gallons of milk.

The tools used in the professional kitchen to measure volume are measuring spoons, dry measuring cups, liquid measuring cups, ladles, and portion-controlled scoops. **See Figure 1-7.** Both dry and liquid ingredients can be measured using volume measurement tools.

Balance Scales

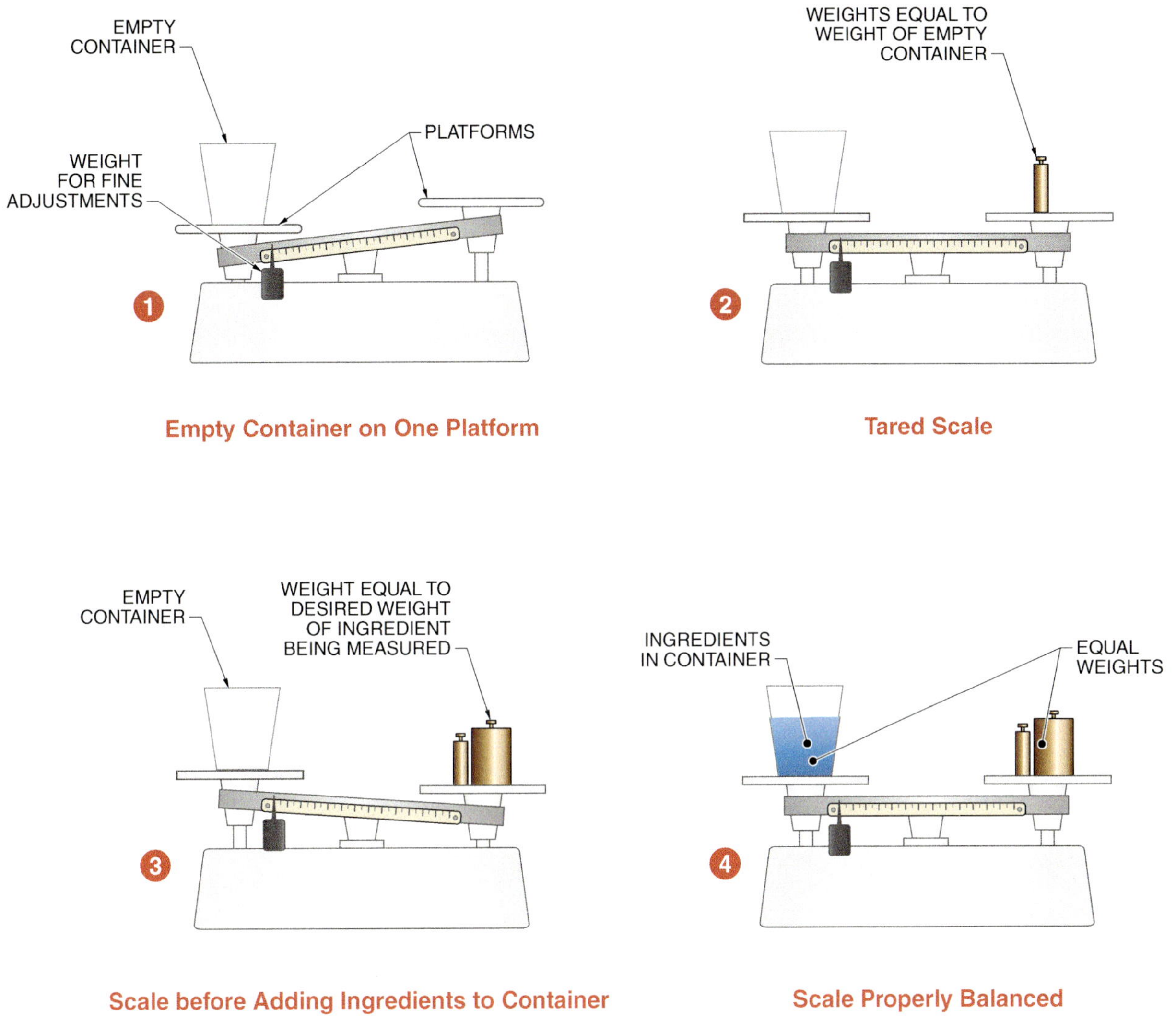

1. An empty container is placed on one platform.
2. Weights are added to the second platform until the scale is tared (zeroed).
3. Weights are added to the second platform equal to the amount of the ingredient to be weighed.
4. Ingredients are added to the empty container until the scale is balanced.

Figure 1-6. A balance scale uses a counterbalance system to measure weight.

Volume Measurement Tools

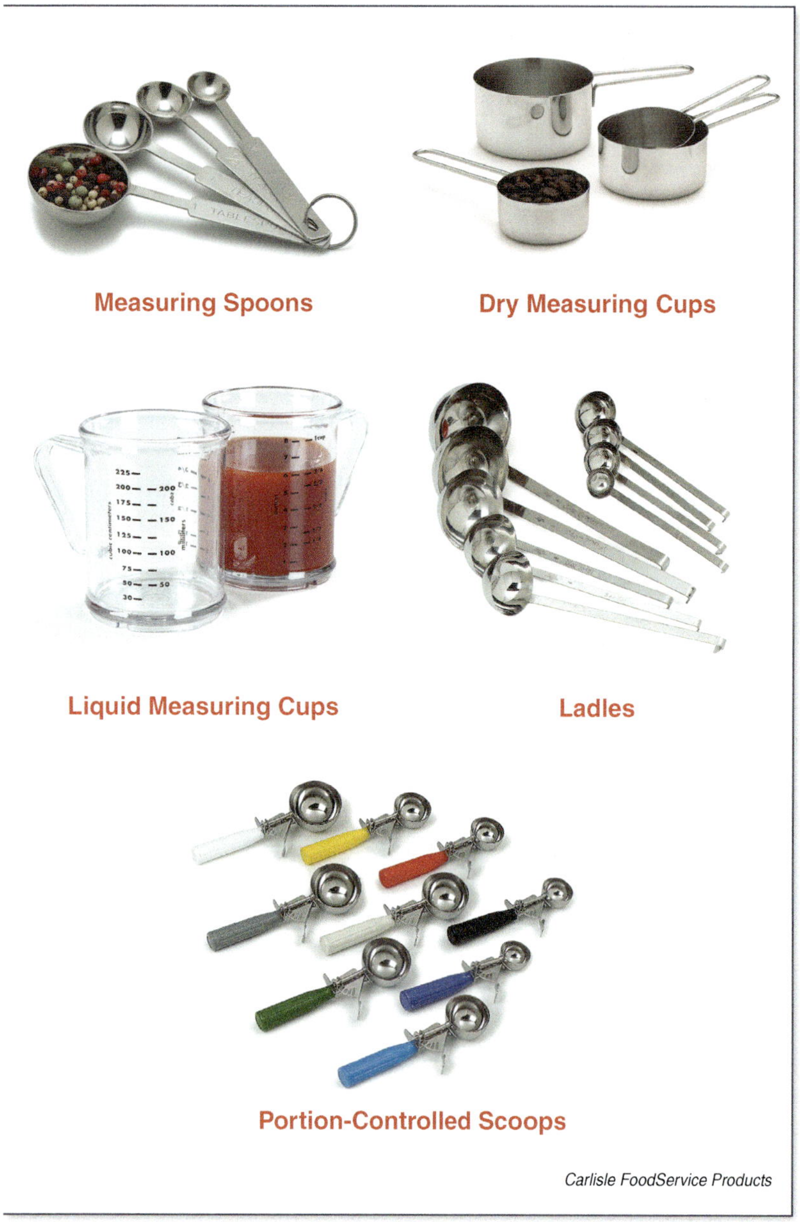

Figure 1-7. A variety of tools for measuring volume are used in the professional kitchen.

Proper techniques must be followed when using these tools in order to make accurate measurements. If a slight distinction in recipe wording is overlooked, it can have a major impact on the quality of the final product. For example, if a recipe calls for "1 cup flour, sifted," measure 1 cup of flour and then sift the flour. However, if a recipe calls for "1 cup sifted flour," sift the flour first and then measure 1 cup of the flour.

Measuring Spoons. A *measuring spoon* is a small volume measurement tool, shaped like a spoon, that is used to measure liquid or dry ingredients. There are usually different sizes in a set. Each customary measuring spoon indicates a capacity of the following:

- one-eighth of a teaspoon (⅛ tsp)
- one-quarter of a teaspoon (¼ tsp)
- one-half of a teaspoon (½ tsp)
- one teaspoon (1 tsp)
- one tablespoon (1 tbsp)

When measuring spoons are used to measure liquid ingredients, the spoons should be filled to the top. When measuring dry ingredients, the spoons should be intentionally overfilled and the ingredient leveled to remove any excess. An ingredient can be leveled by skimming a spatula or the back of a knife across the top of the spoon. Care should be taken not to compress the dry ingredient into the measuring spoon unless directed to do so by the recipe. For example, a recipe may call for 2 tablespoons of brown sugar, firmly packed.

Dry Measuring Cups. A *dry measuring cup* is a volume measurement tool, shaped like a cup, with a short handle used to measure a specific volume of dry ingredients. A dry measuring cup must be filled to the top in order to provide an accurate measurement. Since it is difficult to move a completely filled cup of liquid without spilling some of the contents, liquids should not be measured in dry measuring cups. For the customary system, dry measuring cups are usually kept in a set consisting of the following:

- one-quarter of a cup (1/4 c)
- one-third of a cup (1/3 c)
- one-half of a cup (1/2 c)
- two-thirds of a cup (2/3 c)
- three-fourths of a cup (3/4 c)
- one cup (1 c)

Unless a recipe states otherwise, the proper procedure for measuring dry ingredients in a dry measuring cup is to spoon the ingredient into the cup, initially overfilling it, and then leveling to remove the excess. A dry measuring cup should not be dipped directly into the ingredient being measured, such as a bin of flour, and the cup should not be pressed against the edge of the container to level it. This action compresses the ingredient in the cup, resulting in more of the product being measured than when the proper technique is followed. Therefore, it is best to weigh dry ingredients on a scale to obtain accurate measurements.

Liquid Measuring Cups. A *liquid measuring cup* is a volume measurement tool shaped like a cup or pitcher with graduated markings on the side to indicate the volume of a liquid. For example, a 1-L liquid measuring cup may also be marked to show 100 mL increments. Some liquid measuring cups are also marked to show customary measurements, such as fluid ounces, cups, pints, or quarts. **See Figure 1-8.**

Liquid Measuring Cups

Carlisle FoodService Products

Figure 1-8. Liquid measuring cups have graduated markings on the side that indicate the volume of a liquid.

Liquid measuring cups are the best volume measurement tools for measuring liquid ingredients because they are designed to hold more than the maximum amount to be measured. Since liquid measuring cups are never filled to the very top, a person is less likely to spill the measured ingredients.

Liquid measuring cups are commonly made of aluminum, stainless steel, glass, or plastic. When using them, they should always be placed on a level surface and viewed at eye level so the ingredient is measured accurately. Ingredients should be poured right up to the marking or line on the measuring cup that indicates the desired amount. **See Figure 1-9.**

Using a Liquid Measuring Cup

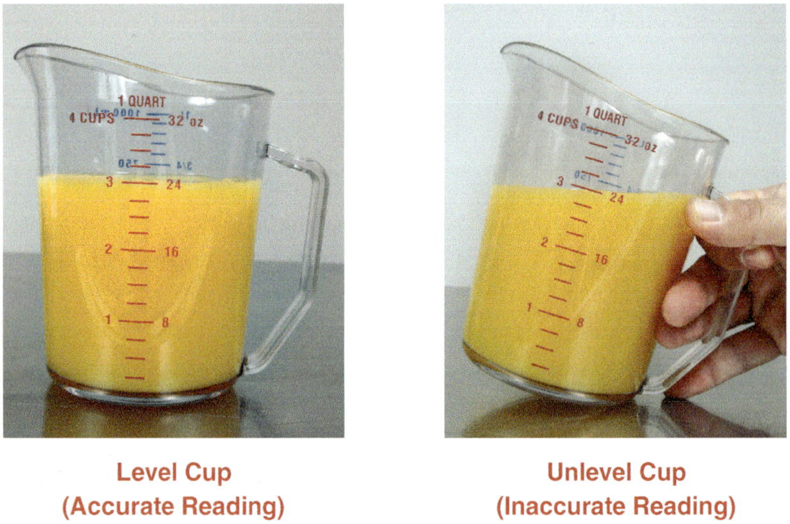

Figure 1-9. To provide an accurate measurement, a liquid measuring cup must be placed on a level surface and viewed at eye level.

Ladles. A *ladle* is a volume measurement tool that consists of a fixed-size cup attached to a long handle. Ladles come in a variety of sizes and are used for serving controlled portions of liquids, such as soups and sauces. The volume (in milliliters or fluid ounces) that can be held by a ladle is stamped on the handle.

Portion-Controlled Scoops. A *portion-controlled scoop,* or a disher, is a volume measurement tool that consists of a handle with a fixed-size scoop at the end. Portion-controlled scoops come in a variety of sizes and are marked with a number indicating how many scoops are required to make 1 customary quart (32 fl oz or 946.35 mL). **See Figure 1-10.** For example, a #32 scoop holds 1 fl oz and would require 32 level-filled scoops to equal 32 fl oz. The lower the number on the scoop, the fewer scoops it takes to empty a container. For example, a #12 scoop holds $2\frac{2}{3}$ fl oz ($32 \div 12 = 2\frac{2}{3}$ fl oz or 78.86 mL), whereas a #6 scoop holds $5\frac{1}{3}$ fl oz ($32 \div 6 = 5\frac{1}{3}$ fl oz or 157.73 mL).

Portion-Controlled Scoops

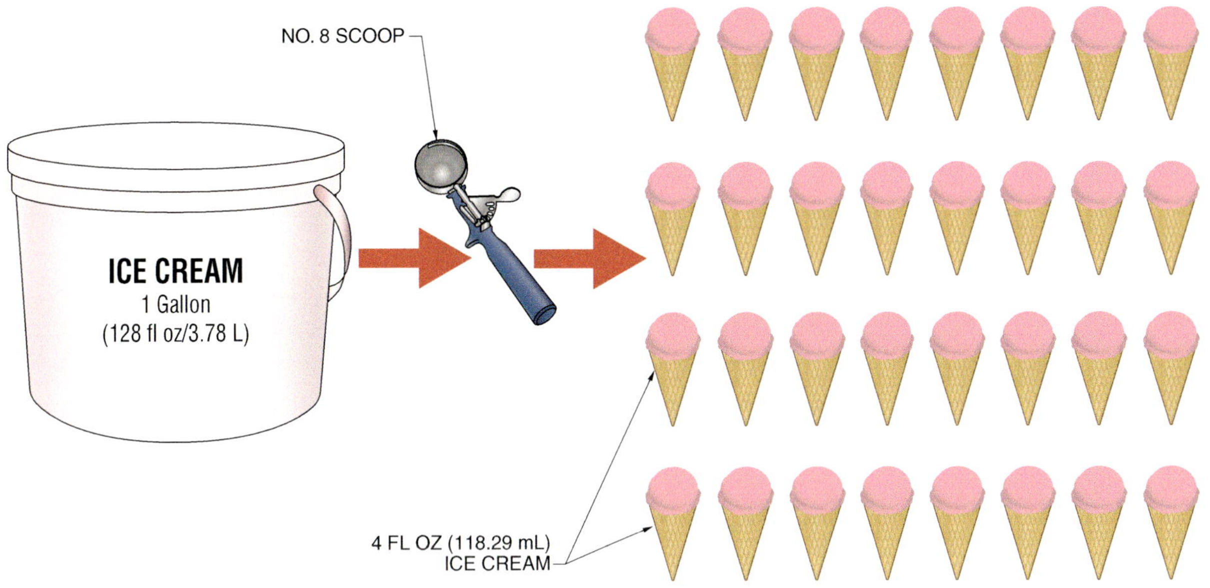

No. 8 scoop: 32 fl oz ÷ 8 = 4 fl oz per scoop (946.35 mL ÷ 8 = 118.29 mL per scoop)

128 fl oz ice cream ÷ 4 fl oz per scoop = 32 scoops ice cream
(3780 mL ice cream ÷ 118.29 mL = 32 scoops ice cream)

Figure 1-10. The number on a portion-controlled scoop indicates how many scoops can be generated from a given volume of food.

Weight Versus Volume

When measuring ingredients, it is important to understand the difference between weight and volume. Grams and kilograms are units of weight, while milliliters and liters are units of volume. Likewise, in the customary and imperial measurement systems, an ounce differs from a fluid ounce. An *ounce* is the smallest weight unit of measure in the customary and imperial systems. A *fluid ounce* is the smallest volume unit of measure in the customary and imperial systems.

When a volume measurement is taken, the measurement can be affected by the technique used to fill the measuring tool. For this reason, weight measurements are considered to be more accurate than volume measurements. For example, 250 mL (1 cup) of brown sugar can vary significantly depending on how tightly or loosely the brown sugar is packed into the measuring tool. In contrast, 250 g (8.82 oz) of brown sugar will always weigh 250 g (8.82 oz). Failure to understand the distinction between weight and volume can lead to costly mistakes.

The only ingredient that always has the same weight and volume is water. For example, 500 mL of water weighs 500 g. Likewise, 1 L of water weighs 1 kg, and 8 fl oz of water weighs 8 oz. However, a few ingredients that are measured by volume in milliliters/liters weigh about the same amount in grams/kilograms. Likewise, if these ingredients are measured by volume in fluid ounces, they will weigh close to the same in ounces because they have a similar density. *Density* is a measurement of how much a given volume of a substance weighs. Ingredients with densities close to water include alcohol, juice, vinegar, oil, milk, butter, eggs, and granulated sugar.

While some ingredients have a density close to water, most ingredients are different. For example, the density of flour is less than the density of water. Therefore, 1 kg of flour would take up more space in a container than 1 kg of water. In other words, even though the flour and water both weigh 1 kg, the container with the water will look like it contains a smaller amount because water is denser than flour.

Ingredients with densities greater than water, such as honey and molasses, weigh more in comparison to their volume. **See Figure 1-11.** For example, while 500 mL of honey weighs approximately 720 g, 500 mL of water weighs 500 g because honey is denser than water. Similarly, 8 fl oz of honey weighs about 12 oz.

Weight and Volume

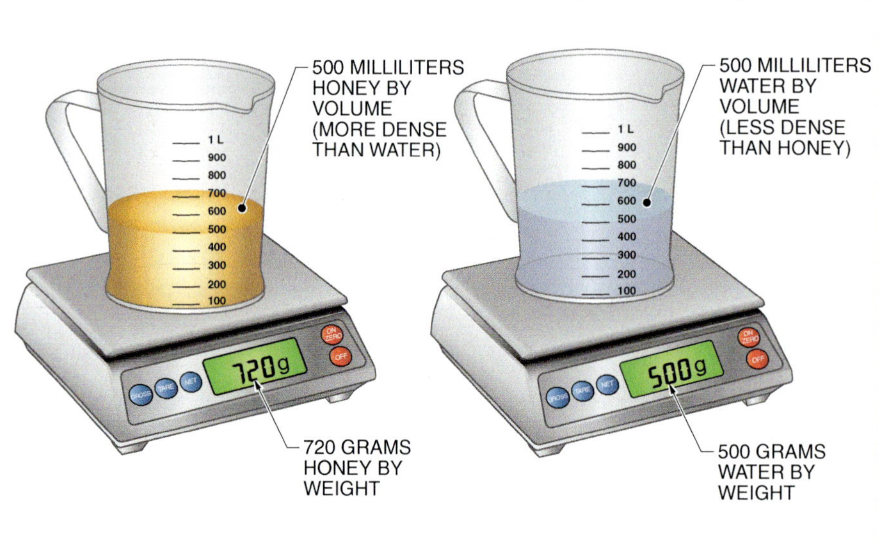

Figure 1-11. The only ingredient that will consistently have the same volume and weight is water.

Much of the confusion between weight and volume is distinguishing between ounces (weight) and fluid ounces (volume). If recipes were carefully written to distinguish between ounces and fluid ounces, this issue would be less important. Unfortunately, some recipes do not distinguish between ounces and fluid ounces. Therefore, it is up to the cook to pay close attention and use the appropriate measuring tool.

Time and Temperature

It is just as important to accurately measure time as it is to measure ingredients. Time is measured in days, hours (hr), minutes (min), or seconds (sec). For example, a recipe may specify that a cake is to bake for 35 min.

Kitchen timers are used in the professional kitchen to sound an alarm when a given amount of time has elapsed. Kitchen timers include hanging timers, countertop timers, and digital timers. **See Figure 1-12.**

Kitchen Timers

Figure 1-12. A kitchen timer can be set to sound an alarm when a certain amount of time has passed.

Temperature is measured in the professional kitchen with a thermometer using either metric units of degrees Celsius (°C) or customary/imperial units of degrees Fahrenheit (°F). Common uses of a thermometer include the following:

- checking the internal temperature of food, such as meat, to ensure it has been cooked to a high enough temperature to be served safely
- monitoring the temperature inside an oven
- monitoring the temperature of oil in a deep fryer
- monitoring the temperature in a freezer or refrigerator
- checking the temperature of foods upon receipt to ensure that the food was stored at the proper temperature during transport
- checking the temperature of food in a steam table to ensure it is held at the proper temperature and safe to serve

Temperature can be measured using different styles of thermometers such as instant-read thermometers, candy/deep fry thermometers, electric probe thermometers, or infrared thermometers. **See Figure 1-13.**

- Instant-read thermometers are the most common type of thermometer used to quickly check food temperatures.
- Candy/deep fry thermometers are used for measuring higher temperatures and can be clipped to the side of a pot to monitor the temperature during the cooking process.
- Electronic probe thermometers have a temperature probe connected to a digital readout and measure a wide range of temperatures.
- Infrared thermometers have sensors to measure the surface temperature of food items without coming in contact with the food.

Kitchen Thermometers

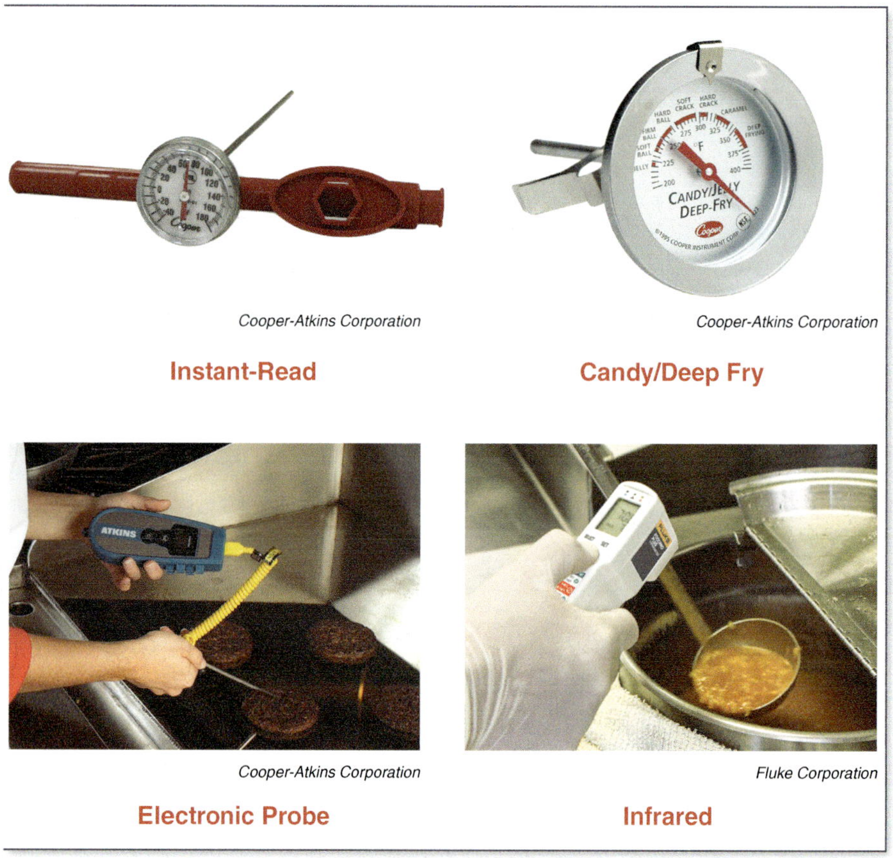

Cooper-Atkins Corporation
Instant-Read
Cooper-Atkins Corporation
Candy/Deep Fry
Cooper-Atkins Corporation
Electronic Probe
Fluke Corporation
Infrared

Figure 1-13. A variety of thermometers are used in the professional kitchen.

Distance

Distance measurements are commonly used when determining room sizes, furniture configurations, tabletop setups, and the sizes of serving platters used at special events. The measurements used for size are also used for distance.

In the professional kitchen, the shape of cooking equipment is often described by its size (20 cm or 8 in. sauté pan) or by the item's capacity (2 L or 2 qt saucepot). Sheet pans and hotel pans are also named according to their size.

Hotel pans come in various shapes and depths to provide flexibility for how they are arranged in steam tables, chafing dishes, and refrigerated tables. The largest hotel pan is referred to as a full pan. The metric standard size for a full hotel pan is 325 mm by 530 mm. The customary standard size for a full hotel pan is 12 in. by 20 in. Hotel pans are commonly described as a fraction of a full pan. For example, three ⅓ pans occupy the same amount of space in a steam table as one full pan. **See Figure 1-14.** The same applies to sheet pans. Two ½ sheet pans equal a full sheet pan.

Hotel Pans

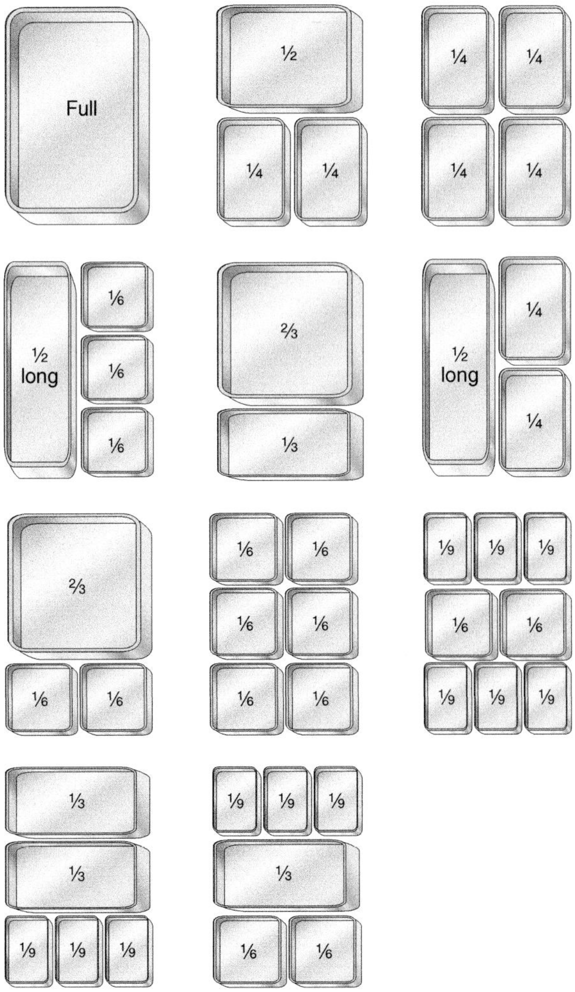

Figure 1-14. The largest hotel pan is a full pan. All other pans are described as a fraction of a full pan.

Checkpoint 1-2

1. Give examples of how count, weight, and volume are used to measure ingredients and serve portions.

2. Why is it important to tare a scale before adding ingredients to an empty container placed on the scale?

3. Describe the proper procedure for measuring ingredients using a dry measuring cup.

4. How many fluid ounces does a #32 portion-controlled scoop hold?

5. Explain why weight measurements are considered more accurate than volume measurements.

6. List eight ingredients that have densities close to water.

7. Identify three types of kitchen timers.

8. Explain how temperature is measured in the professional kitchen.

9. If a steam table can hold two full hotel pans, how many ⅙ pans can the table hold?

Section 1-3 MEASUREMENT EQUIVALENTS

When working with units of measure, cooks must also understand the concept of measurement equivalents. A *measurement equivalent* is an amount in one unit of measure that is equal to another unit of measure. For example, 1000 mL are equal to 1 L, just as 10 dimes are equal to 1 dollar. Other ways of stating this equivalency are to say there are 1000 mL in a liter, there are 1000 mL per liter, or 1000 mL make up 1 L. Likewise, 1 gal. is the equivalent of 4 qt, just as 1 dollar is the equivalent of 4 quarters. Other ways of stating this equivalency are to say there are 4 qt in a gallon, there are 4 qt per gallon, or 4 qt make up 1 gal.

Metric Equivalents

Equivalents within the metric system are easy to remember once metric prefixes are understood. Each prefix has a specific meaning and is used to describe either multiples or fractions of a gram, liter, or meter. **See Figure 1-15.** By using a prefix, the basic units are turned into smaller or larger units. In the professional kitchen, the most common metric equivalents are between grams and kilograms and between liters and milliliters. For example, 2 kg is equivalent to 2000 g because 2 multiplied by 1000 (the meaning of kilo-) equals 2000.

2 kg = 2 × 1000
2 kg = **2000 g**

Likewise, 3000 g is equivalent to 3 kg because 3000 divided by 1000 (the meaning of milli-) equals 3.

3000 g = 3000 ÷ 1000
3000 g = **3 kg**

Similarly, 2 L is equivalent to 2000 mL (2 × 1000 = 2000), and 2000 mL is equivalent to 2 L (2000 ÷ 1000 = 2).

Equivalent Guide

To change a measurement in kilograms to grams, multiply the number of kilograms by 1000 (1 kg = 1000 g).

2 kg = 2000 g

(2 × 1000 = 2000)

To change a measurement in grams to kilograms, divide the number of grams by 1000 (1000 g = 1 kg).

3000 g = 3 kg

(3000 ÷ 1000 = 3)

Metric Unit Equivalents

Prefix	Meaning	Weight	Volume	Length
kilo-	1000	**kilo**gram (kg) = 1000 g	**kilo**liter (kL) = 1000 L	**kilo**meter (km) = 1000 m
hecto-	100	**hecto**gram (hg) = 100 g	**hecto**liter (hL) = 100 L	**hecto**meter (hm) = 100 m
deca-	10	**deca**gram (dag) = 10 g	**deca**liter (daL) = 10 L	**deca**meter (dam) = 10 m
basic unit	1	gram (g)	liter (L)	meter (m)
deci-	1/10 or 0.1	**deci**gram (dg) = 0.1 g	**deci**liter (dL) = 0.1 L	**deci**meter (dm) = 0.1 m
centi-	1/100 or 0.01	**centi**gram (cg) = 0.01 g	**centi**liter (cL) = 0.01 L	**centi**meter (cm) = 0.01 m
milli-	1/1000 or 0.001	**milli**gram (mg) = 0.001 g	**milli**liter (mL) = 0.001 L	**milli**meter (mm) = 0.001 m

Figure 1-15. Metric prefixes are used to describe multiples or fractions of a gram, liter, or meter.

Customary and Imperial Weight Equivalents

The only weight equivalent for both the customary and imperial systems that must be memorized is that 16 oz equals 1 lb (16 oz = 1 lb). When recipes list ingredient weights in customary or imperial units, it is common to see pounds and ounces combined. For example, a recipe may call for 1 lb 2 oz of flour. To change a measurement given in pounds (3 lb) to ounces, the number of pounds is multiplied by 16.

3 lb = 3 × 16
3 lb = **48 oz**

Equivalent Guide

The procedure for changing a measurement in ounces to pounds and ounces is as follows:

Step 1: Divide ounces by 16 (16 oz = 1 lb).

$$\begin{array}{r} 3 \\ 16\overline{)50} \\ -48 \\ \hline 2 \end{array}$$

QUOTIENT = 3; REMAINDER = 2

Step 2: Set the quotient as the number of pounds and the remainder as the number of ounces.

Answer = 3 lb 2 oz

To change a measurement given in ounces (64 oz) to pounds, the number of ounces is divided by 16.

64 oz = 64 ÷ 16
64 oz = **4 lb**

When an ingredient measurement is provided in pounds and ounces, such as 3 lb 2 oz and the measurement must be changed to ounces only, the first step is to multiply the number of pounds in the original measurement by 16 (3 × 16 = 48). Then, that number is added to the number of ounces in the original measurement (48 + 2 = 50). Therefore, in this example, 3 lb 2 oz = 50 oz.

To change a measurement from ounces to pounds and ounces, the number of ounces is divided by 16. The quotient is equal to the number of pounds, and any remainder is equal to the number of additional ounces. For example, 50 oz ÷ 16 = 3 with a remainder of 2. This result equals 3 pounds 2 ounces.

Customary and Imperial Volume Equivalents

Before calculating customary or imperial volume equivalents, it is important to know how they differ. First, the number of fluid ounces in cups, pints, quarts, and gallons is greater in the imperial system than in the customary system. For example, an imperial pint has 20 fl oz, while a customary pint has 16 fl oz.

The second difference between customary and imperial volume measures is that 1 fl oz in the customary system is equivalent to 29.57 mL, while 1 fl oz in the imperial system is equivalent to 28.41 mL. For example, 12 fl oz in the customary system is equivalent to 355 mL, while 12 fl oz in the imperial system is equivalent to 341 mL.

The final difference between customary and imperial volume measures is that cups are not commonly used in the imperial system. Instead, the imperial system uses gills, which is approximately equal to half a cup in the customary system. **See Figure 1-16.**

Customary and Imperial Volume Measurement Differences

Unit of Measure	Customary Measurement	Imperial Measurement
Fluid ounce	1 fl oz (29.57 mL)	1 fl oz (28.41 mL)
Gill	–	5 fl oz
Cup	8 fl oz	10 fl oz (not commonly used)
Pint	16 fl oz	20 fl oz
Quart	32 fl oz	40 fl oz
Gallon	128 fl oz	160 fl oz

Figure 1-16. The customary and imperial systems differ in the number of ounces in a pint, quart, and gallon, and in the size of a fluid ounce.

Recipes should be checked to determine if they are written with customary or imperial measurements because the volume measurement differences between the two systems can alter the recipe's outcome. It will be helpful to use Figure 1-16 to remember the number of fluid ounces in customary and imperial cups, pints, quarts, and gallons. Also, a customary cup equals 8 fl oz while an imperial cup equals 10 fl oz. However, because cups are rarely used in the imperial system—and to avoid confusion—the customary cup (8 fl oz) is the cup used in Canadian food service.

Cooks should know the basic measurement equivalents for volume and be able to calculate the equivalents between any two volume units. **See Figure 1-17.** For example, a cook would be expected to know that 4 qt is equal to 1 gal. and that there are 3 tsp in 1 tbsp. In the customary system, the following six volume measurement equivalents should be memorized:

- 4 qt = 1 gal.
- 2 pt = 1 qt
- 2 c = 1 pt
- 8 fl oz = 1 c
- 2 tbsp = 1 fl oz
- 3 tsp = 1 tbsp

Calculating Volume Equivalents. Using the basic volume equivalents, it is easy to change measurements from one unit to another by following two rules:

- To change from a larger to smaller unit of measure, multiply the number in the original measurement by the number of smaller units that make up the larger unit.
- To change from a smaller to a larger unit, divide the number in the original measurement by the number of smaller units that make up the larger unit.

Customary and Imperial Volume Equivalents

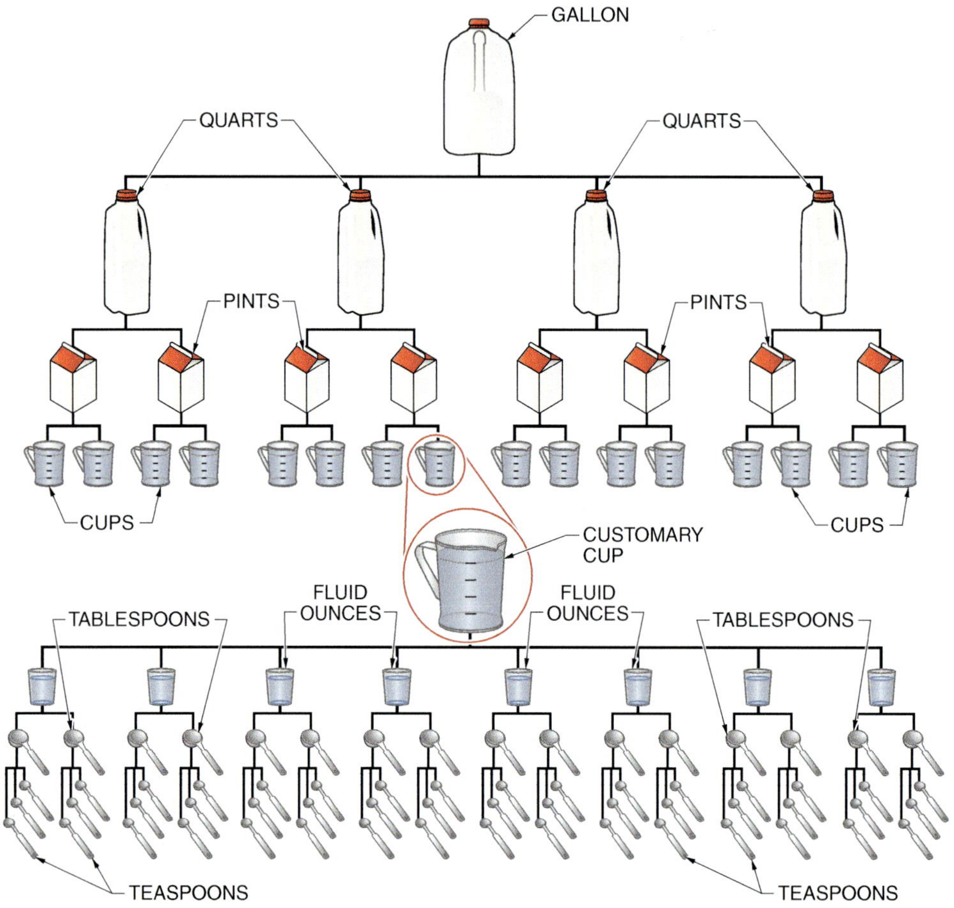

Customary Volume Equivalents

Gallon		Quarts		Pints		Cups		Fluid Ounces		Tablespoons		Teaspoons
1	=	4	=	8	=	16	=	128	=	256	=	768
		1	=	2	=	4	=	32	=	64	=	192
				1	=	2	=	16	=	32	=	92
						1	=	8	=	16	=	48
								1	=	2	=	6
										1	=	3

Imperial Volume Equivalents

Gallon		Quarts		Pints		Cups		Fluid Ounces		Tablespoons		Teaspoons
1	=	4	=	8	=	16	=	160	=	320	=	960
		1	=	2	=	4	=	40	=	80	=	240
				1	=	2	=	20	=	40	=	120
						1	=	10	=	20	=	60
								1	=	2	=	6
										1	=	3

Figure 1-17. Foodservice employees must understand how different volume units of measure relate to one another.

Consider the basic equivalent 4 qt = 1 gal. To change a measurement in gallons to quarts (larger unit to smaller unit), the number of gallons is multiplied by 4 (the number of quarts that make up a gallon). For example, 2 gal. are equivalent to 8 qt (2 × 4 = 8). However, to change a measurement in quarts to gallons (smaller unit to larger unit), the number of quarts is divided by 4. For example, 12 qt are equivalent to 3 gal. (12 ÷ 4 = 3). The same process works using any of the basic volume equivalents. **See Figure 1-18.**

Customary Volume Equivalents

Basic Volume Equivalents	To Change a Larger Unit to a Smaller Unit: Multiply	Example	To Change a Smaller Unit to a Larger Unit: Divide	Example
4 qt = 1 gal.	Gallons to Quarts (multiply by 4)	2 gal. = 8 qt (2 × **4** = 8)	Quarts to Gallons (divide by 4)	8 qt = 2 gal. (8 ÷ **4** = 2)
2 pt = 1 qt	Quarts to Pints (multiply by 2)	2 qt = 4 pt (2 × **2** = 4)	Pints to Quarts (divide by 2)	4 pt = 2 qt (4 ÷ **2** = 2)
2 c = 1 pt	Pints to Cups (multiply by 2)	8 pt = 16 c (8 × **2** = 16)	Cups to Pints (divide by 2)	16 c = 8 pt (16 ÷ **2** = 8)
8 fl oz = 1 c	Cups to Fluid Ounces (multiply by 8)	2 c = 16 fl oz (2 × **8** = 16)	Fluid Ounces to Cups (divide by 8)	16 fl oz = 2 c (16 ÷ **8** = 2)
2 tbsp = 1 fl oz	Fluid Ounces to Tablespoons (multiply by 2)	5 fl oz = 10 tbsp (5 × **2** = 10)	Tablespoons to Fluid Ounces (divide by 2)	10 tbsp = 5 fl oz (10 ÷ **2** = 5)
3 tsp = 1 tbsp	Tablespoons to Teaspoons (multiply by 3)	4 tbsp = 12 tsp (4 × **3** = 12)	Teaspoons to Tablespoons (divide by 3)	12 tsp = 4 tbsp (12 ÷ **3** = 4)

Figure 1-18. Basic volume measurement equivalents can be used to calculate equivalent volume measurements with different units of measure.

Some equivalent measurements may need to be calculated in more than one step. For example, if a standardized recipe calls for 8 tbsp of sugar and the recipe must be made 4 times, the cook would need to measure 32 tbsp (8 × 4 = 32). Since it would take too long to measure 32 tbsp individually, the tablespoons are converted to a larger unit of measure, such as cups. Converting 32 tbsp to 2 c can be done in two steps. Since this conversion is from a smaller unit of measure (tablespoons) to a larger unit of measure (cups), division is used.

First, since 2 tablespoons make up 1 fluid ounce, the measurement in tablespoons is changed to fluid ounces by dividing the number of tablespoons by 2.

32 tbsp = 32 ÷ 2
32 tbsp = **16 fl oz**

Then, since 8 fluid ounces make up 1 cup, the measurement in fluid ounces is changed to cups by dividing the number of fluid ounces by 8.

16 fl oz = 16 ÷ 8 = 2
16 fl oz = **2 c**

Soft Volume Equivalents. Soft equivalents are commonly used when a slight variation in volume measurement will not adversely affect the outcome of a recipe. Soft equivalents are most often used to measure ingredients found in small batch recipes. **See Figure 1-19.** However, soft equivalents should be used with caution. This is especially true in baking because precise measurements are required for a successful outcome.

Soft Equivalents

Customary Measurement	Metric Measurement
¼ teaspoon	1 milliliter
½ teaspoon	2 milliliters
1 teaspoon	5 milliliters
1 tablespoon	15 milliliters
1 fluid ounce	30 milliliters
1 cup	250 milliliters
1 pint	500 milliliters
1 quart	1 liter
1 gallon	4 liters

Figure 1-19. Soft equivalents are commonly used when a slight variation in volume measurement will not adversely affect the outcome of a recipe.

Customary and Imperial Distance Equivalents

The most commonly used customary and imperial units of measure for distance are the inch (in.) and the foot (ft). A customary/imperial measurement equivalent to remember is that 12 in. is equal to 1 ft. Feet can also be represented by a prime symbol (′), and inches can be represented by a double-prime symbol (″). For example, 2 ft 4 in. is the same as 2′-4″.

1-3 Checkpoint

1. Define "measurement equivalent."

2. How many kilograms are equivalent to 6000 g?

3. How many milliliters are equivalent to 8 L?

4. What is the customary/imperial weight measurement equivalent every cook should know?

5. Compare the number of fluid ounces in a customary quart to the number of fluid ounces in an imperial quart.

6. List the six customary measurement equivalents for volume that every cook should memorize.

7. What are the two rules to use when converting a measurement in one unit of measure to a measurement in a different unit?

8. How many inches are equal to 1 ft?

Math Exercises 1

Solve each problem in the space provided. Write the final answer on the blank provided. Note: *Use volume customary measurements for cups.*

Leaf icon indicates a math problem with a sustainability focus.

Example:

2 gal. ________ How many gallons are equivalent to 8 quarts?

Since 4 qt = 1 gal. 8 qt = ***2 gal.*** *(8 ÷ 4 = 2)*

5000 grams ________ **1.** How many grams are equivalent to 5 kg?

5 Kg = 5000 grams

7 Kg ________ **2.** How many kilograms are equivalent to 7000 g?

7000 g = 7 Kg

3000 mL ________ **3.** How many milliliters are equivalent to 3 L?

3 L = 3000 mL

5 L
______ 4. How many liters are equivalent to 5000 mL?

2000 ml
______ 5. If a container has a capacity of 2 L, how many milliliters can the container hold?

210 g
______ 6. A restaurant with a rooftop garden is replanted to change with the seasons. Instead of composting the 7 remaining basil plants, the chef purées their leaves with oil and freezes the purée for later use. How many grams of chopped basil leaves can be puréed if each plant yields 30 g of chopped basil?

7 × 30 g = 210 g

200
______ 7. How many 170 g hamburger patties can be produced from 34 kg of ground beef?

200
______ 8. A cooked ham weighs 11 kg. How many ham slider sandwiches can be made if each sandwich has 55 g of cooked ham?

6.0kg

9. A butcher saves raw beef trimmings to grind up and make into meatballs. How many kilograms of trimmings are needed to make 120 meatballs if each meatball requires 50 g of trimmings?

250

10. Due to a canceled cake order, a local patisserie has 3 kg of prepared buttercream that is no longer needed for the cake. To repurpose the buttercream, the patisserie owner uses it to fill French macarons. If each macaron is filled with 12 g of buttercream, how many macarons can be filled with the leftover buttercream?

20

11. A deli that serves sandwiches on ciabatta bread has 3 loaves left at the end of the day. The owner decides to use the leftover bread in panzanella salads. If each salad requires 120 g of bread and each loaf weighs 800 g, how many salads can be made from the leftover loaves?

8

The Betty Ring moore Bursary

...atoes to serve with their entrées uses ... make creamy potato soup. If the soup ...h prebaked potato weighs 250 g, how ...ded to prepare the soup?

_______________ **13.** A group of 40 people are served a salad topped with grilled chicken for lunch. If each salad includes 125 g of chicken, how many kilograms of chicken are served?

_______________ **14.** A cook mistakenly browned 15 kg of ground beef for burritos instead of 12 kg. To reduce waste, the cook used the extra beef to prepare lasagna. If each pan of lasagna required 600 g of the beef, how many pans of lasagna were prepared?

_______________ **15.** Instead of discarding the leftover rinds from two wheels of Parmesan cheese, a sous chef cuts them into 85 g portions to be repurposed in soups and salads. How many 85 g rind portions can be made if one of the rinds weighs 1 kg and the other weighs 700 g?

_______________ **16.** A foodservice employee places an empty container that weighs 225 g on a digital scale and forgets to tare the scale before adding flour to the container. After the employee adds the flour, the scale reads 455 g. How much flour is in the container?

_______________ **17.** A container with cornmeal mix weighs 1542 g. If the container alone weighs 197 g, what is the weight in grams of the cornmeal mix?

_______________ **18.** A pastry chef needs 90 mL of batter to produce one cupcake. How many cupcakes can be produced from a recipe that yields 18 L of batter?

_______________ **19.** A restaurant that prepares cranberry relish for its turkey lunch special saw fewer lunch customers than usual and had 1 L (1000 mL) of fresh cranberries left over. If it takes 250 mL of fresh cranberries to make a batch of 9 cranberry muffins that could be sold for breakfast the next day, how many cranberry muffins can be made from the leftover cranberries?

_______________ **20.** A bistro replaced its kitchen spray nozzle with a low-flow, prerinse spray nozzle that saves 2 L of water per hour of use. During 4 work shifts, how many liters of water are saved if the spray nozzle is used 6 hr during each shift?

_______________ **21.** If one batch yields 100 cookies and takes 20 min to bake, how many hours would it take to bake 12 batches of cookies, one batch at a time?

_______________ **22.** How many hours will it take a 5 kg rib roast to cook if it is cooked for 36 min per kilogram?

_______________ **23.** A deli replaced two old ovens that each roasted 6 whole chickens in 45 min with a commercial rotisserie oven that roasts 72 whole chickens in 45 min. If 72 chickens are prepared, how many minutes are saved using the rotisserie oven compared to the two old ovens when each oven is filled to capacity?

_______________ **24.** A bakery has one oven that runs hotter than the others by 10°C. If a recipe calls for a cake to be baked at 180°C, what should the temperature setting be for the oven that runs too hot?

_______________ **25.** When a restaurant's deep fryer is not in use between lunch and dinner services, its temperature is reduced to 100°C to save energy. How long will it take the deep fryer to reheat to 180°C if the temperature increases 10°C per minute?

_______________ **26.** What are the dimensions in centimeters of a piece of parchment paper that is 600 mm wide and 900 mm long?

_______________ **27.** At a catered event, 14 sandwiches, 60 cm long each, are served. If each sandwich is cut into 12 cm pieces, how many sandwich pieces can be served?

_______________ **28.** A chafing dish can hold one full hotel pan. How many chafing dishes are needed to hold a total of three ⅓ pans, two ½ pans, and six ⅙ pans?

______________ **29.** How many fluid ounces does a #4 portion-controlled scoop hold?

______________ **30.** How many single-scoop cones can be made from a customary 3 gal. tub of ice cream if a #16 scoop is used? *(Tip: A #16 scoop holds 2 fl oz.)*

______________ **31.** How many ounces are equivalent to 2 lb?

______________ **32.** How many pounds are equivalent to 144 oz?

______________ **33.** What is the equivalent of 36 oz in pounds and ounces?

_______________ **34.** What is the equivalent of 5 lb 2 oz in ounces?

_______________ **35.** How many pounds of cooked Italian sausage are needed to make 32 Italian sausage sandwiches if each sandwich contains 5 oz of cooked sausage?

_______________ **36.** How many gallons are equivalent to 12 qt?

_______________ **37.** How many quarts are equivalent to 5 gal.?

_______________ **38.** How many tablespoons are equivalent to 6 fl oz?

_______________ **39.** How many fluid ounces are equivalent to 8 tbsp?

_______________ **40.** How many cups are equivalent to 4 pt?

_______________ **41.** How many pints are equivalent to 12 c?

_______________ **42.** How many fluid ounces are equivalent to 2 customary pints?

_______________ **43.** How many fluid ounces are equivalent to 2 imperial gallons?

_______________ **44.** How many tablespoons are equivalent to 1 c plus 2 tbsp?

_______________ **45.** Container A has a maximum capacity of 3 gal. Container B has a maximum capacity of 14 qt. How much extra capacity does container B have compared to container A?

_______________ **46.** What is the soft equivalent in milliliters to 2 tsp?

_______________ **47.** What is the soft equivalent in liters to 3 customary gallons?

_______________ **48.** If a recipe calls for 2 customary gallons of cream, how many 8 fl oz containers of cream would be needed to make the recipe? *(Tip: 128 fl oz = 1 gal.)*

_______________ **49.** If a recipe calls for 4 tsp of baking soda, how many cups of baking soda are needed if the recipe is made 12 times?

_______________ **50.** What are the dimensions, in inches, of a piece of puff pastry that is 1′ wide by 2′ long?

Calculating Measurements

2

In food service, measurements are more than just a list of the quantities of ingredients used in a recipe. Measurements also relate to the shape and size of kitchen equipment, the amount of space available in a facility, and the number of servings that can be made from a given amount of food. An understanding of how to perform calculations with measurements is an essential skill for any foodservice professional, especially when calculations involve whole numbers, fractions, and decimals.

Section 2-1: WHOLE NUMBER MEASUREMENTS
- Add and subtract measurements involving whole numbers.
- Multiply and divide measurements involving whole numbers.

Section 2-2: FRACTION MEASUREMENTS
- Convert between improper fractions and mixed numbers.
- Add, subtract, multiply, and divide fractions.

Section 2-3: DECIMAL MEASUREMENTS
- Convert between fractions and decimals.
- Explain how decimals are rounded.
- Add, subtract, multiply, and divide decimals.

Section 2-4: CALCULATING AREA, VOLUME, AND ANGLES
- Calculate the area of a rectangular surface and the area of a circular surface.
- Calculate the volume of a rectangular solid and the volume of a cylinder.
- Explain how angles are used in food service.

Section 2-5: BASIC STATISTICS
- Calculate the average (mean), median, and mode from a set of numbers.
- Generate a data table and a graph.

Key Terms
- measurement
- fraction
- numerator
- denominator
- proper fraction
- improper fraction
- mixed number
- common denominator
- lowest common denominator
- reciprocal
- decimal
- rounding
- area
- diameter
- radius
- capacity
- angle
- average

Learner Resources
atplearningresources.com
access code 267628

Vita-Mix® Corporation

Section 2-1 WHOLE NUMBER MEASUREMENTS

A *measurement* is a number with a corresponding unit of measure that indicates an amount or degree of something. For example, 3 kilograms, 5 liters, 20 centimeters, and 200 degrees Celsius are all metric measurements. Likewise, 2 pounds, 4 gallons, 6 inches, and 350 degrees Fahrenheit are all customary or imperial measurements. Calculations involving only numbers are similar to calculations involving measurements. However, when performing basic math operations with measurements, the unit of measure must be included.

Adding and Subtracting Measurements

Addition and subtraction of measurements are straightforward if the unit of measure is the same for every measurement in the calculation. For example, a recipe for punch calls for 3 L of cranberry juice, 4 L of orange juice, and 2 L of club soda. To determine the size of a punch bowl required to hold the entire recipe, the quantities of the individual ingredients must be added together.

$$3\text{ L} + 4\text{ L} + 2\text{ L} = \mathbf{9\text{ L}}$$

Therefore, a punch bowl that holds at least 9 L of liquid is required. However, different units of measure must be changed to the same unit of measure before they are added or subtracted. For example, if a punch recipe calls for 1 L of club soda and there is only 750 mL of club soda in the bottle, how much more club soda is needed for the punch? To calculate the amount needed, 750 mL must be subtracted from 1 L. First, 1 liter is changed to an equivalent unit of measure in milliliters.

$$1\text{ L} = 1000\text{ mL } (1 \times 1000)$$

Then, 750 mL is subtracted from 1000 mL to determine that an additional 250 mL of club soda is needed.

$$1000\text{ mL} - 750\text{ mL} = \mathbf{250\text{ mL}}$$

Similarly, a punch recipe written in customary/imperial volume measurements calls for 3 qt of cranberry juice, 1 gal. of orange juice, and 4 pt of club soda. To determine the size of a punch bowl required to hold the entire recipe, the quantities of the individual ingredients must be changed to the same unit of measure before they can be added. **See Figure 2-1.**

If the 9 qt of punch are prepared and 1 pt of the punch is left over after a bridal shower, how much was consumed? To calculate the amount of punch consumed, 1 pt must be subtracted from 9 qt. First, 9 quarts is changed to an equivalent unit of measure in pints (2 pt = 1 qt).

$$9\text{ qt} = 18\text{ pt } (9 \times 2 = 18)$$

Then, the 1 pt of punch that was left over is subtracted from the 9 qt prepared, which results in 17 pt consumed.

18 pt − 1 pt = **17 pt**

Adding Measurements

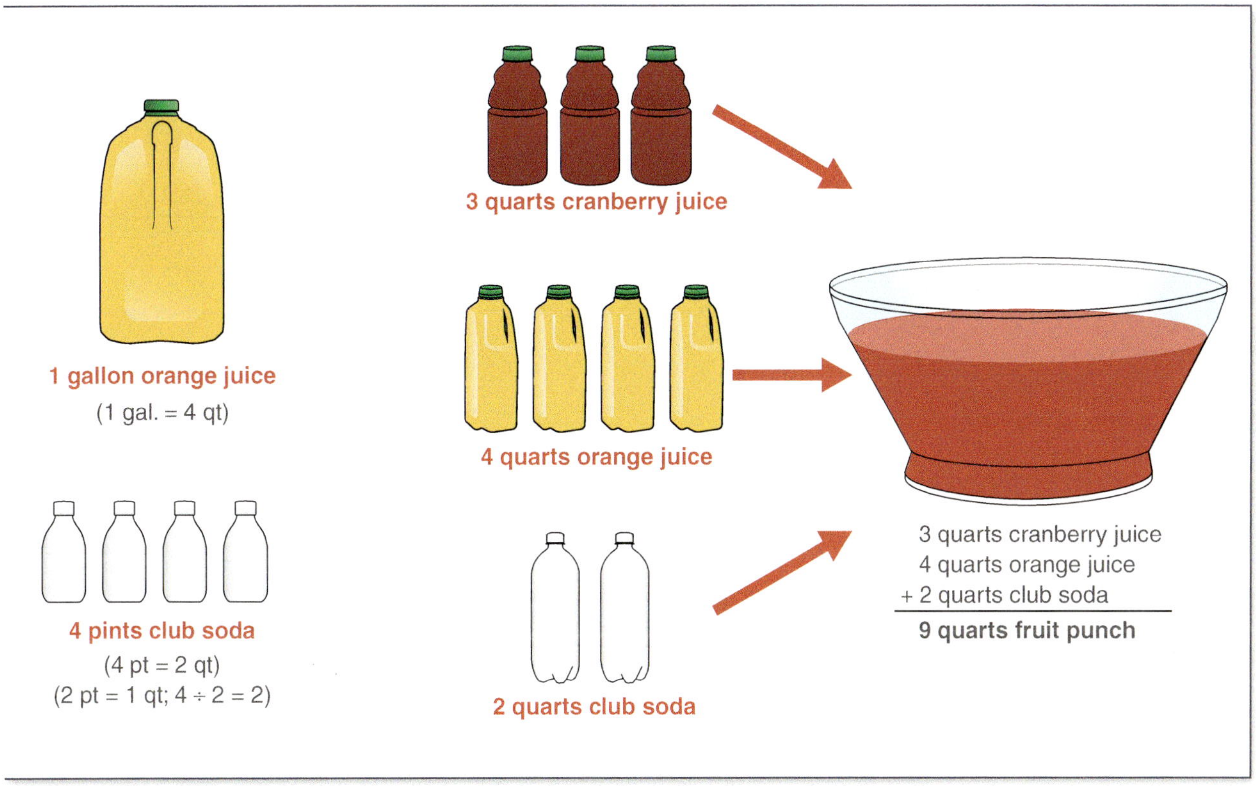

Figure 2-1. Measurements must be changed to the same unit of measure before they can be added.

Multiplying and Dividing Measurements

In food service, multiplication and division are used when increasing or decreasing a measurement and when changing a measurement from one unit to another. When a measurement is multiplied or divided by a number, the unit of measure stays the same. For example, 5 L multiplied by 2 is 10 L. Likewise, 10 L divided by 2 is 5 L.

5 L × 2 = **10 L**

and

10 L ÷ 2 = **5 L**

2-1 Checkpoint

1. What is the sum of 2 kg, 250 g, and 750 g? *(Provide the answer in grams.)*

2. Subtract 565 mL from 1 L. *(Provide the answer in milliliters.)*

3. What is the sum of 6 c and 4 pt? *(Provide the answer in cups.)*

4. Subtract 2 pt from 2 qt. *(Provide the answer in quarts.)*

5. Multiply 4 L by 6.

Section 2-2 FRACTION MEASUREMENTS

Many measurements in the professional kitchen involve fractions. In food service, fraction measurements are commonly used with customary and imperial units of measure when working with volume measuring tools and weight. A *fraction* is a part of a whole. A fraction is written as two numbers (a numerator and a denominator) separated by a line (or fraction bar). A *numerator* is the number in a fraction at the top (or to the left) of a fraction bar that represents the parts of a whole. A *denominator* is the number in a fraction at the bottom (or to the right) of a fraction bar that represents the number of parts into which a whole is divided. For example, a quarter-cup dry measuring cup is represented by the fraction ¼ with 1 as the numerator and 4 as the denominator. Since a fraction represents part of a whole, the fraction ¼ represents one part out of four, 2/4 represents two parts out of four, ¾ represents three parts out of four, and 4/4 represents four parts out of four. **See Figure 2-2.**

When the numerator and denominator are equal, such as 3/3 or 4/4, the value of the fraction is always 1. Any whole number can also be written as a fraction by using the whole number as the numerator and 1 as the denominator. For example, the whole number 4 written as a fraction is 4/1.

Fractions are classified as proper or improper. A *proper fraction* is a fraction in which the numerator is smaller than the denominator. An *improper fraction* is a fraction in which the numerator is larger than the denominator. For example, 3/4 is a proper fraction, and 4/3 is an improper fraction.

A *mixed number* is a combination of a whole number and a fraction. For example, 1½ c of milk is 1 c of milk plus ½ c of milk. Improper fractions and mixed numbers are related to each other. For example, the improper fraction 7/3 can be converted to the mixed number 2⅓ by dividing the numerator by the denominator. Likewise, the mixed number 2⅓ can be converted to the improper fraction 7/3.

Fractions (Parts of a Whole)

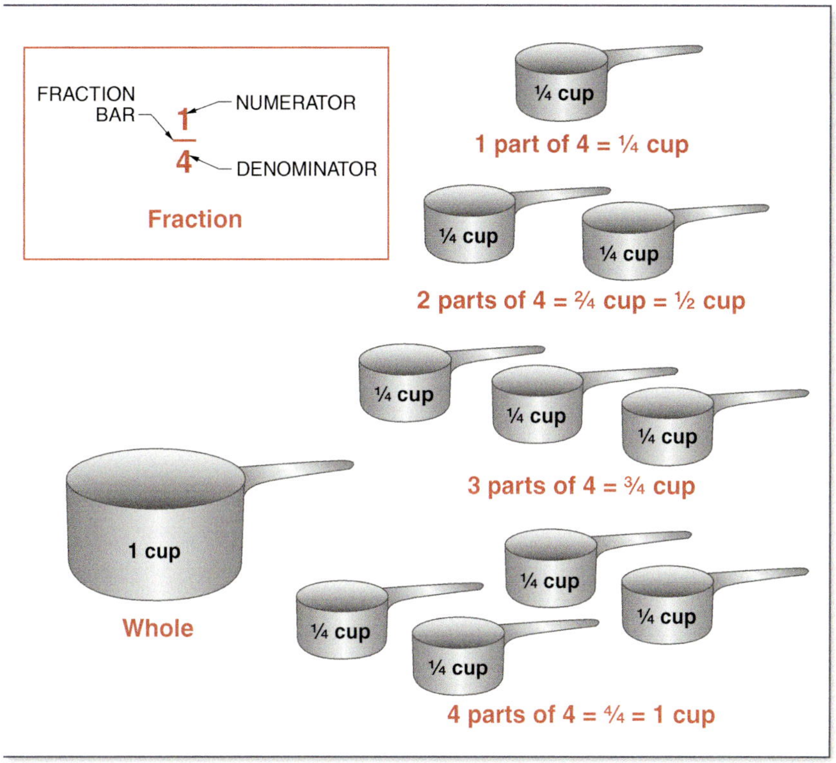

Figure 2-2. A fraction represents part of a whole. The numerator represents the part, and the denominator represents the whole.

To convert a mixed number to an improper fraction, first the whole number is multiplied by the denominator. For example, in the mixed number 2⅓, the whole number is 2, the denominator is 3, and their product is 6 ($2 \times 3 = 6$). Next, the original numerator (1) is added to that product to calculate the numerator of the improper fraction ($6 + 1 = 7$). Finally, the calculated numerator (7) is placed over the original denominator (3) to form the improper fraction 7/3. **See Figure 2-3.**

Fractions where both the numerator and denominator can be divided evenly by the same number may be reduced (or simplified) to an equivalent fraction. This is called reducing (simplifying) a fraction to its lowest terms. For example, the fraction 6/8 can be reduced to ¾ by dividing the numerator and the denominator by 2. In the professional kitchen, fractions should be reduced to the lowest terms possible to make measuring and calculations easier.

Reducing Guide

Step 1: Determine the largest number by which both the numerator and denominator can be evenly divided.

$$\frac{6}{8} = \frac{3 \times 2}{4 \times 2}$$

Step 2: Divide the numerator and denominator by that number. The resulting fraction has been reduced to its lowest terms.

$$\frac{6 \div 2}{8 \div 2} = \frac{3}{4}$$

Converting between Improper Fractions and Mixed Numbers

Example: Convert 7⁄3 to a mixed number.

1. Arrange the numerator as the dividend and the denominator as the divisor.

NUMERATOR $\frac{7}{3}$ DENOMINATOR

DIVISOR $3\overline{)7}$ DIVIDEND

2. Divide the numerator by the denominator.

QUOTIENT 2; $3\overline{)7}$; 6; 1 REMAINDER

3. Write the mixed number using the quotient as the whole number and the remainder over the divisor as the fraction.

QUOTIENT 2⅓ REMAINDER DIVISOR

Answer: 2⅓

Example: Convert 2⅓ to an improper fraction.

1. Multiply the whole number by the denominator.

WHOLE NUMBER 2⅓ NUMERATOR DENOMINATOR

$2 \times 3 = 6$ PRODUCT

2. Add the product to the numerator, and place the sum over the original denominator.

$$\frac{6+1}{3} = \frac{7}{3}$$

Answer: 7⁄3

Figure 2-3. Improper fractions can be converted into mixed numbers, and mixed numbers can be converted into improper fractions.

Adding and Subtracting Fractions

Adding and subtracting fractions that have a common denominator is simple. A *common denominator* is a denominator that is the same in two or more fractions. A common denominator must be determined before fractions with unlike denominators can be added or subtracted.

Common Denominators. To add two or more fractions that have a common denominator, the numerators are added together, and the sum is placed over the common denominator. For example, if a fruit salad recipe calls for ¼ c of strawberries, ¼ c of blueberries, and ¼ c of raspberries, the total amount of berries required is ¾ c. **See Figure 2-4.**

Likewise, two fractions that have a common denominator are subtracted by simply subtracting one numerator from the other numerator. The difference is placed over the common denominator. For example, if a fish fillet weighs ⅝ lb and ⅛ lb of skin is removed, the final weight of the fish fillet is ½ lb.

$$\frac{5}{8}\text{lb} - \frac{1}{8}\text{lb} = \frac{4}{8}\text{lb} = \mathbf{\frac{1}{2}lb}$$

Adding and Subtracting Fractions with Common Denominators

Adding

Example: A fruit salad recipe calls for ¼ c of strawberries, ¼ c of blueberries, and ¼ c of raspberries. What is the total amount of berries required?

$$\frac{1}{4} + \frac{1}{4} + \frac{1}{4} = \frac{1+1+1}{4} = \frac{3}{4}$$

SUM OF NUMERATORS

DENOMINATOR STAYS THE SAME

Answer: ¾ c

Subtracting

Example: A fish fillet weighing ⅝ lb has ⅛ lb of skin removed. What is the final weight of the fish fillet?

$$\frac{5}{8} - \frac{1}{8} = \frac{5-1}{8} = \frac{4}{8} = \frac{4 \div 4}{8 \div 4} = \frac{1}{2}$$

DIFFERENCE BETWEEN NUMERATORS

DENOMINATOR STAYS THE SAME

Answer: ½ lb

Figure 2-4. When all the fractions in a calculation involving addition or subtraction have a common denominator, the numerators are added or subtracted, and the denominator stays the same.

Unlike Denominators. To add or subtract fractions with unlike denominators, the fractions must be rewritten so they have a common denominator. Rewriting the fractions begins by finding the lowest common denominator. The *lowest common denominator* is the smallest number into which each of the denominators of a group of fractions can divide evenly.

For example, if a spice mixture recipe requires ½ c of black pepper, ⅔ c of garlic powder, and ¾ c of salt, how many total cups of the spice mixture will the recipe make? To add the three fractions, the lowest common denominator among the three denominators (2, 3, and 4) must be found first. Since 12 is the smallest number that 2, 3, and 4 all divide into evenly, 12 is the lowest common denominator. **See Figure 2-5.**

The next step is to rewrite all the fractions so they include the lowest common denominator. To rewrite each fraction as a fraction of equal value with a common denominator of 12, the numerator and denominator must be multiplied by the same number. For example, since 2 × 6 = 12, ½ is multiplied by 6/6.

$$\frac{1}{2} \times \frac{6}{6} = \frac{1 \times 6}{2 \times 6} = \mathbf{\frac{6}{12}}$$

Finding the Lowest Common Denominator

Example: What is the lowest common denominator of the fractions $\frac{1}{2}$, $\frac{2}{3}$, and $\frac{3}{4}$?

1. List all the denominators and multiples of the denominators.
2. Identify the smallest multiple that appears as a multiple of all three denominators. This is the lowest common denominator.

MULTIPLES OF DENOMINATORS

DENOMINATORS									
2 —	2	4	6	8	10	12	14	16
3 —	3		6	9		12		15	
4 —		4		8		12			16

LOWEST COMMON DENOMINATOR: 12

Answer: 12

Figure 2-5. Before fractions with unlike denominators can be added or subtracted, a lowest common denominator must first be determined.

Then, $\frac{2}{3}$ is multiplied by $\frac{4}{4}$ to get $\frac{8}{12}$ ($\frac{2}{3} \times \frac{4}{4} = \frac{8}{12}$). Finally, $\frac{3}{4}$ is multiplied by $\frac{3}{3}$ to get $\frac{9}{12}$ ($\frac{3}{4} \times \frac{3}{3} = \frac{9}{12}$). Now that the fractions $\frac{6}{12}$, $\frac{8}{12}$, and $\frac{9}{12}$ have a common denominator, they can be added by adding the numerators ($6 + 8 + 9 = 23$) and placing the sum (23) over the common denominator (12). Therefore, the total amount of spice mix the recipe makes is $\frac{23}{12}$ c. Then, $\frac{23}{12}$ c can be converted to a mixed number by dividing the numerator by the denominator ($23 \div 12 = 1$ with a remainder of 11 or $1\frac{11}{12}$ c). **See Figure 2-6.**

Adding Fractions with Unlike Denominators

Example: A spice mixture recipe requires $\frac{1}{2}$ c of black pepper, $\frac{2}{3}$ c of garlic powder, and $\frac{3}{4}$ c of salt. How many total cups of the spice mixture will the recipe make?

$$\frac{1}{2} + \frac{2}{3} + \frac{3}{4} =$$

UNLIKE DENOMINATORS

1. Find the lowest common denominator (12).
2. Divide the lowest common denominator by each of the unlike denominators.

$$12 \div 2 = 6$$
$$12 \div 3 = 4$$
$$12 \div 4 = 3$$

QUOTIENTS

3. Multiply the numerator and denominator of each fraction by the corresponding quotients from Step 2 to rewrite the fractions as equivalent fractions with a common denominator.

$$\frac{1}{2} \times \frac{6}{6} = \frac{1 \times 6}{2 \times 6} = \frac{6}{12}$$
$$\frac{2}{3} \times \frac{4}{4} = \frac{2 \times 4}{3 \times 4} = \frac{8}{12}$$
$$\frac{3}{4} \times \frac{3}{3} = \frac{3 \times 3}{4 \times 3} = \frac{9}{12}$$

COMMON DENOMINATOR

4. Add the numerators of the equivalent fractions, and record the sum over the common denominator.

$$\frac{6 + 8 + 9}{12} = \frac{23}{12}$$

5. Convert the answer to a mixed number if necessary.

$$12\overline{)23} = 1\frac{11}{12} \quad (23 - 12 = 11)$$

Answer: $\frac{23}{12}$ c or $1\frac{11}{12}$ c

Figure 2-6. Fractions with unlike denominators must be rewritten as fractions of equivalent values with common denominators before they can be added.

Finally, if ½ c of the spice mix is set aside for use during lunch service and only ⅓ c is used, how much spice mix is left? To calculate this amount, ⅓ c must be subtracted from ½ c. As with addition, subtraction cannot be performed until a common denominator is found. The same steps are followed as for addition except the numerators of the rewritten fractions are subtracted instead of added. **See Figure 2-7.**

Subtracting Fractions with Unlike Denominators

Example: If ½ c of a spice mixture is prepared and ⅓ c of the mixture is used during lunch service, how much spice mixture remains?

$$\frac{1}{2} - \frac{1}{3} =$$

UNLIKE DENOMINATORS

1. Find the lowest common denominator (6).

$$6 \div 2 = 3$$
$$6 \div 3 = 2$$

QUOTIENTS

2. Divide the lowest common denominator by each of the unlike denominators.

3. Multiply the numerator and denominator of each fraction by the corresponding quotients from Step 2 to rewrite the fractions as equivalent fractions with a common denominator.

$$\frac{1}{2} \times \frac{3}{3} = \frac{1 \times 3}{2 \times 3} = \frac{3}{6}$$
$$\frac{1}{3} \times \frac{2}{2} = \frac{1 \times 2}{3 \times 2} = \frac{2}{6}$$

COMMON DENOMINATOR

4. Subtract the numerators of the equivalent fractions and record the difference over the common denominator.

$$\frac{3 - 2}{6} = \frac{1}{6}$$

Answer: ⅙ c

Figure 2-7. Fractions with unlike denominators must be rewritten as fractions of equivalent values with common denominators before they can be subtracted.

Multiplying Fractions

When multiplying fractions, the numerators and the denominators are multiplied separately. Any mixed number must be converted to an improper fraction before multiplying. If necessary, the resulting fraction can be converted back to a mixed number after multiplying.

For example, if a recipe calls for 2⅓ c of flour and 1½ times the recipe needs to be prepared, how much flour is needed? To multiply the mixed numbers 2⅓ and 1½, they are first converted to the improper fractions 7/3 and 3/2. Next, the numerators are multiplied, and the denominators are multiplied. The resulting fraction (21/6) can then be converted to a mixed number (3 3/6). The fraction 3/6 can be reduced to ½. Therefore, 3½ c of flour is needed for the recipe. **See Figure 2-8.**

Multiplying Fractions

Example: A recipe calls for 2⅓ c of flour, and 1½ times the recipe needs to be made. How much flour will be needed?

$$2\frac{1}{3} \times 1\frac{1}{2} =$$

1. Convert both mixed numbers to improper fractions.

$$2\frac{1}{3} = \frac{(2 \times 3) + 1}{3} = \frac{6 + 1}{3} = \frac{7}{3}$$

$$1\frac{1}{2} = \frac{(1 \times 2) + 1}{2} = \frac{2 + 1}{2} = \frac{3}{2}$$

2. Multiply the numerators by each other and the denominators by each other.

$$\frac{7}{3} \times \frac{3}{2} = \frac{7 \times 3}{3 \times 2} = \frac{21}{6}$$

PRODUCT

3. Convert the product to a mixed number, and reduce to lowest terms.

$$\frac{21}{6} = 6\overline{)21} = 3\frac{3}{6} = 3\frac{1}{2}$$

(21 ÷ 6 = 3, 18, remainder 3)

Answer: 3½ c

Figure 2-8. When multiplying fractions, the numerators are multiplied, and the denominators are multiplied.

Dividing Fractions

Dividing one fraction by another fraction involves using a reciprocal. A *reciprocal* is a fraction that is the result of switching the numerator and denominator in the fraction. For example, the reciprocal of ⅔ is 3⁄2. The product of a fraction and its reciprocal is always 1.

$$\frac{2}{3} \times \frac{3}{2} = \frac{6}{6} = \mathbf{1}$$

To divide fractions, the first fraction (the dividend) is multiplied by the reciprocal of the second fraction (the divisor). For example, ½ can be divided by ⅗ by simply multiplying ½ by the reciprocal of ⅗, which is 5⁄3. The result is ⅚.

$$\frac{1}{2} \div \frac{3}{5} = \frac{1}{2} \times \frac{5}{3} = \mathbf{\frac{5}{6}}$$

Likewise, in order to calculate how many ¼ lb hamburger patties a butcher can make out of 12½ lb of ground beef, 12½ is divided by ¼. **See Figure 2-9.** The first step in dividing the fractions is to convert the mixed number 12½ to an improper fraction, which is 25⁄2. Next, 25⁄2 can be divided by ¼. This is done by multiplying 25⁄2 by 4⁄1 (the reciprocal of ¼), which results in 100⁄2. In this case, the result is equal to the whole number 50. Therefore, the butcher can make 50 hamburger patties at ¼ lb each out of 12½ lb of ground beef.

Dividing Fractions

Example: How many ¼ lb hamburger patties can be made from 12½ lb of ground beef?

$$12\frac{1}{2} \div \frac{1}{4} =$$

DIVIDEND — $12\frac{1}{2}$; DIVISOR — $\frac{1}{4}$

1. Convert the mixed number to an improper fraction.

$$12\frac{1}{2} = \frac{(12 \times 2) + 1}{2} = \frac{24 + 1}{2} = \frac{25}{2}$$

2. Multiply the dividend by the reciprocal of the divisor.

$$\frac{25}{2} \times \boxed{\frac{4}{1}} = \frac{25 \times 4}{2 \times 1} = \frac{100}{2}$$

(RECIPROCAL OF DIVISOR: $\frac{4}{1}$; PRODUCT: $\frac{100}{2}$)

3. Reduce the product to lowest terms.

$$\frac{100}{2} = \frac{50}{1} = 50$$

Answer: 50 hamburger patties

Figure 2-9. Dividing fractions requires converting the divisor fraction into its reciprocal.

Checkpoint 2-2

1. What is a fraction?

____

____

2. A fraction contains a numerator and a denominator. Which is above the fraction bar, and which is below the fraction bar?

____

____

3. What is a mixed number?

____

____

4. Convert 25⁄3 to a mixed number.

____

____

2-2

Checkpoint (continued)

5. Convert $2\frac{5}{8}$ to an improper fraction.

6. Reduce $\frac{9}{12}$ to its lowest possible terms.

7. A recipe calls for $12\frac{1}{2}$ c of oats. If 2 times the recipe needs to be made, how many cups of oats will be required?

8. How many $\frac{1}{3}$ lb portions of potato salad can be made from $9\frac{2}{3}$ lb of potato salad?

Section 2-3 DECIMAL MEASUREMENTS

Just as with fractions, calculations that involve decimals require more advanced math skills. In food service, decimal measurements are used with metric units of measure and when working with digital scales. An understanding of decimals is also required when performing calculations involving money. A *decimal* is a number that represents part of a whole and can be expressed as a fraction with a denominator that is a power of 10 (such as 10, 100, 1000, and so on). For example, 0.1 is a decimal and is equal to $\frac{1}{10}$. Similarly, 0.25 is equal to $\frac{25}{100}$ and 0.575 is equal to $\frac{575}{1000}$, which are all parts of the whole number 1.

$$\frac{1}{10} = \mathbf{0.1} \qquad \frac{25}{100} = \mathbf{0.25} \qquad \frac{575}{1000} = \mathbf{0.575}$$

The period in the decimal is called a decimal point. The whole number is written to the left of the decimal point, and the decimal part is written to the right of the decimal point. The first digit to the left of the decimal is the ones place; the second digit to the left of the decimal place is the tens place; the third number to the left of the decimal place is the hundreds place, and so on. In other words, as the number moves to the left, each place is 10 times larger. Similarly, each place to the right of the decimal is 10 times smaller. Therefore, the first digit to the right of the decimal is the tenths place, followed by the hundredths place, followed by the thousandths place, and so on. **See Figure 2-10.** For example, 2.3 represents the whole number 2 and $3/10$, 14.35 represents the whole number 14 and $35/100$, and 342.567 represents the whole number 342 and $567/1000$.

$$2\frac{3}{10} = \mathbf{2.3} \qquad 14\frac{35}{100} = \mathbf{14.35} \qquad 342\frac{567}{1000} = \mathbf{342.567}$$

Decimal Numbers

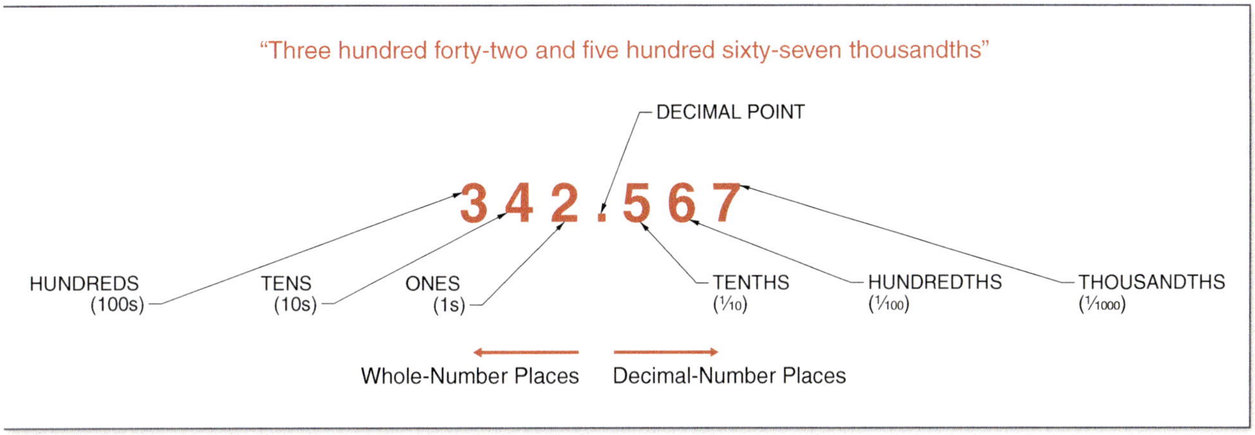

Figure 2-10. In a decimal, whole-number places are located to the left of the decimal point, and decimal-number places are located to the right of the decimal point.

Many monetary values are based on decimals. For example, the dollar ($1.00) is valued at 100 cents. Each cent is $1/100$ of a dollar ($0.01), and each nickel is $5/100$ of a dollar ($0.05). Likewise, each dime is $10/100$ or $1/10$ of a dollar ($0.10). Each quarter is $25/100$ or $1/4$ of a dollar ($0.25).

Converting between Fractions and Decimals

To change a fraction to a decimal, the numerator is divided by the denominator. For example, if $5/8$ oz of salt needs to be measured on a digital scale that displays weight in decimals, the fraction $5/8$ can be converted to a decimal by dividing the numerator by the denominator. **See Figure 2-11.** Since the decimal equivalent of $5/8$ is 0.625, then $5/8$ oz of salt can be measured as 0.625 oz on a digital scale.

To change a decimal to a fraction, the decimal is set as the numerator in a fraction without a decimal point. Then the denominator is calculated as a power of 10 depending on how many places there are in the decimal being converted. For example, to convert the measurement

0.75 lb of sugar to a fraction, use 75 as the numerator. Since there are two places in the decimal 0.75, the denominator is calculated as two powers of 10 (10 × 10 = 100). With the denominator set as 100, the fraction becomes 75⁄100. After reducing the fraction 75⁄100 to the lowest terms, the final answer is ¾. **See Figure 2-12.**

Converting Fractions to Decimals

Example: Convert ⅝ oz to a decimal.

1. Arrange the numerator as the dividend and the denominator as the divisor.
2. If the divisor is greater than the dividend, add a decimal point and a zero to the right of the dividend.
3. Divide the numerator by the denominator, adding zeros as necessary. Place a decimal point in the quotient above the decimal point in the dividend.

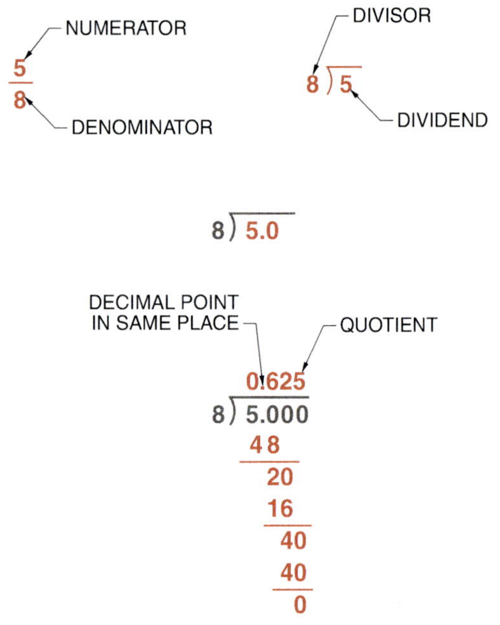

Answer: 0.625 oz

Figure 2-11. To convert a fraction to a decimal, divide the numerator by the denominator.

Converting Decimals to Fractions

Example: Convert 0.75 lb to a fraction.

1. Set the decimal as the numerator in a fraction (without a decimal point).
2. Set the denominator equal to a power of 10 based on the number of decimal places in the decimal being converted.
3. Reduce the fraction to lowest possible terms. (Convert an improper fraction to a mixed number if necessary.)

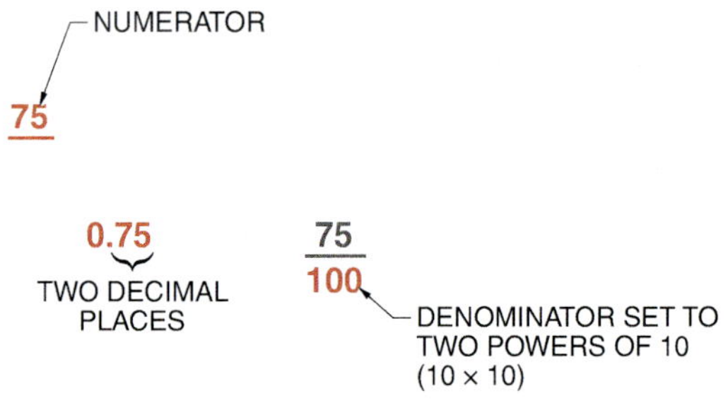

$$\frac{75}{100} = \frac{75 \div 25}{100 \div 25} = \frac{3}{4}$$

Answer: ¾ lb

Figure 2-12. Any decimal can be converted to a fraction by setting the denominator as a power of 10.

Rounding Decimals

Rounding is the process of replacing a number with another number of similar value. Numbers, including decimals, are often rounded to make calculations easier, but it is important to remember that rounded numbers are less accurate than unrounded numbers.

The first step in rounding a decimal is to decide which digit to round to. Then, look at the next digit to the right. If the next digit to the right is less than five (4, 3, 2, 1, or 0), drop that digit and any others that follow. This is referred to as rounding down. If the next digit to the right is five or more (5, 6, 7, 8, or 9), increase the rounding digit by one and drop any digits that follow. This is referred to as rounding up. **See Figure 2-13.**

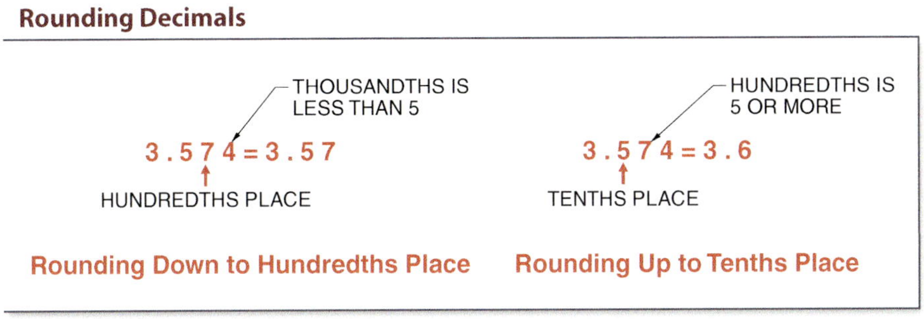

Figure 2-13. To round decimals, decide which digit to keep, and then round that digit up or down based on the value of the next digit to the right.

For example, if the decimal 3.574 is rounded to the hundredths place, it would be rounded down to 3.57 since the next digit to the right of the hundredths place is 4. If 3.574 is rounded to the tenths place, it would be rounded up to 3.6 since the next digit to the right of the tenths place is 7.

Also, the more digits there are in a rounded decimal, the more accurate it is. For example, a decimal rounded to three places (the thousandths place) represents a higher degree of accuracy than a decimal rounded to two places (the hundredths place).

Decimal numbers are often rounded to whole numbers. The process is the same, and the rounding digit is in the ones place. The next digit to the right is the digit in the tenths place. If the tenths digit is less than five, round down. If it is five or greater, round up. The decimal point can be dropped in either case. For example, 62.3 rounded to a whole number is 62, and 62.7 rounded to a whole number is 63.

Adding and Subtracting Decimals

To add or subtract decimals, the decimal points are first aligned. Then, either addition or subtraction is performed normally as with whole numbers. The decimal point does not move.

For example, three honeydew melons are weighed separately on a digital scale. The results are 2.35 kg, 2.7 kg, and 2.24 kg. The total weight when added is 7.29 kg. **See Figure 2-14.** If a total of 6.1 kg of edible honeydew melon is left after peeling and deseeding, the amount of waste is calculated to be 1.19 kg by subtracting 6.1 kg from the original 7.29 kg.

Adding and Subtracting Decimals

Adding

Example: **Three honeydew melons weigh 2.35 kg, 2.7 kg, and 2.24 kg. What is the total weight of all three honeydew melons?**

2.35 + 2.7 + 2.24 =

1. Stack numbers and align on decimal points.

$$\begin{array}{r} 2.35 \\ 2.7 \\ +\,2.24 \\ \hline \end{array}$$

2. Add digits column by column.

$$\begin{array}{r} {}^{1} \\ 2.35 \\ 2.7 \\ +\,2.24 \\ \hline 7.29 \end{array}$$

Answer: 7.29 kg

Subtracting

Example: **After trimming 7.29 kg of honeydew melon, 6.1 kg of edible fruit is obtained. How much waste was generated?**

7.29 − 6.1 =

1. Stack numbers and align on decimal points.

$$\begin{array}{r} 7.29 \\ -\,6.1 \\ \hline \end{array}$$

2. Subtract digits column by column.

$$\begin{array}{r} 7.29 \\ -\,6.1 \\ \hline 1.19 \end{array}$$

Answer: 1.19 kg

Figure 2-14. Decimals are added and subtracted in the same way as whole numbers.

Multiplying Decimals

Decimals are multiplied in the same way as whole numbers. However, placement of the decimal point in the final product is based on the total number of decimal places in the original calculation. For example, to find the total amount of peanut butter in 2.5 containers when each container holds 2.26 kg of peanut butter, 2.5 is multiplied by 2.26. The total is determined by multiplying 2.26 and

2.5 as if they were whole numbers (226 × 25 = 5650). Since there are a total of three decimal places (two in 2.26 and one in 2.5), the decimal point is inserted three places to the left (5.650). Note that when one or more zeroes are at the end of the decimal portion of a number, they can be dropped. Therefore, the final answer is 5.65 kg. **See Figure 2-15.**

Multiplying Decimals

Example: One container holds 2.26 kg of peanut butter. How much peanut butter is there in 2.5 containers?

2.26 × 2.5 =

1. Multiply decimals the same as whole numbers.

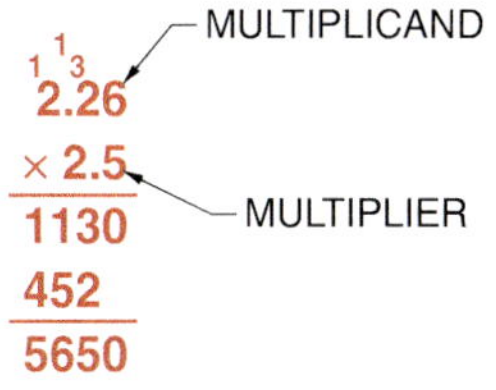

2. Add the number of decimal places to the right of the decimal point in the multiplicand to the number of decimal places to the right of the decimal point in the multiplier (2 + 1 = 3).

3. Insert a decimal point in the final product a number of spaces to the left that is equal to the number of spaces calculated in Step 2.

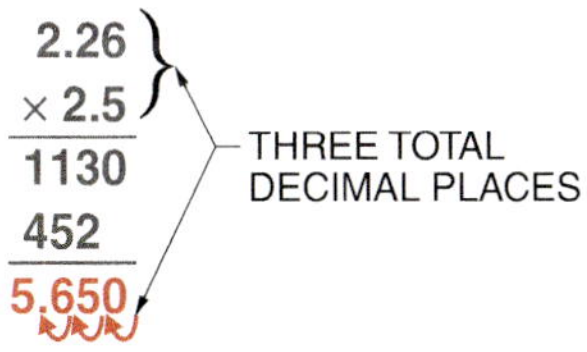

Answer: 5.65 kg

Figure 2-15. When multiplying decimals, the location of the decimal point in the product is based on the number of decimal places in the multiplicand and multiplier.

Dividing Decimals

To divide decimals, the first step is to move the decimal point in the divisor to the right until the divisor becomes a whole number. Next, the decimal point in the dividend is moved the same number of places to the right. If there are not enough digits in the dividend, zeroes are added to the places created by moving the decimal point.

For example, to divide 7.5 by 0.25, the decimal point is moved to the right two places in each number (0.25 becomes 25 and 7.5 becomes 750).

$$0.25\overline{)7.5} = 0.25\overline{)7.50} = 25.\overline{)750.}$$

Then, the decimal point in the dividend is brought up to the quotient, and division is performed the same way as with whole numbers.

$$25\overline{)750.} = 25\overline{)750.} = \begin{array}{r} 3\,0. \\ 25\overline{)7\,5\,0} \\ \underline{7\,5} \\ 0 \end{array}$$

Likewise, to determine the number of 150 g portions that can be obtained from 13.8 kg of sliced mushrooms, the first step is to keep the units of measure the same. Since 1 kg is equivalent to 1000 g, 150 g is equivalent to 0.15 kg (150 ÷ 1000 = 0.15). Then 13.8 is divided by 0.15. Thus, 92 portions can be made from 13.8 kg of sliced mushrooms. **See Figure 2-16.**

Dividing Decimals

Example: How many 0.15 kg portions of sliced mushrooms can be obtained from 13.8 kg of sliced mushrooms?

13.8 ÷ 0.15 =

1. Move the decimal point in the divisor to the right enough places to make the divisor a whole number.

   DIVISOR: $15.\overline{)13.8}$

2. Move the decimal point in the dividend the same number of places to the right.

   DIVIDEND: $15.\overline{)1380.}$

3. Bring the decimal point in the dividend up to the quotient.

   $15.\overline{)1380.}$

4. Divide the dividend by the divisor.

   QUOTIENT:
   $$\begin{array}{r} 92.0 \\ 15.\overline{)1380.} \\ \underline{135} \\ 30 \\ \underline{30} \\ 0 \end{array}$$

Answer: 92 portions

Figure 2-16. When the divisor and dividend in a division calculation are both multiplied by the same factor of 10, the value of the quotient does not change.

The process of moving the decimal point to the right in both the divisor and the dividend is the same as multiplying both numbers by powers of 10. For example, moving the decimal point one place to the right is the same as multiplying by 10. Moving it two places to the right is the same as multiplying by 100. Since both the divisor and the dividend are multiplied by the same power of 10, the value of the quotient is not affected.

2-3 Checkpoint

1. Define "decimal."

2. A recipe calls for 0.375 lb of sugar. What fraction represents the same amount of sugar?

3. A recipe calls for ⅔ lb of cornstarch. If the cornstarch is weighed on a digital scale, what decimal number would be equal to ⅔ lb? *(Round the answer to two decimal places.)*

4. Define "rounding."

5. Which represents a higher degree of accuracy: a decimal rounded to the tenths place or a decimal rounded to the hundredths place?

6. Write out the decimal 12.56 in words.

7. Write down the decimal that represents six and two tenths.

8. Round the decimal 34.6575 to the thousandths place.

9. Three beef tenderloins are to be prepared. One weighs 3.9 kg, another weighs 3.4 kg, and the last weighs 3.2 kg. What is the total weight of the three beef tenderloins?

2-3

Checkpoint (continued)

10. If a pork roast weighed 6.2 kg before being trimmed and 5.6 kg afterward, how much was trimmed off the roast?

____

____

11. If one can of ketchup contains 12.96 c of ketchup, how many cups of ketchup are in 3.5 cans?

____

____

12. How many 2.5 oz portions of salad dressing can be created from 62.5 oz of salad dressing?

____

____

Section 2-4 CALCULATING AREA, VOLUME, AND ANGLES

Measurements can be multiplied to calculate the area of a two-dimensional (flat) surface or the volume of a three-dimensional object. In food service, examples of two-dimensional surfaces include baking sheets, tabletops, and the floor space of a banquet room. Three-dimensional objects include items such as food containers and stockpots as well as walk-in coolers. Angles are used in food service to describe how to cut or portion certain foods and how to properly use some kitchen tools.

Calculating Area

Area is the size of a two-dimensional (flat) surface. Distance measurements with the same unit of measure must be used to calculate the area of a surface. To calculate the area of a square or rectangle, the following formula is applied:

$$A = L \times W$$

where

A = area

L = length

W = width

Area = Length × Width

When calculating area, the numbers in the two measurements are multiplied, and the units of measure are multiplied. Therefore, the area unit of measure is the square of the original unit. For example, 3 meters × 2 meters = 6 square meters, 20 centimeters × 10 centimeters = 200 square centimeters, 2 feet × 2 feet = 4 square feet, and 3 inches × 3 inches = 9 square inches. Square units of measure are abbreviated two different ways. **See Figure 2-17.**

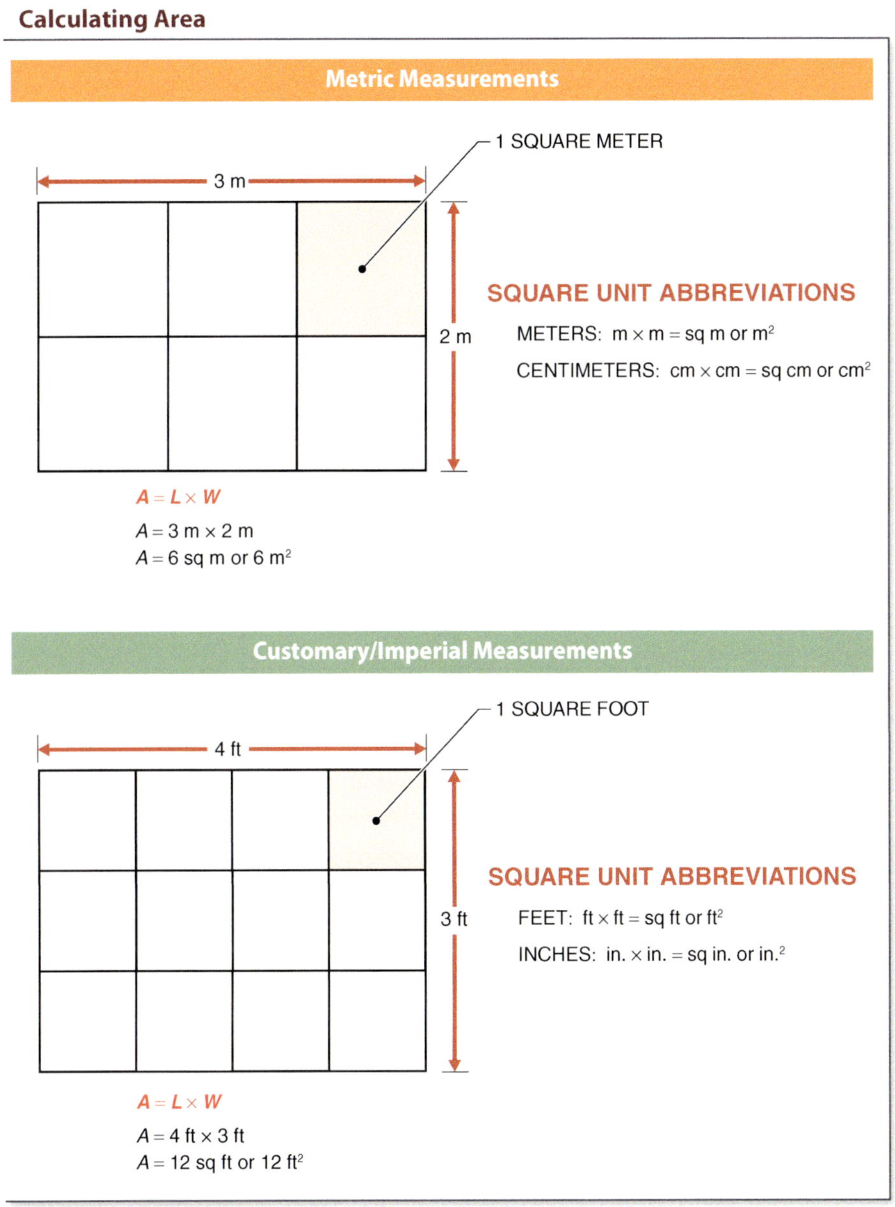

Figure 2-17. The area of a rectangle or square is equal to the length multiplied by the width and is expressed in square units of measure.

To calculate the area of the floor space of a given banquet room, the formula for the area of a rectangle is applied using the following problem-solving steps:

Problem-Solving Steps

Metric Measurements	Customary/Imperial Measurements
1. Determine the length and width of the banquet room.	
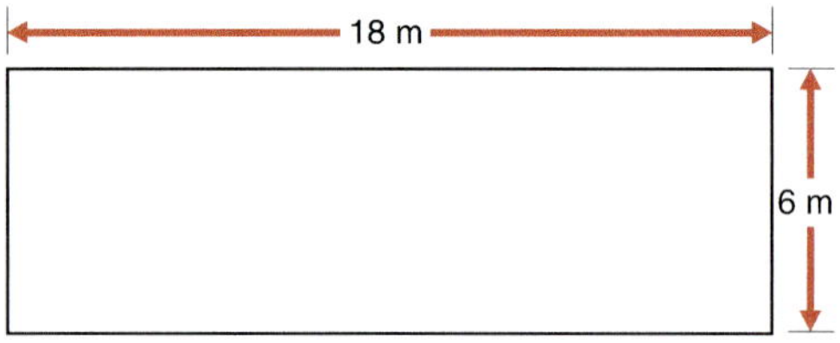	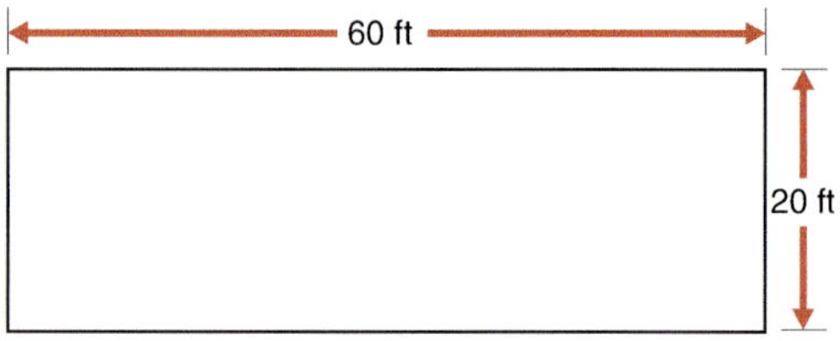
length = 18 m	length = 60 ft
width = 6 m	width = 20 ft
2. Apply the formula to calculate the area of the banquet room.	
A = L × W	**A = L × W**
A = 18 m × 6 m	A = 60 ft × 20 ft
A = **108 sq m**	A = **1200 sq ft**

Diameter and Radius of a Circle

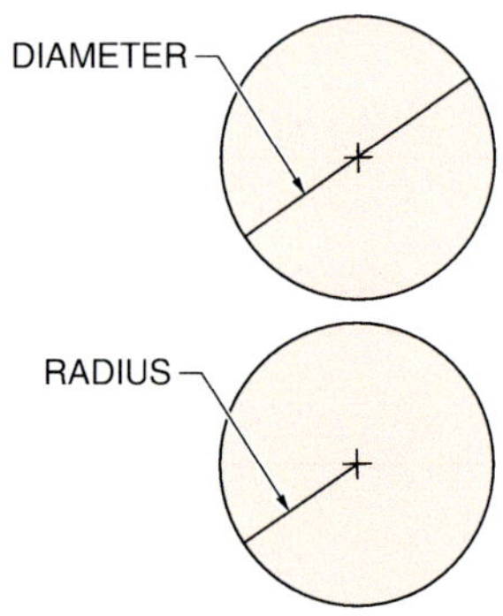

Figure 2-18. The radius of a circle is equal to one-half the diameter of the circle.

To calculate the area of a circle, the radius of the circle is first multiplied by itself (squared) and then multiplied by the constant number 3.14, shown in formulas as the Greek letter pi (π). The *radius* is the distance from the center of a circle to the edge of the circle and is equal to one-half the diameter of the circle. The *diameter* is the length of a line drawn through the center of a circle to both edges. **See Figure 2-18.** To calculate the area of a circle, the following formula is applied:

$$A = \pi \times r^2$$

Area = 3.14 × Radius²

where

A = area

π = 3.14 (constant number)

r = radius

To calculate the area of a given dining table, the formula for the area of a circle is applied using the following problem-solving steps:

Problem-Solving Steps

Metric Measurements

1. Determine the radius of the dining table.

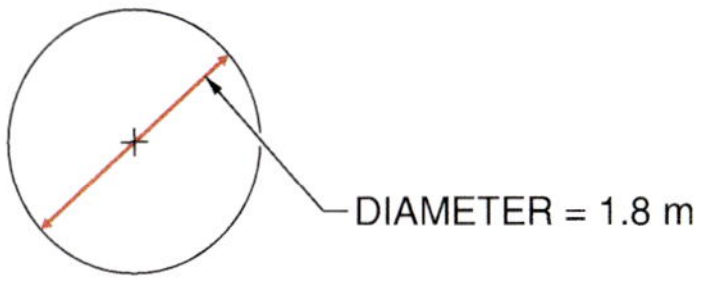

Diameter = 1.8 m
r = diameter ÷ 2
r = 1.8 m ÷ 2
r = 0.9 m

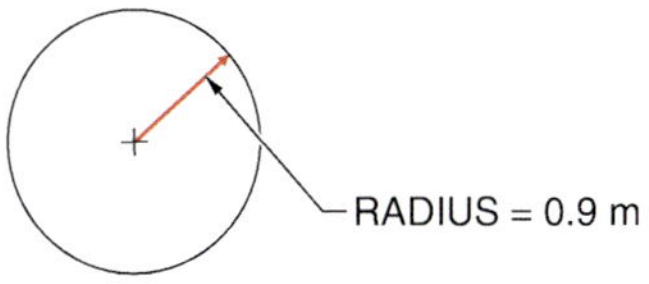

2. Apply the formula to calculate the area of the dining table.

$\mathbf{A} = \pi \times \mathbf{r}^2$

$A = 3.14 \times (0.9 \text{ m})^2$

$A = 3.14 \times 0.81$ sq m

$A =$ **2.54 sq m**

Customary/Imperial Measurements

1. Determine the radius of the dining table.

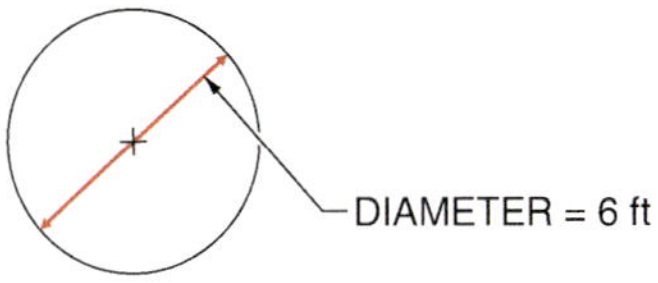

Diameter = 6 ft
r = diameter ÷ 2
r = 6 ft ÷ 2
r = 3 ft

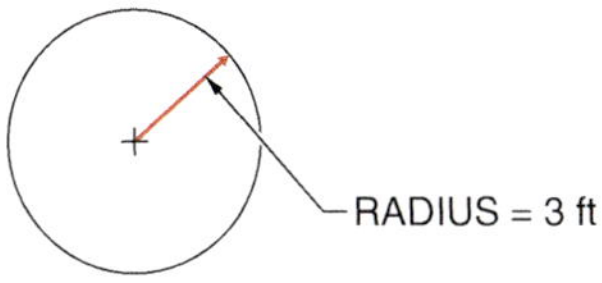

2. Apply the formula to calculate the area of the dining table.

$\mathbf{A} = \pi \times \mathbf{r}^2$

$A = 3.14 \times (3 \text{ ft})^2$

$A = 3.14 \times 9$ sq ft

$A =$ **28.26 sq ft**

Calculating Volume

Volume represents the amount of physical space a substance occupies or the amount of physical space inside an object. Distance measurements with the same unit of measure can be used to calculate the volume of a three-dimensional object, such as a food container. When calculating volume, the resulting unit of measure is the cube of the original unit. For example, meters × meters × meters = cubic meters, centimeters × centimeters × centimeters = cubic centimeters, feet × feet × feet = cubic feet, and inches × inches × inches = cubic inches. Cubic units of measure are abbreviated two different ways:

m × m × m = cu m or m^3

cm × cm × cm = cu cm or cm^3

ft × ft × ft = cu ft or ft^3

in. × in. × in. = cu in. or $in.^3$

In food service, it is common to refer to some equipment by capacity, such as a 9 L stockpot or a 250 cu ft walk-in cooler. *Capacity* is the volume that can be placed inside an empty three-dimensional object. For example, a steam kettle with a capacity of 30 L can hold a volume of liquid equal to 30 L. Likewise, a 20 cu ft refrigerator can hold 10 boxes of food that are 2 cu ft each (10 × 2 = 20).

The volume equivalent between cubic centimeters and liters is 1000 cu cm = 1 L. Therefore, to change a volume measured in cubic centimeters to liters (a smaller unit to a larger unit), the number of cubic centimeters is divided by 1000. For example, to calculate the volume, in liters, of a stockpot with a volume of 10,000 cu cm, 10,000 is simply divided by 1000.

10,000 cu cm = **10 L** (10,000 ÷ 1000 = 10)

Similarly, the volume equivalent between cubic inches and quarts is 57.8 cu in. = 1 qt. Therefore, to change a volume measured in cubic inches to quarts (a smaller unit to a larger unit), the number of cubic inches is divided by 57.8. For example, to calculate the volume, in quarts, of a stockpot with a volume of 1000 cu in., 1000 is simply divided by 57.8.

1000 cu in. = **17.3 qt** (1000 ÷ 57.8 = 17.3)

To calculate the volume of a rectangular object, the following formula is applied:

$$V = L \times W \times H$$

Volume = Length × Width × Height

where

V = volume

L = length

W = width

H = height (or depth)

To calculate the volume (capacity) of a given walk-in cooler, the formula for calculating the volume of a rectangular object is applied using the following problem-solving steps:

Problem-Solving Steps

Metric Measurements	Customary/Imperial Measurements

1. Determine the length, width, and height of the walk-in coolers shown below.

Metric Measurements	Customary/Imperial Measurements
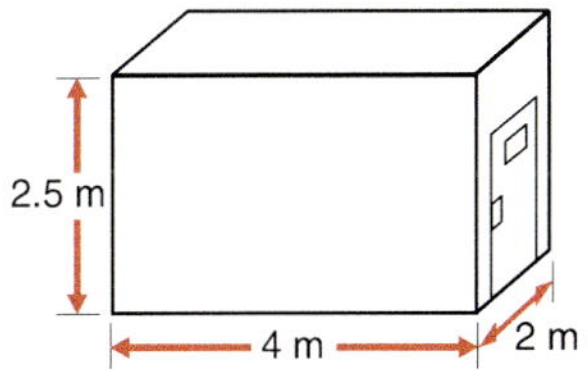	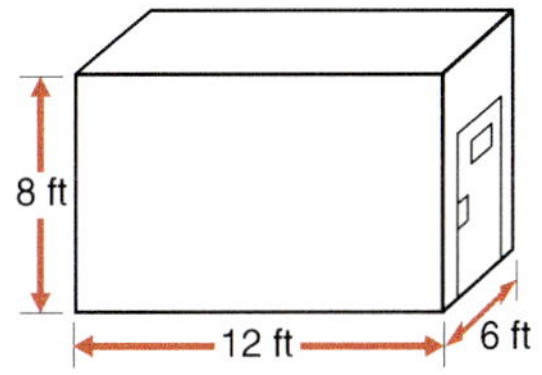
L = 4 m W = 2 m H = 2.5 m	L = 12 ft W = 6 ft H = 8 ft

2. Apply the formula for determining the volume of the walk-in coolers.

Metric Measurements	Customary/Imperial Measurements
$V = L \times W \times H$	$V = L \times W \times H$
V = 4 m × 2 m × 2.5 m	V = 12 ft × 6 ft × 8 ft
V = **20 cu m**	V = **576 cu ft**

To calculate the volume of an object shaped like a cylinder, such as a stockpot, the area of the circular base (or opening) of the object is multiplied by the height (or depth) of the object. The following formula is used to calculate the volume of a cylinder:

$$V = \pi \times r^2 \times H$$

$$\text{Volume} = 3.14 \times \text{Radius}^2 \times \text{Height}$$

where

V = volume

π = 3.14 (constant number)

r = radius of the base

H = height

To calculate the volume in liters of a given stockpot, the formula for calculating the volume of a cylinder is applied using the following problem-solving steps:

Problem-Solving Steps

Metric Measurements

1. Determine the radius and height of the stockpot shown below.

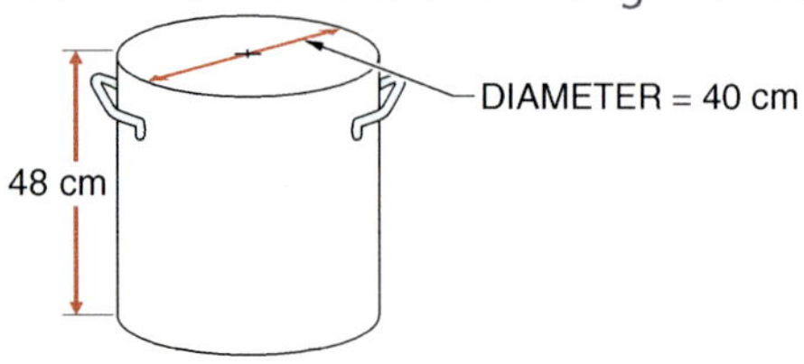

r = diameter ÷ 2
r = 40 cm ÷ 2 = 20 cm
H = 48 cm

2. Apply the formula for calculating the volume of the stockpot.

$V = \pi \times r^2 \times H$
$V = 3.14 \times (20\text{ cm})^2 \times 48\text{ cm}$
$V = 3.14 \times 20\text{ cm} \times 20\text{ cm} \times 48\text{ cm}$
$V = 3.14 \times 19{,}200$ cu cm
$V = 60{,}288$ cu cm

3. Change 60,288 cubic centimeters to liters (1000 cu cm = 1 L).

60,288 cu cm ÷ 1000 = 60.288
60.288 = **60.3 L**

Customary/Imperial Measurements

1. Determine the radius and height of the stockpot shown below.

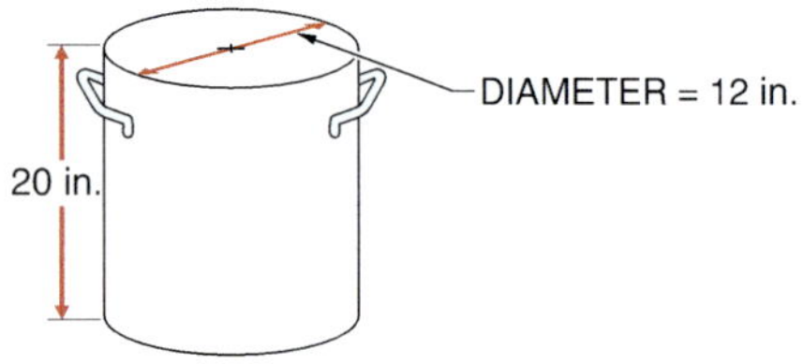

r = diameter ÷ 2
r = 12 in. ÷ 2 = 6 in.
H = 20 in.

2. Apply the formula for calculating the volume of the stockpot.

$V = \pi \times r^2 \times H$
$V = 3.14 \times (6\text{ in.})^2 \times 20\text{ in.}$
$V = 3.14 \times 6\text{ in.} \times 6\text{ in.} \times 20\text{ in.}$
$V = 3.14 \times 720$ cu in.
$V = 2260.8$ cu in.

3. Change 2260.8 cubic inches to quarts (57.8 cu in. = 1 qt).

2260.8 ÷ 57.8 = 39.1
39.1 qt

Calculating Angles

An *angle* is a figure consisting of two straight lines that intersect (cross) at a common point. For example, a circle can be divided into four equal parts by drawing a horizontal line and a vertical line through the center, such as when a pizza is cut into four equal slices. Angles are created where the lines intersect at the center (common point) of the circle.

The size of an angle is measured in degrees and is abbreviated using the degree symbol (°). **See Figure 2-19.** A full circle has 360 degrees (360°). A circle divided into two equal pieces has two angles, each measuring 180° (360° ÷ 2 = 180°). A circle divided into four equal pieces has four angles, each measuring 90° (360° ÷ 4 = 90°). A circle divided into eight equal pieces has eight angles, each measuring 45° (360° ÷ 8 = 45°). When a circle is divided into equal pieces with the center as its common point, each piece will have the same angle measurement.

Degrees and Angles

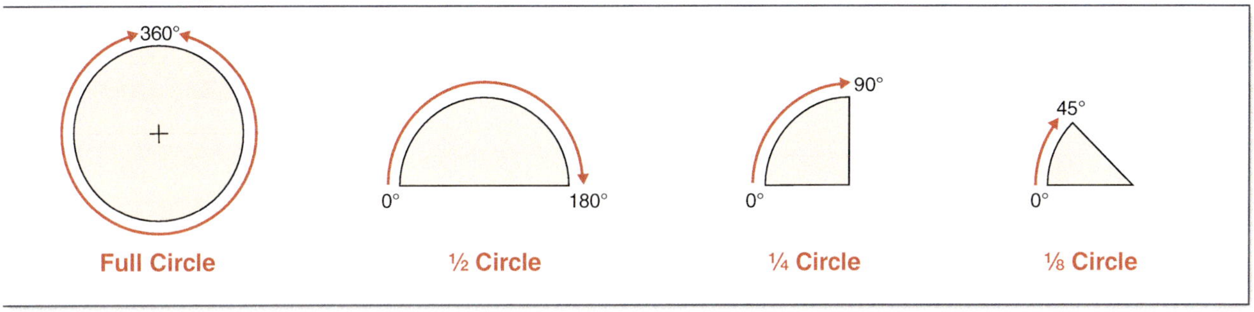

Figure 2-19. The size of an angle is measured in degrees and is abbreviated using the degree symbol (°).

Angles are also used in food service to specify how to position a kitchen tool. For example, a recipe instruction may state to "hold the immersion blender at a 60° angle when puréeing the soup" or to "cut the carrots on a bias by holding the knife at a 45° angle." **See Figure 2-20.**

Using Angles

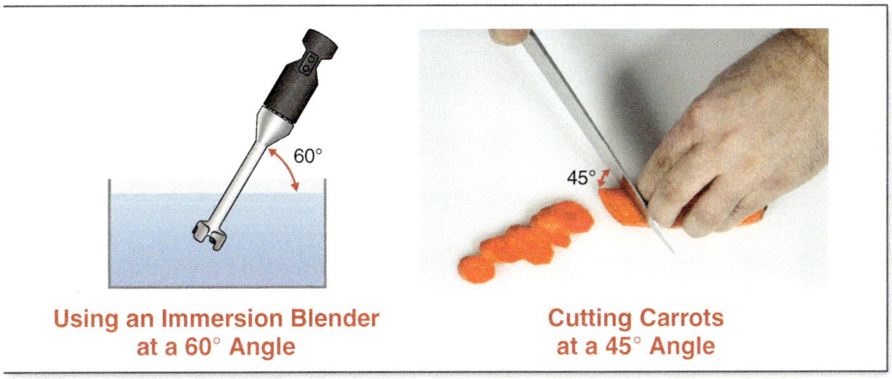

Figure 2-20. Angles can be used in recipe instructions to explain how to hold kitchen equipment when performing different tasks.

2-4 Checkpoint

1. Define "area."

2. Stove top A measures 90 cm long by 66 cm wide. Stove top B measures 98 cm long by 62 cm wide. Which stove top has the larger area?

3. How is the radius of a circle related to the diameter of a circle?

4. What is the area of a round serving platter that measures 14 in. in diameter?

5. What is capacity?

6. A storage room measures 5 m long by 4 m wide by 2.5 m high. What is the total capacity of the storage room in cubic meters?

7. What is the capacity (in liters) of a stockpot with a diameter of 24 cm and a height of 18 cm? *(Round the answer to a whole number.)*

8. How many equal pieces has a circle been cut into if each piece has an angle of 90 degrees?

Section 2-5 BASIC STATISTICS

Statistics is a mathematical system for evaluating sets of numbers. The three most common statistical measurements of a set of numbers are the average (or mean), the median, and the mode.

An *average* is the sum of a set of numbers divided by how many numbers there are in the set. Another term for average is "mean." A *median* is the middle value within a set of numbers that are arranged in numerical order. The median can be pictured as a set of numbers where half of the set are numbers less than the median and the other half of the set are numbers greater than the median. The *mode* is the value that appears most frequently within a set of numbers.

> **Average Guide**
>
> **To calculate the average of a set of numbers such as:**
>
> 10 14 11 13
>
> Step 1: Add the numbers in the set.
>
> $10 + 14 + 11 + 13 = 48$
>
> Step 2: Divide the sum (48) by how many numbers are in the set (4).
>
> $48 \div 4 = 12$

Statistics are most commonly used in food service to calculate averages, such as the following:

- the average number of each menu item ordered per day
- the average number of customers per day
- the average number of hours worked per month per employee
- the average amount of a guest check
- the average amount of an operation's utility bills

Statistical measurements are often used with counts in the professional kitchen. For example, shrimp are packaged by count (number per pound) for a given size. A bag of 16/20 count jumbo shrimp contains between 16 and 20 shrimp per pound. A 5 lb bag of 16/20 count colossal shrimp contains between 80 shrimp ($5 \times 16 = 80$) and 100 shrimp ($5 \times 20 = 100$).

If the shrimp in 9 bags of 16/20 count shrimp that are 5 lb each were actually counted, the average, median, and mode of those numbers could be calculated. If the bags of shrimp each contain between 16 and 20 shrimp per pound, each 5 lb bag should contain between 80 and 100 shrimp ($16 \times 5 = 80$ and $20 \times 5 = 100$). Therefore, the average, median, and mode should all be between 80 and 100.

Creating Data Tables

When analyzing a group of numbers, it is sometimes helpful to write them down in a data table. A *data table* is a collection of information that is organized into a set of rows and columns. The top row of each column contains a heading that describes the data in that column. **See Figure 2-21.**

Data Tables

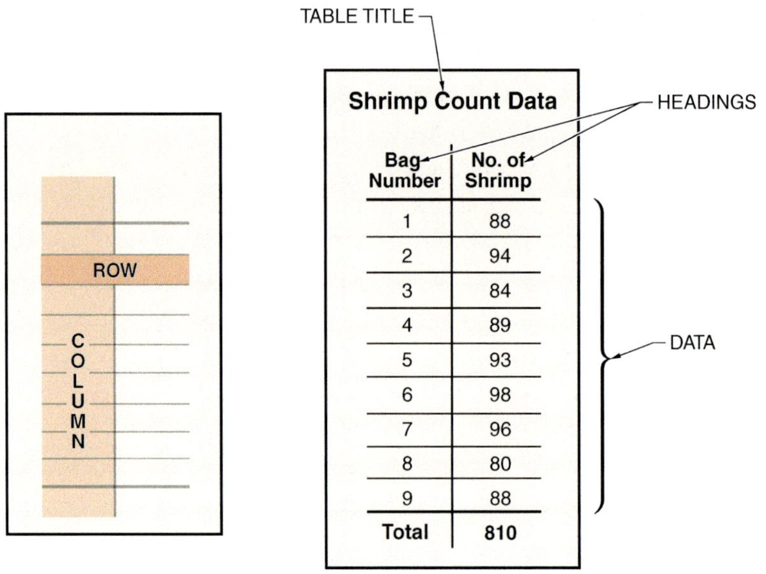

Shrimp Count Data

Bag Number	No. of Shrimp
1	88
2	94
3	84
4	89
5	93
6	98
7	96
8	80
9	88
Total	**810**

Figure 2-21. A data table is a good tool for organizing sets of numerical information.

According to the data table, the total of shrimp counted is 810, and the total number of bags is 9. The total number of shrimp is required in order to calculate the average number of shrimp in each bag. In this case, there is an average of 90 shrimp per 5 lb bag.

810 shrimp ÷ 9 bags = **90 shrimp per bag**

To find the median of the number of shrimp per bag, the data in the column for number of shrimp are listed in order from lowest to highest.

80 84 88 88 **89** 93 94 96 98

The median is 89 because it is the value that falls between the lower half of numbers (80, 84, 88, and 88) and the upper half of numbers (93, 94, 96, and 98). The mode is 88 shrimp since it is the most common number in the group.

80 84 **88 88** 89 93 94 96 98

By reviewing these statistics, it is confirmed that a 5 lb bag of 16/20 count shrimp from this seafood vendor will contain an average of 90 shrimp. Also, about half the bags will contain less than 89 shrimp (the median), and the other half will contain more than 89 shrimp. It will be most common to find 88 shrimp (the mode) in any given bag.

Graphing Data

When dealing with a large group of numbers, it may be easier to interpret data by looking at it in a graph rather than a data table. For example, a line graph consists of an *x*-axis (horizontal axis), a *y*-axis (vertical axis), and data. In the shrimp example, the two sets of data are the individual bag numbers and the number of shrimp per bag.

To represent data from the table in a graph, the bag numbers are placed along the *x*-axis, and the counts of shrimp are placed along the *y*-axis. To make the graph easy to read, the lowest number on each axis should be slightly less than the lowest data value in the table. Likewise, the highest number on each axis should be slightly more than the highest data value in the table. Since the smallest bag number is 1 and the highest bag number is 9, a range of 0 to 10 would be used for the *x*-axis. Since the smallest shrimp count is 80 and the highest is 98, a range of 76 to 100 would be a good range to use for the *y*-axis.

Data points are placed on the graph to match the information in the data table. For example, bag 1 has a count of 88, so a data point is placed on the graph where the number 1 on the *x*-axis intersects with number 88 on the *y*-axis. Bag 2 has a count of 94, so a data point is placed where the number 2 on the *x*-axis intersects with number 94 on the *y*-axis, and so forth. Lines are drawn to connect the data points. The average (mean), median, and mode are calculated and represented by horizontal lines. **See Figure 2-22.**

Graphs

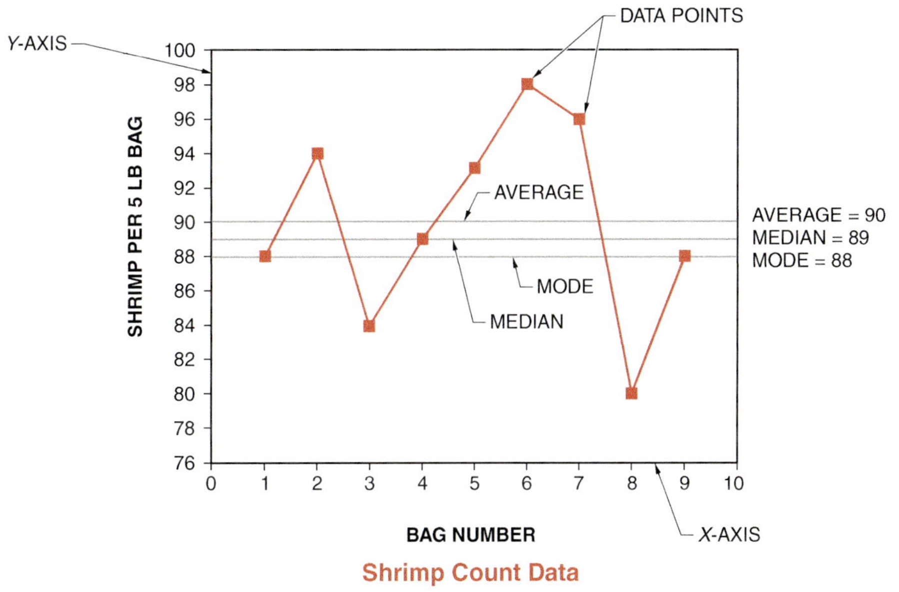

Figure 2-22. A graph is a visual representation of data.

2-5 Checkpoint

1. Explain how to calculate a statistical average.

---

2. Define "median."

---

3. Define "mode."

Use the following data table to answer the remaining questions. The number of tortilla chips were counted in 11 different 1.5 oz bags of tortilla chips.

Bag Number	1	2	3	4	5	6	7	8	9	10	11	**Total**
Number of Chips	12	14	16	22	16	16	18	17	19	20	18	**188**

4. What is the average number of tortilla chips found in the 11 bags? *(Round the answer to a whole number.)*

---

5. What is the median of the number of tortilla chips found in the 11 bags?

---

6. What is the mode of the number of tortilla chips found in the 11 bags?

Math Exercises 2

Work each problem in the space provided. Write the final answer on the blank provided. Round all decimal answers to the hundredths place, and reduce all fraction answers to lowest terms. Unless otherwise noted, keep answers to fraction problems in fraction form and answers to decimal problems in decimal form.

Leaf icon indicates a math problem with a sustainability focus.

Example:

170 grams A cheese plate for two is served with 35 grams of Gorgonzola, 40 grams of Muenster, 45 grams of Gouda, and 50 grams of white Cheddar. How many grams of cheese are on the plate?

35 grams + 40 grams + 45 grams + 50 grams = ***170 grams***

__________ **1.** If an appetizer with 140 g of buffalo chicken wings and 85 g of blue cheese dressing are served in a basket that weighs 55 g, what is the combined weight of the chicken wings, dressing, and basket?

__________ **2.** If 6 L of soup was prepared and 300 mL of soup remains, how much soup was served?

__________ **3.** A restaurant reduces expenses and leftovers by preparing cured meats in-house and shopping locally for the fruits and cheeses used on their charcuterie boards. If a filled charcuterie board weighs 42 oz and the board alone weighs 23 oz, what is the weight in pounds and ounces of the foods on the board?

_______________ **4.** A Caprese salad recipe uses 2 kg of mozzarella cheese, 1 kg of heirloom tomatoes, and 2 cans, 250 g each, of black olives. What is the combined weight in kilograms of the cheese, tomatoes, and olives if the recipe is doubled?

_______________ **5.** If a server brews 12 L of coffee per day 7 days a week, how many total liters of coffee does the server brew per week?

_______________ **6.** If a cook peeled 96 kg of potatoes in 4 hours, how many kilograms of potatoes did the cook peel per hour on average?

_______________ **7.** What is the total amount of salt and pepper in a recipe that requires $\frac{3}{8}$ oz of salt and $\frac{1}{8}$ oz of pepper?

_______________ **8.** If a spice container holds $\frac{7}{8}$ oz of oregano and $\frac{5}{8}$ oz is used, how much oregano is left in the container?

_______________ **9.** A meatloaf recipe calls for ½ lb of ground beef, ½ lb of ground veal, and ½ lb of ground pork. How many total pounds of meat does the recipe require?

_______________ **10.** A prep cook needs to grate cheese for three different recipes. The first recipe calls for 1⅜ lb, the second calls for 2½ lb, and the third calls for 1¼ lb. What is the total amount of cheese that must be grated?

_______________ **11.** A coffeehouse prepares a pumpkin-spice iced latte with a 2 fl oz shot of espresso, 1½ fl oz of pumpkin-spice syrup, 3¼ fl oz of milk, and 5¼ fl oz of crushed ice. How many fluid ounces are in each pumpkin-spice iced latte?

_______________ **12.** A chef purchases whole beef chuck rolls and grinds them in-house to lower costs. If the week's menu requires 12½ lb of ground beef for meatloaf, 15⅜ lb for hamburgers, and 6¾ lb for chili, how many total pounds of ground beef does the chef need?

_______________ **13.** A server starts a shift with 20½ L of iced tea available for beverage service. After lunch, 2⅓ L of iced tea are left. How much iced tea did the server use during lunch?

______________ **14.** If $17\frac{3}{4}$ lb of stew meat are needed but a chef only has $5\frac{7}{8}$ lb, how many more pounds of stew meat are needed?

______________ **15.** A recipe calls for $4\frac{2}{3}$ c of stock. If $4\frac{1}{2}$ times the recipe needs to be made, how much stock is needed?

______________ **16.** If each container holds 3.5 kg of salad dressing, how many kilograms of salad dressing are there in 6.5 containers?

______________ **17.** If each potato weighs $\frac{2}{3}$ lb, how many potatoes are there in a 50 lb case?

honn
______________ **18.** How many $\frac{1}{4}$ lb pork chops can be cut from a $9\frac{1}{2}$ lb boneless pork loin?

Trick

_______________ **19.** A quick-service restaurant stopped serving meals on disposable, nonbiodegradable plates in favor of more eco-friendly, washable plates. Prior to the switch, how many of the nonbiodegradable plates had the restaurant been using each day if a disposable plate weighed 1⁄60 lb and 5 lb were typically used each day?

_______________ **20.** A café will use the 6 zucchinis that remain in inventory to make one loaf of zucchini bread and a spiralized zucchini "noodle" salad. How many zucchinis are available to make the salad if 2 c of grated zucchini are needed for the bread and a zucchini yields ⅔ c of grated zucchini?

_______________ **21.** How many ¼ c portions can be served from 12 qt of potato salad?

_______________ **22.** How many gallons of soup are needed if 96 people at an event will be served a ½ c portion of soup?

_______________ **23.** The owner of a concession stand lowers costs by using sustainably farmed, local ingredients to prepare lemonade and sun tea that are then served in 250 mL recyclable cups. If the day's sales include 12.125 L of lemonade, 3.5 L of unsweetened sun tea, and 4.375 L of sweetened sun tea, how many 250 mL cups of these beverages were sold?

_______________ **24.** After trimming 200 g of surface fat from a 7.2 kg strip loin, how many 280 g New York strip steaks can be cut from the loin?

_______________ **25.** The surface fat from trimming beef loins is placed in a freezer bag and frozen for later use in beef stock preparation. If 1 c of water is needed for every ½ lb of surface fat, how many pounds of surface fat are needed to make 3½ gal. of beef stock?

_______________ **26.** A chicken breast weighs 1.375 lb on a digital scale. What is that same weight as a mixed number?

____________ **27.** What will be the decimal reading on a digital scale for a $1\frac{5}{8}$ lb steak?

____________ **28.** If a cantaloupe weighs $2\frac{3}{8}$ lb, a watermelon weighs 6.25 lb, and a honeydew melon weighs $3\frac{1}{2}$ lb, what is the total weight of all of the melons? (*Show the answer as a mixed number.*)

1026.5

____________ **29.** A restaurant receives an electric bill for \$245.67, a gas bill for \$734.90, and a water bill for \$45.93. What is the total amount of the three utility bills?

245.67 + 734.90 + 45.93 = 1026.5

2.38Kg

____________ **30.** If a whole turkey weighs 8.24 kg before the breasts are removed and 5.86 kg after the breasts are removed, what is the weight of the turkey breasts?

8.24 Kg − 5.86Kg = 2.38 Kg.

614.10

____________ **31.** A manager in a restaurant earns \$17.25 per hour. How much will the manager earn for 35.6 hours worked?

\$17.25 X 35.6 = \$614.10

_______________ **32.** To meet consumer demand and promote sustainability, a fast-casual restaurant adds more plant-based menu items and reduces meat portions from 225 g to 170 g per dish. On average, 69 portions of the 225 g meat dishes priced at $8.95 had sold daily, while 87 portions of the 170 g meat dishes priced at $7.25 now sell daily. How much more daily revenue results from this menu change?

~~69 × 8.95 = 617.55~~

~~87 × 7.25 = 628.52~~

_______________ **33.** A restaurant purchases a new ENERGY STAR-certified conveyer-rack dishwasher that uses 1.44 L of water per rack compared to the old dishwasher that used 3.37 L per rack. If the restaurant washes 243 racks per hour, how many liters of water will be saved after 8 hours of dishwasher use?

1.44 − 3.37 = 1.93

1.93 × 243 × 8 = 375 192L

_______________ **34.** If 16.4 kg of cheese is cut into 400 g pieces, how many pieces of cheese will there be?

50g

_______________ **35.** If 7.2 kg of cookie dough is prepared and the dough is portioned into 144 identically sized cookies before baking, how many grams does each unbaked cookie weigh?

_______________ **36.** A restaurant's switch to earth-friendly, to-go containers has been worth the higher costs, as it has resulted in increased business. The earth-friendly containers cost $20 for 30 containers, while the previously used plastic containers cost $32 for 50 containers. If 1200 containers were used last month, how much more was spent on the earth-friendly containers than on the plastic containers?

_______________ **37.** A restaurant purchases a new ENERGY STAR-certified washing machine, which uses less water and energy to launder their kitchen towels and aprons. The new washing machine uses 2 tbsp of detergent per load, while the old washing machine used 1/4 c per load. If the restaurant washes 42 loads in one month, how many tablespoons of detergent will be saved monthly?

_______________ **38.** Based on the chart below, if a recipe calls for 2.3 kg of asparagus, 1.4 kg of broccoli crowns, and 2 packages, 250 g each, of mushrooms, how much more will be spent if organic vegetables are used instead of nonorganic vegetables? (*Round each price to the nearest cent.*)

Vegetable Prices

Vegetable Type	*Regular Price*	*Organic Price*
Asparagus	$7.57/kg	$9.98/kg
Broccoli crowns	$1.38/kg	$3.34/kg
Mushrooms (250-gram package)	$1.50 ea.	$2.00 ea.

759 ________ **39.** If brownies are baked in a pan measuring 33 cm long by 23 cm wide, how many square centimeters of brownies will the pan hold?

________ **40.** A rectangular buffet that measures 0.9 m by 5 m long has a hot-foods section and cold-foods section. If the cold-foods section requires a space of 0.9 m by 2 m, how many square meters remain for the hot-foods section?

________ **41.** If the base of a round wedding cake is 20 cm in diameter, what is the area of the base of the wedding cake?

________ **42.** What is the difference in square centimeters between the area of a 26 cm circular plate and the area of a 26 cm square plate?

________ **43.** If a rectangular chafing dish holds a container that measures 38 cm long by 20 cm wide by 8 cm deep, how many liters of food will the chafing dish hold? (*Tip: 1 L = 1000 cu cm.*)

______ **44.** If a soup warmer holds a cylinder-shaped container that measures 22 cm in diameter and is 30 cm high, how many liters of soup will the container hold? (*Tip: 1 L = 1000 cu cm.*)

______ **45.** A cook is to prepare 8 L of soup and needs to determine which stockpot has the capacity to appropriately hold the soup. Based on the information below, should the cook use stockpot A or stockpot B to prepare the soup? (*Tip: 1000 cu cm = 1 L.*)

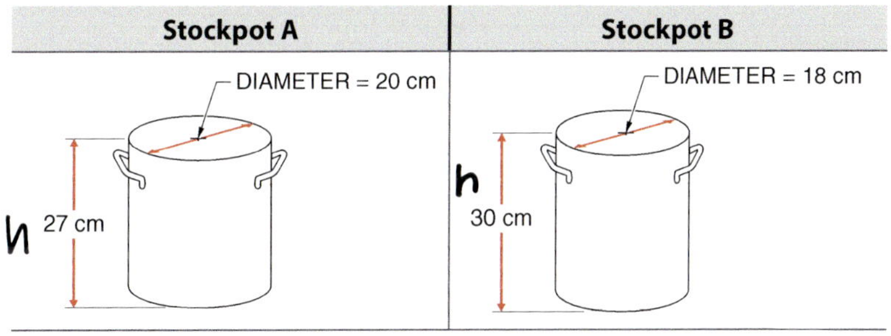

______ **46.** If a round pizza is cut into 12 equal pieces through the center, what is the angle measurement of each piece?

______ **47.** If all of the apples in 6 bags, 5 kg each, are counted and the total number of apples is 150, what is the average number of apples per bag?

_______________ **48.** If four customers in a restaurant are presented with checks in the amounts of \$54.32, \$67.90, \$89.25, and \$32.50, what is the average check amount per customer?

_______________ **49.** If four whole chickens weigh 1.15 kg, 1.28 kg, 1.37 kg, and 1.52 kg respectively, what is the average weight of the chickens?

_______________ **50.** The chart below shows one week of daily sales for a sandwich shop's smoked brisket sandwiches. Based on the chart, what is the mean, median, and mode of the smoked brisket sandwich sales for the week? (*Round each answer to the nearest whole number.*)

Day of the Week	Monday	Tuesday	Wednesday	Thursday	Friday	Saturday	Sunday
Sandwiches Sold	90	87	91	87	98	91	87

3

Converting Measurements and Scaling Recipes

Recipes are often changed to produce more or less food to meet the demands of a particular kitchen. Foodservice employees must be able to calculate new ingredient measurements for those changes in recipes. Often, measurements may need to be converted to different units of measure. Factors such as cooking times and temperatures also need to be considered when recipes are changed. By using solid math skills and paying close attention to detail, foodservice employees can make accurate changes to recipes while maintaining the quality of the food prepared.

Section 3-1: CONVERTING MEASUREMENTS

- Convert measurements within the metric, customary, and imperial measurement systems.
- Convert measurements between the metric, customary, and imperial measurement systems.
- Convert between volume and weight measurements.
- Explain why it is important to estimate answers when using a kitchen calculator.

Section 3-2: SCALING RECIPES

- Identify the most common elements of a standardized recipe.
- Calculate scaling factors based on recipe yield.
- Calculate scaling factors based on product availability.
- Multiply recipe ingredients by scaling factors.
- Explain how other scaling considerations of a recipe are affected when the yield is changed.

Key Terms

- converting
- cancelling
- conversion factor
- scaling
- standardized recipe
- yield
- portion size
- scaling factor

Learner Resources
atplearningresources.com
access code 267628

All-Clad Metalcrafters

Section 3-1 CONVERTING MEASUREMENTS

With a working knowledge of the standard units of measure used in the professional kitchen and an understanding of how measurements are calculated, foodservice employees can convert measurements. *Converting* is the process of changing a measurement with one unit of measure to an equivalent measurement with a different unit of measure. Three different types of measurement conversions are often performed in the professional kitchen:

- **Converting weight or volume measurements within the metric, customary, and imperial systems.** Converting grams to kilograms, liters to milliliters, ounces to pounds, and gallons to quarts are examples of this type of conversion.
- **Converting between metric and customary or imperial measurements.** Converting grams to ounces, kilograms to pounds, quarts to liters, and Fahrenheit to Celsius are examples of this type of conversion.
- **Converting between volume and weight measurements.** Converting teaspoons to grams, liters to kilograms, cups to ounces, and gallons to pounds are examples of this type of conversion. These conversions are unique because volume-to-weight equivalents are approximations and differ depending on the ingredient being measured.

Converting within the Metric System

The basic units of measure in the metric system include the gram (weight), the liter (volume), and the meter (length). These basic units are often accompanied by metric prefixes. Metric prefixes indicate multiples or fractions of ten. **See Figure 3-1.** Therefore, converting from one metric unit to another is accomplished by multiplying or dividing the measurement by a power of 10, or by simply moving the decimal point the correct number of places.

Metric Prefix Conversions								
Weight			**Volume**			**Length**		
1 kilogram (kg)	=	1000 g	1 kiloliter (kL)	=	1000 L	1 kilometer (km)	=	1000 m
1 hectogram (hg)	=	100 g	1 hectoliter (hL)	=	100 L	1 hectometer (hm)	=	100 m
1 decagram (dag)	=	10 g	1 decaliter (daL)	=	10 L	1 decameter (dam)	=	10 m
1 gram (g)			1 liter (L)			1 meter (m)		
1 decigram (dg)	=	0.1 g	1 deciliter (dL)	=	0.1 L	1 decimeter (dm)	=	0.1 m
1 centigram (cg)	=	0.01 g	1 centiliter (cL)	=	0.01 L	1 centimeter (cm)	=	0.01 m
1 milligram (mg)	=	0.001 g	1 milliliter (mL)	=	0.001 L	1 millimeter (mm)	=	0.001 m

Figure 3-1. Metric prefixes indicate multiples or fractions of ten.

To convert a smaller unit of measure to a larger unit of measure, the decimal point can be moved to the left the required number of spaces. Zeros are added as place holders when necessary. For example, to convert

1500 grams to kilograms, the decimal point is moved three spaces to the left. This produces the same result as dividing the number by three powers of 10 (10 × 10 × 10 = 1000). Therefore, 1500 g converts to 1.5 kg (1500 g ÷ 1000 = 1.5 kg).

Problem-Solving Steps

Example: Convert 1500 grams to kilograms.

1. Starting at grams on the chart, move three spaces to the left to get to kilograms.
2. Count each space as one decimal place.
3. Convert the measurement from grams to kilograms by moving the decimal point three places to the left.

Weight	1000 g	100 g	10 g	1	0.1 g	0.01 g	0.001 g
Unit	kilogram (kg)	hectogram (hg)	decagram (dag)	gram (g)	decigram (dg)	centigram (cg)	milligram (mg)

1500.

1500 g = **1.5 kg**

To convert a larger unit of measure to a smaller unit of measure, the decimal point can be moved to the right the required number of spaces. Zeros are added as place holders when necessary. For example, to convert 2.25 liters to milliliters, the decimal point is moved three spaces to the right. This produces the same result as multiplying the number by three powers of 10 (10 × 10 × 10 = 1000). Therefore, 2.25 L converts to 2250 mL (2.25 L × 1000 = 2250 mL).

Problem-Solving Steps

Example: Convert 2.25 liters to milliliters.

1. Starting at liters on the chart, move three spaces to the right to get to millilters.
2. Count each space as one decimal place.
3. Convert the measurement from liters to milliliters by moving the decimal point three places to the right.

Weight	1000 L	100 L	10 L	1	0.1 L	0.01 L	0.001 L
Unit	kiloliter (kL)	hectoliter (hL)	decaliter (daL)	liter (L)	deciliter (dL)	centiliter (cL)	milliliter (mL)

2.250

2.25 L = **2250 mL**

Converting within the Customary and Imperial Systems

To convert a measurement to a different unit within the customary or imperial measurement system, the measurement is first written as a fraction. For example, to convert 8 quarts to gallons, the first step is to write the original measurement as a fraction.

$$\frac{8\text{ qt}}{1}$$

The next step is to identify the conversion factor that the original measurement can be multiplied by to convert quarts to gallons and then write it as a fraction. In this case, the common equivalent of 4 qt = 1 gal. can be used. The equivalent can be written as a fraction in two ways, just like it is equally correct to say that "1 gallon is equivalent to 4 quarts" or "4 quarts are equivalent to 1 gallon."

$$\frac{1\text{ gal.}}{4\text{ qt}} \text{ or } \frac{4\text{ qt}}{1\text{ gal.}}$$

The equivalent is written so that the unit in the denominator is the same as the unit in the original measurement. Then, the original measurement is multiplied by the equivalent.

$$\frac{8\text{ qt}}{1} \times \frac{1\text{ gal.}}{4\text{ qt}}$$

When multiplied, the unit in the numerator of the original measurement (8 qt) cancels the matching unit in the denominator of the written equivalent (4 qt). *Cancelling* is the process of crossing out and eliminating matching units in the numerators and denominators of fractions in a calculation. Cancelling is shown by drawing a line through the matching units. In this example, the quarts cancel each other.

$$\frac{8\text{ }\cancel{\text{qt}}}{1} \times \frac{1\text{ gal.}}{4\text{ }\cancel{\text{qt}}} = \frac{8}{1} \times \frac{1\text{ gal.}}{4}$$

When multiplying fractions, the numerators are multiplied by each other, and the denominators are multiplied by each other.

$$\frac{8 \times 1\text{ gal.}}{1 \times 4} = \frac{8\text{ gal.}}{4}$$

Then, the numerator is divided by the denominator to obtain the final answer.

8 gal. ÷ 4 = **2 gal.**

> **Cancelling Guide**
>
> **Convert 4 pints to quarts.**
>
> **Step 1:** Write the measurement and the conversion factor as fractions in a multiplication calculation.
>
> $$\frac{4\text{ pt}}{1} \times \frac{1\text{ qt}}{2\text{ pt}}$$
>
> **Step 2:** Cancel the matching units in the numerators and denominators, and then multiply the resulting fractions.
>
> $$\frac{4\text{ }\cancel{\text{pt}}}{1} \times \frac{1\text{ qt}}{2\text{ }\cancel{\text{pt}}} = \frac{4}{1} \times \frac{1\text{ qt}}{2} = \frac{4\text{ qt}}{2}$$
>
> **Step 3:** Divide the numerator by the denominator to obtain the final answer.
>
> **4 qt ÷ 2 = 2 qt**

The cancelling method works for any measurement conversion within the same measurement system as long as the appropriate conversion factor is known. For example, 20 ounces of chocolate can be converted to pounds of chocolate. **See Figure 3-2.**

Converting Weight Measurements within the Customary or Imperial System

Example: Convert 20 ounces of chocolate to pounds of chocolate.

1. Write the original measurement as a fraction with the measurement as the numerator and 1 as the denominator.

   $\frac{20\text{ oz}}{1}$ (ORIGINAL MEASUREMENT)

2. Identify the equivalent between the original measurement and the desired measurement and write it as a fraction with the original measurement unit in the denominator.

   $\frac{1\text{ lb}}{16\text{ oz}}$ (TO CONVERT OUNCES TO POUNDS)

3. Set up a multiplication calculation with the measurement and the equivalent. Cancel the matching units in the numerators and denominators of the calculation.

   $\frac{20\,\cancel{\text{oz}}}{1} \times \frac{1\text{ lb}}{16\,\cancel{\text{oz}}}$ (CANCEL MATCHING UNITS)

4. Multiply the resulting fractions.

   $\frac{20}{1} \times \frac{1\text{ lb}}{16} = \frac{20 \times 1\text{ lb}}{1 \times 16} = \frac{20\text{ lb}}{16}$

5. Divide the numerator by the denominator to obtain the final answer.

   $20\text{ lb} \div 16 = \mathbf{1.25\text{ lb}}$

Answer: 1.25 lb

Figure 3-2. Converting measurements involves expressing the measurements and equivalents as fractions and cancelling the matching units of measure.

Because the cancellation method can be used to convert measurements within the same measurement system, it can also be used when converting within the metric system. For example, the cancellation method can be used to convert 4000 mL to 4 L.

$$\frac{4000\,\cancel{\text{mL}}}{1} \times \frac{1\text{L}}{1000\,\cancel{\text{mL}}} = \frac{4000}{1} \times \frac{1\text{L}}{1000} = \frac{4000 \times 1\text{L}}{1 \times 1000} = \frac{4000\text{L}}{1000} = \mathbf{4\,L}$$

Converting between Metric and Customary or Imperial Measurements

When converting between metric and customary or imperial measurements, it is important to remember that weight is measured the same in both the customary and imperial systems. For example, in the customary and imperial systems, 1 lb is equivalent to 454 g, 1 oz is equivalent to 28.35 g, and 1 kg is equivalent to 2.2 lb. However, customary and imperial volume measurements differ. For example, 1 L is slightly larger than a customary quart but slightly smaller than an imperial quart. **See Figure 3-3.**

When converting between metric and customary or imperial measurements, it is common to calculate answers as decimals. Decimal answers are rounded based on the degree of accuracy required for that ingredient in the recipe.

Metric and Customary/Imperial Equivalents

Weight

Metric and Customary or Imperial Equivalents

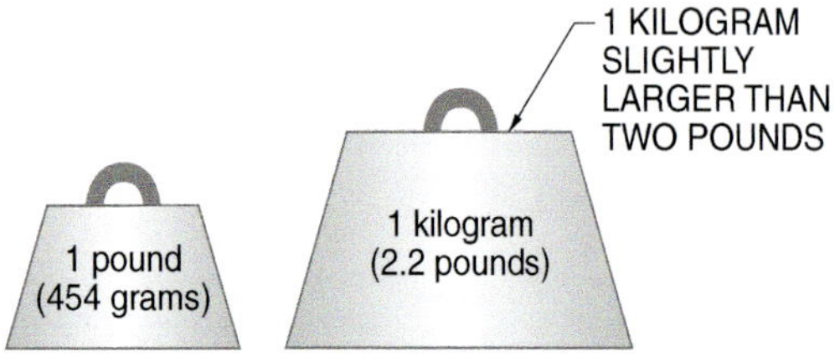

1 pound	=	0.454 kilograms
1 pound	=	454 grams
1 ounce	=	28.35 grams
1 kilogram	=	2.2 pounds

Volume

Metric and Customary Equivalents

1 gallon	=	3.79 liters
1 quart	=	0.95 liters
1 pint	=	473.18 milliliters
1 cup	=	236.59 milliliters
1 fluid ounce	=	29.57 milliliters
1 teaspoon	=	4.93 milliliters
1 liter	=	1.06 quarts
1 liter	=	33.8 fluid ounces

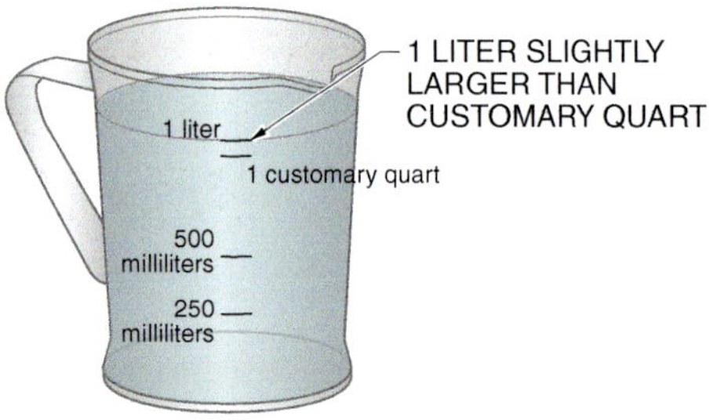

Metric and Imperial Equivalents

1 gallon	=	4.55 liters
1 quart	=	1.14 liters
1 pint	=	568.26 milliliters
1 gill	=	142.07 milliliters
1 fluid ounce	=	28.41 milliliters
1 teaspoon	=	5.92 milliliters
1 liter	=	0.88 quart
1 liter	=	35.2 fluid ounces

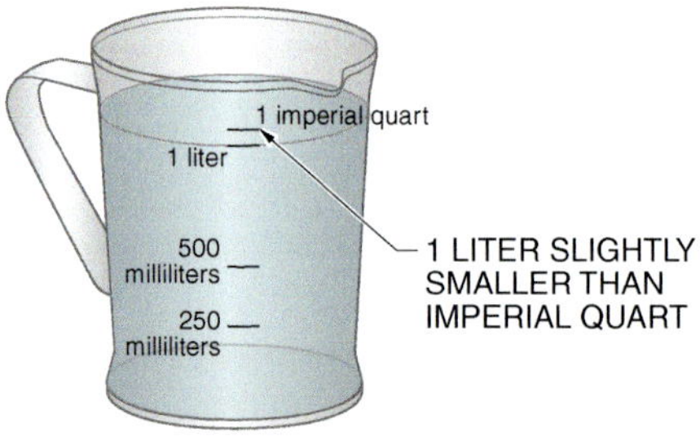

Figure 3-3. Equivalents between metric and customary/imperial units of measure for weight and volume are used to perform calculations in the professional kitchen.

Weight and Volume Conversions. The process for converting between metric and customary or imperial measurements for weight and volume is the same as for other conversions. For example, to convert 800 grams to pounds, the first step is to write 800 grams as a fraction.

$$\frac{800\text{ g}}{1}$$

The second step is to identify the equivalent between grams and pounds. The equivalent 1 lb = 454 g is found in Figure 3-3. This equivalent is written as a fraction with grams in the denominator so the units will cancel each other.

$$\frac{800\,\cancel{\text{g}}}{1}\times\frac{1\text{ lb}}{454\,\cancel{\text{g}}}=\frac{800}{1}\times\frac{1\text{ lb}}{454}$$

Next, the numerators of each fraction are multiplied, and the denominators of each fraction are multiplied.

$$\frac{800 \times 1\,\text{lb}}{1 \times 454} = \frac{800\,\text{lb}}{454}$$

Then, the numerator is divided by the denominator to obtain the final answer.

$$800\ \text{lb} \div 454 = \mathbf{1.76\ lb}$$

In some instances, two measurement equivalents will need to be used in one conversion calculation. For example, if a restaurant has 2 L of soy sauce in storage and a recipe requires 3 pt of soy sauce, is there enough soy sauce to make the recipe? To answer this question, two equivalents are required. The first equivalent is used to convert liters to quarts, and the second equivalent is used to convert quarts to pints. **See Figure 3-4.**

Converting between Metric and Customary or Imperial Measurements

Example: If a restaurant has 2 L of soy sauce in storage and a recipe requires 3 pt of soy sauce, is there enough soy sauce to make the recipe?

	Customary Measurements	Imperial Measurements
1. Write the original measurement as a fraction.	$\frac{2\ \text{L}}{1}$	$\frac{2\ \text{L}}{1}$
2. Identify the equivalents between the original measurement and the desired measurement and write them as fractions.	TO CONVERT LITERS TO CUSTOMARY QUARTS: $\frac{1\ \text{qt}}{0.95\ \text{L}}$ and TO CONVERT QUARTS TO PINTS: $\frac{2\ \text{pt}}{1\ \text{qt}}$	TO CONVERT LITERS TO IMPERIAL QUARTS: $\frac{1\ \text{qt}}{1.14\ \text{L}}$ and TO CONVERT QUARTS TO PINTS: $\frac{2\ \text{pt}}{1\ \text{qt}}$
3. Set up a multiplication calculation with the measurement and the equivalents. Cancel the matching units in the numerators and denominators of the calculation.	$\frac{2\ \cancel{\text{L}}}{1} \times \frac{1\ \cancel{\text{qt}}}{0.95\ \cancel{\text{L}}} \times \frac{2\ \text{pt}}{1\ \cancel{\text{qt}}}$	$\frac{2\ \cancel{\text{L}}}{1} \times \frac{1\ \cancel{\text{qt}}}{1.14\ \cancel{\text{L}}} \times \frac{2\ \text{pt}}{1\ \cancel{\text{qt}}}$
4. Multiply the resulting fractions.	$\frac{2}{1} \times \frac{1}{0.95} \times \frac{2\ \text{pt}}{1} = \frac{4\ \text{pt}}{0.95}$	$\frac{2}{1} \times \frac{1}{1.14} \times \frac{2\ \text{pt}}{1} = \frac{4\ \text{pt}}{1.14}$
5. Divide the numerator by the denominator to obtain the final answer (rounded to the tenths place).	$4\ \text{pt} \div 0.95 = 4.2\ \text{pt}$	$4\ \text{pt} \div 1.14 = 3.5\ \text{pt}$

Answer: Yes, there are 4.2 customary pt or 3.5 imperial pt of soy sauce.

Figure 3-4. Volume measurements in metric units can be converted to volume measurements in customary or imperial units.

Temperature Conversions. Temperature is measured in degrees Celsius (°C) or degrees Fahrenheit (°F). On the Celsius scale, the freezing point of water is 0°C, and the boiling point is 100°C. On the Fahrenheit scale, the freezing point of water is 32°F, and the boiling point is 212°F.

Use the following formula when converting from Celsius to Fahrenheit:

$$°F = (1.8 \times °C) + 32$$

where

°F = degrees Fahrenheit

°C = degrees Celsius

$$\text{Degrees Fahrenheit} = (1.8 \times \text{Degrees Celsius}) + 32$$

For example, if a recipe requires that an oven be set to 180°C but the oven is programmed in degrees Fahrenheit, then 180°C would need to be converted to degrees Fahrenheit. The result of this conversion is 356°F. Because it is not practical to set an oven to 356°F, the temperature would typically be rounded down to 350°F.

$$°F = (1.8 \times °C) + 32$$

$$°F = (1.8 \times 180) + 32$$

$$°F = 324 + 32$$

$$°F = \mathbf{356}$$

Similarly, 350°F would convert to 176.67°C and typically be rounded up to 180°C by applying the following formula:

$$°C = \frac{(°F - 32)}{1.8}$$

$$°C = \frac{(350 - 32)}{1.8}$$

$$°C = \frac{318}{1.8}$$

$$°C = \mathbf{176.67}$$

$$\text{Degrees Celsius} = \frac{\left(\text{Degrees Fahrenheit} - 32\right)}{1.8}$$

Conversion Factors. Instead of using fractions to convert between metric and customary or imperial measurements, a shortcut is simply to multiply or divide by the appropriate conversion factor in decimal form. A *conversion factor* is a number used to change one set of measurement units to an equivalent set of measurement units by multiplying or dividing. **See Figure 3-5.**

Metric and Customary/Imperial Conversion Factors

When Instructions Show:	Divide by the Conversion Factor:	To Get:	When Instructions Show:	Multiply by the Conversion Factor:	To Get:
Metric and Customary Volume Conversion Factors					
milliliters	4.93	teaspoons	teaspoons	4.93	milliliters
milliliters	14.79	tablespoons	tablespoons	14.79	milliliters
milliliters	29.57	fluid ounces	fluid ounces	29.57	milliliters
milliliters	236.59	cups	cups	236.59	milliliters
liters	0.236	cups	cups	0.236	liters
liters	0.473	pints	pints	0.473	liters
liters	0.95	quarts	quarts	0.95	liters
liters	3.79	gallons	gallons	3.79	liters
Metric and Imperial Volume Conversion Factors					
milliliters	5.92	teaspoons	teaspoons	5.92	milliliters
milliliters	17.76	tablespoons	tablespoons	17.76	milliliters
milliliters	28.41	fluid ounces	fluid ounces	28.41	milliliters
milliliters	142.07	gills	gills	142.07	milliliters
liters	0.568	pints	pints	0.568	liters
liters	1.14	quarts	quarts	1.14	liters
liters	4.55	gallons	gallons	4.55	liters
Metric and Customary/Imperial Weight Conversion Factors					
grams	28.35	ounces	ounces	28.35	grams
grams	454	pounds	pounds	454	grams
kilograms*	0.454	pounds	pounds*	0.454	kilograms
Metric and Customary/Imperial Distance Conversion Factors†					
millimeters	25.4	inches	inches	25.4	millimeters
centimeters	2.54	inches	inches	2.54	centimeters
Metric and Customary/Imperial Temperature Conversion Factors					
degrees Celsius	multiply by 1.8 and add 32	degrees Fahrenheit	degrees Fahrenheit	subtract 32 and divide by 1.8	degrees Celsius

*Since 1 kg = 2.2 lb, another way to convert kilograms to pounds is to multiply by 2.2, and to convert pounds to kilograms, divide by 2.2.
† When meters are known, multiply by 3.28 to get feet, and when feet are known, divide by 3.28 to get meters.

Figure 3-5. Conversion factors are used to change one set of measurement units to an equivalent set of measurement units by multiplying or dividing.

Converting between Volume and Weight Measurements

Converting between volume and weight measurements is often necessary because food products cannot always be purchased in the same units that are called for in a recipe. **See Figure 3-6.** Equivalents between volume and weight units are approximations based on how much a given volume of an ingredient will weigh on a scale. Two ingredients of the same volume may not weigh the same due to differences in density.

Volume vs. Weight Units

Blueberry Pie

Yield: 1 (23-cm/9-in. pie)

Ingredients	
680 g (24 oz)	Blueberries, fresh
170 g (6 oz)	Sugar, granulated
180 mL (6 fl oz)	Water
2 tsp	Lemon juice

Recipe Calls for Grams (Ounces)

Product Sold in Pints

Figure 3-6. Food products are not always sold in the same units as those used in a recipe.

For example, 8 fl oz of water will weigh 8 oz, but 8 fl oz of all-purpose flour will only weigh about 4.5 oz, while 8 fl oz of honey will weigh about 12 oz. Volume-to-weight equivalents tables can be referenced as needed. **See Appendix.**

It is important to remember that volume-to-weight equivalents are approximate and care must be taken to reference the most appropriate entry in an equivalents table. For example, there may be more than one volume-to-weight equivalent listed for grapes depending on whether the grapes are sliced or whole. A cup of sliced grapes will weigh more than a cup of whole grapes because the sliced grapes will fill the cup more compactly. **See Figure 3-7.**

Referencing Volume-to-Weight Equivalents

Volume-to-Weight Equivalents		
Ingredient	**Volume**	**Weight**
Grapes		
sliced	1 c	163 g (5¾ oz)
whole	1 c	106 g (3¾ oz)

1 Cup Grapes, Sliced

1 Cup Grapes, Whole

Figure 3-7. When referencing volume-to-weight equivalents, there may be more than one entry for an ingredient.

Volume-to-weight equivalents can be used to convert volume measurements to weight measurements. For example, how many ounces of frozen peas are there in 10 c? The first step is to write the original measurement as a fraction.

$$\frac{10\text{ c}}{1}$$

Based on the equivalents table, the volume-to-weight equivalent for frozen peas is 1 c = 3.5 oz. This equivalent is written with cups in the denominator so the cups will cancel each other.

$$\frac{10\,\cancel{c}}{1}\times\frac{3.5\,\text{oz}}{1\,\cancel{c}}=\frac{10}{1}\times\frac{3.5\,\text{oz}}{1}$$

The numerators of each fraction and the denominators of each fraction are then multiplied. Then, the numerator is divided by the denominator to obtain the final answer.

$$\frac{10\times 3.5\,\text{oz}}{1\times 1}=\frac{35\,\text{oz}}{1}=\mathbf{35\,oz}$$

Volume-to-weight equivalents can also be used to convert weight measurements to volume measurements. Consider the example of a recipe that requires 680 grams (24 ounces) of fresh blueberries. If the blueberries are only available by the pint, how many pints should be ordered? To answer this question, 680 grams (24 ounces) of blueberries is converted to pints. **See Figure 3-8.**

Converting between Volume and Weight Measurements

Example: A recipe requires 680 g (24 oz) of fresh blueberries and fresh blueberries are purchased in 1 pt containers. How many pints of blueberries should be ordered?

Tip: 1 c of fresh blueberries weighs 200 g (7 oz).

	Metric Measurements	Customary/Imperial Measurements
1. Write the original measurements as a fraction.	$\frac{680\text{ g}}{1}$	$\frac{24\text{ oz}}{1}$
2. Identify the equivalents between the original measurement and the desired measurement and write as fraction with the original measurement unit in the denominator.	$\frac{1\text{ c}}{200\text{ g}}$ (TO CONVERT GRAMS TO CUPS) and $\frac{1\text{ pt}}{2\text{ c}}$ (TO CONVERT CUPS TO PINTS)	$\frac{1\text{ c}}{7\text{ oz}}$ (TO CONVERT OUNCES TO CUPS) and $\frac{1\text{ pt}}{2\text{ c}}$ (TO CONVERT CUPS TO PINTS)
3. Set up a multiplication calculation with the original measurement and the equivalents. Cancel the matching units in the numerators and denominators of the calculation.	$\frac{680\,\cancel{g}}{1}\times\frac{1\,\cancel{c}}{200\,\cancel{g}}\times\frac{1\text{ pt}}{2\,\cancel{c}}$	$\frac{24\,\cancel{oz}}{1}\times\frac{1\,\cancel{c}}{7\,\cancel{oz}}\times\frac{1\text{ pt}}{2\,\cancel{c}}$
4. Multiply the resulting fractions.	$\frac{680}{1}\times\frac{1}{200}\times\frac{1\text{ pt}}{2}=\frac{680\text{ pt}}{400}$	$\frac{24}{1}\times\frac{1}{7}\times\frac{1\text{ pt}}{2}=\frac{24\text{ pt}}{14}$
5. Divide the numerator by the denominator to obtain the final answer.	680 pt ÷ 400 = **1.7 pt**	24 pt ÷ 14 = **1.7 pt**

Answer: Since 1.7 pt are required, 2 pt should be ordered.

Figure 3-8. Weight measurements can be converted to volume measurements using approximate volume-to-weight equivalents.

Using a Kitchen Calculator

A handheld or online kitchen calculator can be used to quickly convert units of measure, scale recipes, and alter the number of servings for a recipe. **See Figure 3-9.** However, it is important to be able to mentally estimate answers to all conversion and scaling calculations even when a calculator is used. Otherwise, any error made by inputting an incorrect number or unit of measure or by using an incorrect key on the calculator keypad can result in one or more wrong answers.

Kitchen Calculator Functions

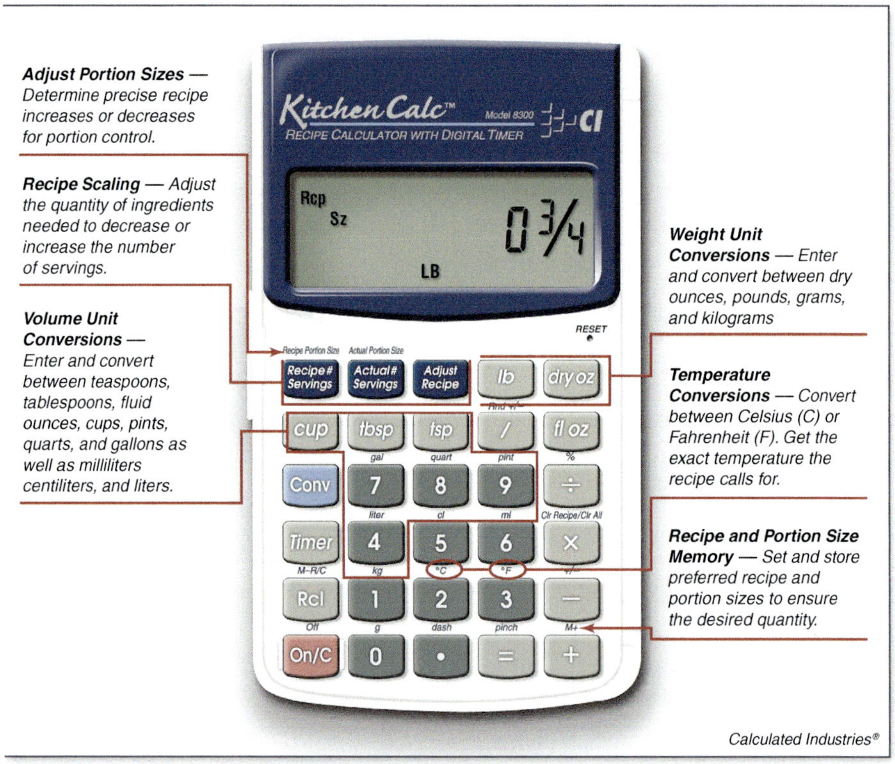

Figure 3-9. A kitchen calculator can be used to quickly convert units of measure, scale recipes, and alter the number of servings for a recipe.

It is also important to remember that a calculator cannot be used to covert volume to weight nor weight to volume because of differences in density. In the customary and imperial systems, ounces can be used to measure both volume and weight but with very different results. Ounces of liquids are typically measured by volume, but ounces of solids are best measured by weight. If a recipe lists 6 oz of grated cheese, it means 6 oz by weight. If grated cheese were poured into a measuring cup to the 6 oz mark, the cheese would only weigh about 3 oz. Once it is understood when and how to apply these mathematical procedures, a kitchen calculator can be an efficient tool.

3-1 Checkpoint

1. Define "cancelling."

2. Convert 4.25 kilograms to grams.

3. Convert 6 cups to quarts.

4. Convert 10 cups to liters and round the answer to the tenths place. (*Tip: 1 qt = 0.95 L.*)

5. Convert 425 degrees Fahrenheit to degrees Celsius. (*Round the answer as per common industry practice.*)

6. Why would it be important to distinguish between chopped pecans and whole pecans when looking up a volume-to-weight equivalent for pecans?

7. Why is it important to estimate calculations before using a kitchen calculator?

Section 3-2 SCALING RECIPES

Converting measurements is often done when scaling recipes. *Scaling* is the process of calculating new amounts for each ingredient in a recipe when the total amount of food the recipe makes is changed. For example, a recipe that serves 4 people may be scaled for use in a restaurant that plans to make 50 servings of the recipe. Similarly, a recipe used by a banquet hall that normally serves 100 people may need to be scaled to make only 12 servings for a small party.

A recipe may also need to be scaled based on the availability of an ingredient. For example, a recipe may require 7 kg of minced lamb, but only 3 kg of minced lamb are available. A foodservice employee needs to know how to adjust all of the other ingredient amounts in a recipe to account for the available amount of the key ingredient. They also need to understand how scaling can affect other elements of a recipe. For example, depending on how significantly the recipe is scaled, the units of measure used for some ingredients may need to be converted to make measuring the ingredients more practical. In addition, cooking times or temperatures may need to be adjusted, or cooking equipment of a different size may be required. A well-written, standardized recipe will contain all of the information that needs to be considered when a recipe is scaled.

Standardized Recipes

A *standardized recipe* is a list of ingredients, ingredient amounts, and procedural steps for preparing a specific quantity of a food item. A standardized recipe includes a list of ingredients and uses standard units of measure to represent a specific amount of each ingredient. When used properly, standardized recipes help ensure consistency and control costs regardless of who prepares the food or beverage. The benefits of using a standardized recipe include the following:

- Assures consistency in quality and quantity
- Provides reliable portion sizes
- Serves as a reference for addressing nutritional concerns
- Helps reduce waste
- Assists with employee training
- Helps with pricing forms and purchase orders

The exact look and format of a standardized recipe will vary from one foodservice operation to another. **See Figure 3-10.** However, most standardized recipes usually contain the following common elements:

- **Recipe Name.** The name of a recipe should be descriptive of the dish being prepared and should reflect the name used on the menu.
- **Yield.** *Yield* is the total quantity of a food or beverage item that is made from a standardized recipe. Yields can be expressed as a count, a total volume or weight, or a number of portions. For example, 12 biscuits, 4 L, 10 kg, and 24 portions, 150 g each, are all valid recipe yields. Likewise, 24 cookies, 3 gal., 50 lb, and 36 portions, 8 oz each, are also valid recipe yields.
- **Portion Size.** *Portion size* is the amount of a food or beverage item that is served to an individual person. Portion size is related to yield. For example, a soup recipe that yields 4 L (4000 mL) can also be said to yield 16 portions of 250 mL each (4000 mL ÷ 16 = 250 mL). Likewise, a soup recipe that yields 1 customary gallon (128 fl oz) can also be said to yield 16 portions of 8 fl oz each (128 fl oz ÷ 16 = 8 fl oz). However, if the soup recipe yields 1 imperial gallon (160 fl oz), then each of the 16 portions will have 10 imperial fluid ounces (160 fl oz ÷ 16 = 10 fl oz). **See Figure 3-11.**

- **Ingredients and Procedures.** The amount of each ingredient used in the recipe is listed next to the name of the ingredient. If an ingredient is to be prepared in a certain way prior to being measured, such as minced, that information is also provided. The ingredients are usually listed in the order that they are incorporated into the recipe. Procedures are listed in sequential order.
- **Cooking Temperature.** The temperature at which food is cooked greatly affects the outcome of the final product.
- **Cooking Time.** Cooking times provided in standardized recipes are often guidelines. Many professional cooks rely on the appearance or feel of an item and on exact measurements, such as an internal temperature checked with a thermometer, to determine when a food item is done.
- **Nutrition Information.** While nutrition information is not required to prepare a recipe, it is important information to have for menu planning and for customer inquiries.

Standardized Recipe Elements

Meatloaf

Yield: 10 Servings

Cooking Temperature: 180°C (350°F)

Portion Size: 170 g (6 oz)

Cooking Time: 1 hour

Amount	Ingredients	Procedure
15 mL (1 tbsp)	vegetable oil	1. Heat oil in small sauté pan and sauté celery and onions until tender. Allow to cool.
85 g (3 oz)	celery, small dice	2. Combine remaining ingredients and mix well.
115 g (4 oz)	onion, small dice	3. Form mixture into a loaf and place in a greased bread pan.
60 mL (2 fl oz)	milk	4. Bake at 180°C (350°F) for about 1 hour or until a thermometer inserted in the center of the loaf registers 75°C (165°F).
2	eggs, beaten	5. Remove from oven, cover, and let rest for 15 minutes before slicing into 170 g (6 oz) portions.
115 g (4 oz)	breadcrumbs	
15 mL (1 tbsp)	salt	
7 mL (1½ tsp)	black pepper	
500 g (1 lb)	ground beef	
500 g (1 lb)	ground pork	
500 g (1 lb)	ground veal	

Nutrition info (per serving): 309 calories; 10.7 g total fat; 3.7 g saturated fat; 145 mg cholesterol; 881 mg sodium; 582 mg potassium; 9.7 g carbohydrates; 0.9 g fiber; 1.6 g sugar; 40.8 g protein.

Figure 3-10. Most standardized recipes include the same common elements.

Yield and Portion Size

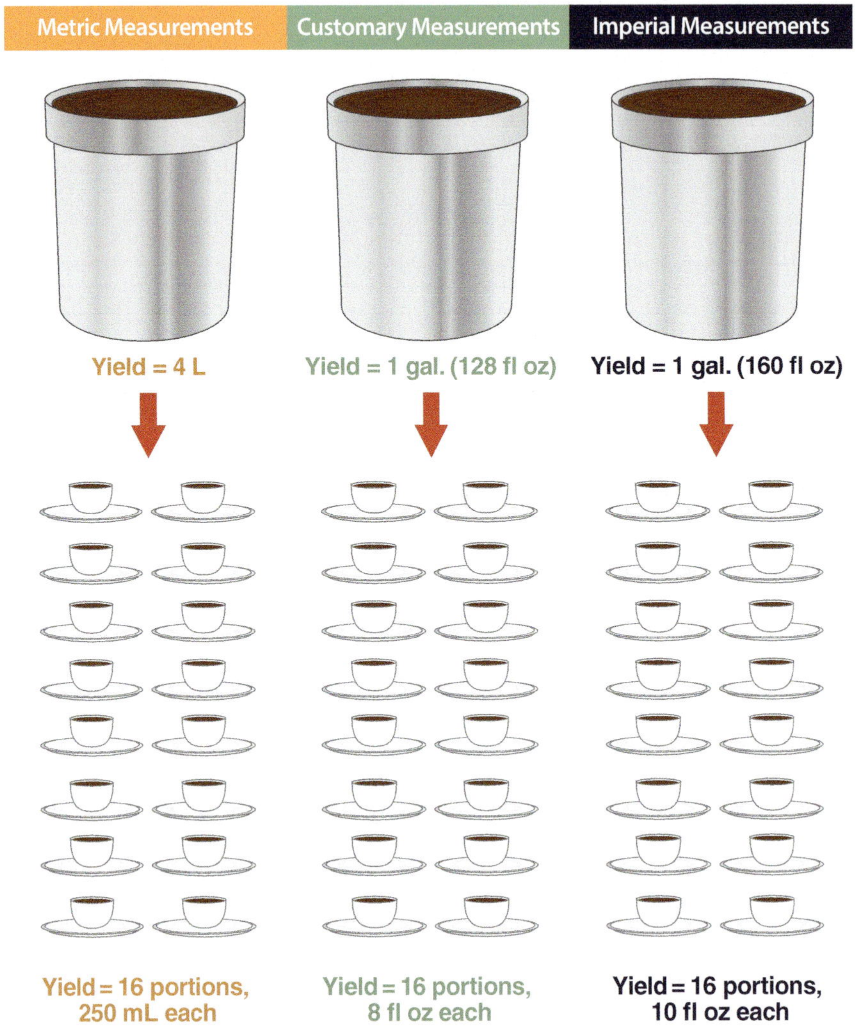

Figure 3-11. Total recipe yield can be expressed as a number of portions and a portion size.

Scaling Based on Yield

The most straightforward examples of scaling a recipe are doubling the yield where all the ingredient amounts are simply multiplied by 2 or halving the yield by dividing all the ingredient amounts by 2.

Scaling becomes more challenging when the yield is changed by a factor that is not as simple as doubling or halving the recipe. For example, a recipe that normally yields 3 L may need to be scaled to yield 10 L. Likewise, a recipe that makes 12 portions, 170 g each, may need to be scaled to make 30 portions, 250 g each.

Regardless of the reason for scaling a recipe, the scaling process starts out by calculating a scaling factor. A *scaling factor* is the number that each ingredient amount and the recipe yield are multiplied by in order to increase or decrease a recipe. The formula for calculating a scaling factor based on yield is as follows:

$$SF = DY \div OY$$

where

SF = scaling factor

DY = desired yield

OY = original yield

$$\text{Scaling Factor} = \frac{\text{Desired Yield}}{\text{Original Yield}}$$

Scaling Based on Count. If a cookie recipe that makes 24 cookies is scaled to make 84 cookies, the scaling factor is calculated by dividing the desired yield (84 cookies) by the original yield (24 cookies). **See Figure 3-12.**

$$SF = DY \div OY$$

SF = 84 cookies ÷ 24 cookies

SF = **3.5**

Calculating Scaling Factors

$$\text{Scaling Factor} = \frac{\text{Desired Yield}}{\text{Original Yield}}$$

Type of Yield	Original Yield	Desired Yield	Scaling Factor
 Count Yield	24 cookies	84 cookies	84 ÷ 24 = **3.5**
 Volume Yield	8 L	3 L	3 ÷ 8 = **0.375**
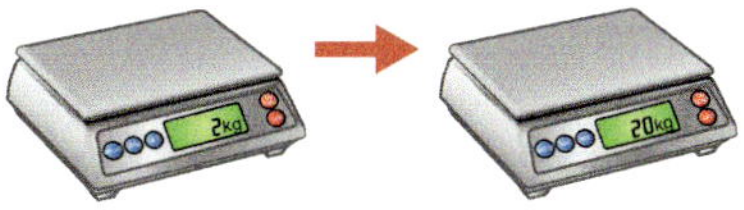 Weight Yield	2 kg	20 kg	20 ÷ 2 = **10**
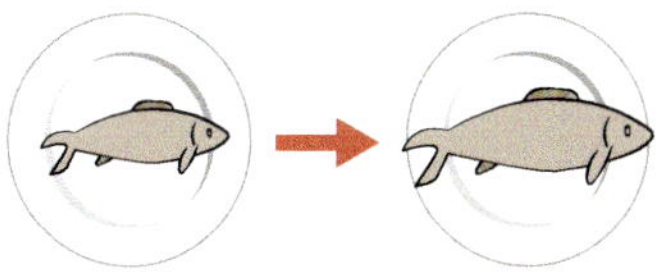 Portion Yield	10 portions, 150 g each (10 × 150 g = 1500 g)	30 portions, 200 g each (30 × 200 g = 6000 g)	6000 ÷ 1500 = **4**

Figure 3-12. When a recipe is scaled based on yield, the scaling factor is calculated by dividing the desired yield by the original yield.

Scaling Based on Volume. If a soup recipe that makes 8 L of soup is scaled to make 3 L of soup, the scaling factor is calculated by dividing the desired yield (3 L) by the original yield (8 L).

$$SF = DY \div OY$$

$$SF = 3 \text{ L} \div 8 \text{ L}$$

$$SF = \mathbf{0.375}$$

Scaling Based on Weight. If a potato salad recipe that makes 2 kg of salad is scaled to make 20 kg of salad, the scaling factor is calculated by dividing the desired yield (20 kg) by the original yield (2 kg).

$$SF = DY \div OY$$

$$SF = 20 \text{ kg} \div 2 \text{ kg}$$

$$SF = \mathbf{10}$$

Scaling Based on Portion Size. If a fish recipe that makes 10 portions, 150 g each, is scaled to make 30 portions, 200 g each, the yields must first be converted to a total number of grams.

$$OY = 10 \times 150 \text{ g} = 1500 \text{ g}$$

$$DY = 30 \times 200 \text{ g} = 6000 \text{ g}$$

Then, the scaling factor formula can be applied.

$$SF = DY \div OY$$

$$SF = 6000 \text{ g} \div 1500 \text{ g}$$

$$SF = \mathbf{4}$$

Scaling Based on Product Availability

In some cases, a recipe is scaled because the amount of one ingredient needs to be changed based on availability. For example, if a beef stew recipe that calls for 5 kg of beef stew meat needs to be made with only 3 kg of beef stew meat, the scaling factor is calculated by dividing the available ingredient amount (desired yield) by the original ingredient amount (original yield).

$$SF = DY \div OY$$

$$SF = 3 \text{ kg beef stew meat} \div 5 \text{ kg beef stew meat}$$

$$SF = \mathbf{0.6}$$

Multiplying Scaling Factors

Once a scaling factor is known, every ingredient amount in the original recipe is multiplied by the scaling factor. **See Figure 3-13.** Using the new ingredient amounts will produce the desired yield of the scaled recipe. For example, a meatloaf recipe that normally yields 10 servings is scaled to make 80 servings. The scaling factor (based on count) is calculated first.

$SF = DY \div OY$

$SF = 80 \text{ servings} \div 10 \text{ servings}$

$SF = \mathbf{8.0}$

Then, the new amount of each ingredient is calculated using the following formula:

$NA = OA \times SF$

New Amount = Original Amount × Scaling Factor

where

NA = new amount

OA = original amount

SF = scaling factor

For example, the original meatloaf recipe requires 15 mL of vegetable oil. The new amount of vegetable oil required is calculated as follows:

$NA = OA \times SF$

$NA = 15 \text{ mL} \times 8.0$

$NA = \mathbf{120 \text{ mL}}$

The new amounts for the remaining ingredients are then calculated using the same formula. *Note:* It may be necessary to convert some of the new ingredient amounts to a different unit of measure to make measuring the ingredients more efficient.

In general, it is most efficient to measure ingredients using the largest appropriate unit of measure. For example, the customary measurement in the original meatloaf recipe in Figure 3-10 calls for 1 tablespoon of vegetable oil. The new amount based on a scaling factor of 8 is calculated as follows:

$NA = OA \times SF$

$NA = 1 \text{ tbsp} \times 8.0$

$NA = \mathbf{8 \text{ tbsp}}$

However, measuring 8 tbsp individually is time consuming. Instead, 8 tbsp can be converted to a larger unit of measure such as ounces. Measuring 4 fl oz (or ½ c) is more efficient than measuring 8 tbsp.

$$\frac{8 \cancel{\text{tbsp}}}{1} \times \frac{1 \text{ fl oz}}{2 \cancel{\text{tbsp}}} = \frac{8 \times 1 \text{ fl oz}}{1 \times 2} = \frac{8 \text{ fl oz}}{2} = 8 \text{ fl oz} \div 2 = \mathbf{4 \text{ fl oz}} (\tfrac{1}{2}\mathbf{c})$$

Multiplying Measurements by a Scaling Factor

Ingredient	Original Amount × Scaling Factor*	New Amount	Adjust New Amounts as Needed	Scaled Recipe
Metric Measurements				
Vegetable oil	15 mL × 8	120 mL	—	**120 mL**
Celery, small dice	85 g × 8	680 g	—	**680 g**
Onion, small dice	115 g × 8	920 g	—	**920 g**
Milk	60 mL × 8	480 mL	—	**480 mL**
Eggs, beaten	2 × 8	16	—	**16**
Breadcrumbs	115 g × 8	920 g	—	**920 g**
Salt	15 mL × 8	120 mL	—	**120 mL**
Pepper	7 mL × 8	56 mL	—	**56 mL**
Ground beef	500 g × 8	4000 g	$\frac{4000\,\cancel{g}}{1} \times \frac{1\text{ kg}}{1000\,\cancel{g}} = \frac{4000\text{ kg}}{1000} = 4\text{ kg}$	**4 kg**
Ground pork	500 g × 8	4000 g	$\frac{4000\,\cancel{g}}{1} \times \frac{1\text{ kg}}{1000\,\cancel{g}} = \frac{4000\text{ kg}}{1000} = 4\text{ kg}$	**4 kg**
Ground veal	500 g × 8	4000 g	$\frac{4000\,\cancel{g}}{1} \times \frac{1\text{ kg}}{1000\,\cancel{g}} = \frac{4000\text{ kg}}{1000} = 4\text{ kg}$	**4 kg**
Customary Measurements				
Vegetable oil	1 tbsp × 8	8 tbsp	$\frac{8\,\cancel{\text{tbsp}}}{1} \times \frac{1\,\cancel{\text{fl oz}}}{2\,\cancel{\text{tbsp}}} \times \frac{1\text{ c}}{8\,\cancel{\text{fl oz}}} = \frac{8\text{ c}}{16} = \frac{1}{2}\text{ c}$	**½ c**
Celery, small dice	3 oz × 8	24 oz	$\frac{24\,\cancel{\text{oz}}}{1} \times \frac{1\text{ lb}}{16\,\cancel{\text{oz}}} = \frac{24\text{ lb}}{16} = 1.5\text{ lb} = 1\frac{1}{2}\text{ lb} = 1\text{ lb }8\text{ oz}$	**1 lb 8 oz**
Onion, small dice	4 oz × 8	32 oz	$\frac{32\,\cancel{\text{oz}}}{1} \times \frac{1\text{ lb}}{16\,\cancel{\text{oz}}} = \frac{32\text{ lb}}{16} = 2\text{ lb}$	**2 lb**
Milk	2 fl oz × 8	16 fl oz	$\frac{16\,\cancel{\text{fl oz}}}{1} \times \frac{1\,\cancel{\text{c}}}{8\,\cancel{\text{fl oz}}} \times \frac{1\text{ pt}}{2\,\cancel{\text{c}}} = \frac{16\text{ pt}}{16} = 1\text{ pt}$	**1 pt**
Eggs, beaten	2 × 8	16	—	**16**
Breadcrumbs	4 oz × 8	32 oz	$\frac{32\,\cancel{\text{oz}}}{1} \times \frac{1\text{ lb}}{16\,\cancel{\text{oz}}} = \frac{32\text{ lb}}{16} = 2\text{ lb}$	**2 lb**
Salt	1 tbsp × 8	8 tbsp	$\frac{8\,\cancel{\text{tbsp}}}{1} \times \frac{1\,\cancel{\text{fl oz}}}{2\,\cancel{\text{tbsp}}} \times \frac{1\text{ c}}{8\,\cancel{\text{fl oz}}} = \frac{8\text{ c}}{16} = \frac{1}{2}\text{ c}$	**½ c**
Pepper	1½ tsp × 8	12 tsp	$\frac{12\,\cancel{\text{tsp}}}{1} \times \frac{1\text{ tbsp}}{3\,\cancel{\text{tsp}}} = \frac{12\text{ tbsp}}{3} = 4\text{ tbsp}$	**4 tbsp**
Ground beef	1 lb × 8	8 lb	—	**8 lb**
Ground pork	1 lb × 8	8 lb	—	**8 lb**
Ground veal	1 lb × 8	8 lb	—	**8 lb**

* Meatloaf recipe scaled from 10 servings to 80 servings (scaling factor = 80 ÷ 10 = 8).

Figure 3-13. When recipe ingredients are multiplied by a scaling factor, it may be necessary to adjust the new measurements to a different unit of measure.

Additional Scaling Considerations

When recipes are scaled, additional considerations must be taken into account before actually preparing the recipe. Addressing these considerations will help to ensure that the final product is the same quality as the original recipe.

Adjusting Measurements. If a new measurement is calculated that is not easily measured, such as 3.7 c, the measurement will need to be adjusted to make measuring more practical. However, to avoid affecting the final result, the amount should only be adjusted slightly to ensure a quality product. For example, 3.7 c should only be adjusted to 3¾ c (3.75 c). Also, care should be taken when substantially increasing the amount of spices and seasonings in a recipe. For best results, use less than is called for and then adjust the spices and seasonings as needed.

Adjusting Cooking Temperature. In certain circumstances, such as when a recipe yield is significantly decreased, it may be necessary to reduce the cooking temperature. This will keep the food from drying out.

Adjusting Cooking Time. The cooking time for a recipe may need to be increased or decreased. For example, if a larger roast is used for a recipe, a longer cooking time will be required. Likewise, if a cake recipe that makes cake layers is scaled to make one sheet cake, the thinner sheet of cake may bake faster than the thicker cake layers.

Checkpoint 3-2

1. List the elements found in most standardized recipes.

____

____

2. What is the yield of a recipe in liters that makes 20 portions, 240 mL each?

____

____

3. If a standardized recipe that yields 500 mL of sauce is scaled to yield 2 L, what is the scaling factor?

____

____

3-2

Checkpoint (continued)

4. If a standardized recipe for stew that yields 20 portions, 170 g each, is scaled to yield 10 portions, 225 g each, what is the scaling factor?

5. If a standardized recipe for chicken pot pie calls for 4 kg of cooked chicken meat and is scaled to use 5 kg of available cooked chicken meat, what is the scaling factor?

6. If a standardized recipe calls for 85 g of Cheddar cheese and the recipe is scaled by a scaling factor of 16, how many kilograms of cheese are required?

7. If a scaled measurement is 1.45 c, how should the measurement be changed to make measuring in cups more practical?

Solve each problem in the space provided. Write the final answer on the blank provided. Round any decimal answers to the hundredths place.

Leaf icon indicates a math problem with a sustainability focus.

Example:

64 portions ______

If a soup recipe yields 3 gallons, how many 6-fluid-ounce portions will the recipe make? *(Tip: 1 gal. = 128 fl oz)*

$$\frac{3\text{ gal}}{1} \times \frac{128\text{ fl oz}}{1\text{ gal}} = 384\text{ fl oz, then}$$

$$\frac{384\text{ fl oz}}{1} \times \frac{1\text{ portion}}{6\text{ fl oz}} = \frac{384\text{ portions}}{6} = 64\text{ portions}$$

______ **1.** How many 240 mL servings are in a lemonade recipe that yields 12 L?

$$\frac{240\text{mL}}{1} \times \frac{0.001}{1} = 0.24$$

______ **2.** How many 425 g jumbo chocolate chip cookies can be prepared from 34 kg of cookie dough?

______ **3.** If a stir-fry recipe requires 120 mL of teriyaki sauce per serving, how many servings of stir-fry can be made from 3 L of teriyaki sauce?

________________ **4.** If a soup recipe written in imperial measurements yields 20 gal., how many 5 fl oz portions will the recipe make? *(Tip: 1 gal. = 160 fl oz.)*

________________ **5.** If a chowder recipe yields 50 portions, 100 mL each, what is the total yield of the recipe in liters?

________________ **6.** If 25 mL of extra-virgin olive oil is drizzled over finished pasta dishes, how many pasta dishes can be finished from a 3 L container of extra-virgin olive oil?

________________ **7.** How many 12 oz bags of frozen peaches are needed to make a peach sorbet that calls for 3 customary pints of frozen peaches. *(Tip: 1 c of frozen peaches weighs about 6 oz.)*

________________ **8.** A recipe calls for an oven temperature of 275°F. What temperature should the oven be set to if it is programmed in degrees Celsius?

______________ **9.** A recipe calls for an oven temperature of 150°C. What temperature should the oven be set to if it is programmed in degrees Fahrenheit? *(Round the answer as per common industry practice.)*

______________ **10.** How many grams of sugar are in a 4 lb bag of sugar? *(Tip: 1 lb = 454 g.)*

______________ **11.** A produce stand where fresh items are brought in daily uses day-old spinach and overripe bananas in their signature green smoothie recipe. If one serving of the green smoothie is 300 mL, what is one serving of the smoothie in cups? *(Tip: 1 c = 236.59 mL. Round the answer to the tenths place.)*

______________ **12.** If a salad dressing recipe calls for 3.5 L of olive oil, is 4 customary quarts of olive oil enough to make the salad dressing? *(Tip: 1 qt = 0.95 L.)*

______________ **13.** If a meatball recipe calls for 10 lb of ground beef, is 5 kg of ground beef enough to make the meatballs? *(Tip: 1 kg = 2.2 lb.)*

_______________ **14.** If 20 L of lemon juice are needed for a punch recipe and one case of lemons yields 4 imperial quarts of lemon juice, will 4 cases provide enough lemon juice to make the punch? *(Tip: 1 qt = 1.14 L.)*

_______________ **15.** How many ounces of cornstarch are there in a box containing 300 g of cornstarch? *(Tip: 1 oz = 28.35 g.)*

_______________ **16.** Trimmed produce leaves are saved for composting and used for the flower beds in front of a deli. If 4.5 lb of leaves are trimmed from produce every week, how many kilograms of trimmed leaves will be composted in a year? *(Tip: 1 lb = 0.454 kg.)*

_______________ **17.** If a brownie recipe yields 36 brownies, what scaling factor is needed to scale the recipe to yield 396 brownies?

_______________ **18.** If a recipe yields 2 kg of quinoa-kale salad, what scaling factor would be used to make 6 kg of the salad?

______________ **19.** After picking apples at a local orchard, the owner of a bakery adds apple fritters to the menu. At the end of the day, 20 apple fritters are left over and set aside to make bread pudding. If 6 fritters make one pan of bread pudding, what is the scaling factor that the other ingredients need to be multiplied by in order to use all 20 fritters? *(Show the answer as a mixed number.)*

______________ **20.** If a tiramisu recipe yields 12 servings, what scaling factor would be used to make 156 servings?

______________ **21.** If a recipe yields 72 minimuffins, what scaling factor would be used to make 45 minimuffins?

______________ **22.** A chef with a nose-to-tail cooking approach purchases whole turkeys since it is cost-effective and helps eliminate food waste. The chef uses the bones for stock, various parts for gravy, and different cuts for entrées, including 87 pot pies. If the recipe for turkey pot pie yields 116 pot pies, what scaling factor would be used to make 87 pot pies?

_______________ **23.** If a recipe yields 4 L of pasta sauce, what scaling factor is needed to scale the recipe to yield 750 mL of pasta sauce?

_______________ **24.** If a bread recipe yields 7 kg of dough, what scaling factor is needed to scale the recipe to yield 22 kg?

_______________ **25.** A restaurant that serves roasted cauliflower as a side dish has five cauliflower heads left over. To use the leftover cauliflower, the chef will make crispy battered cauliflower bites for an appetizer the next day. If the recipe yields 20 servings, what scaling factor would be used to yield 30 servings?

_______________ **26.** If a chicken fajita recipe yields 20 fajitas, 85 g each, what scaling factor is needed to scale the recipe to yield 50 fajitas, 115 g each?

_______________ **27.** If a kombucha tea recipe yields 60 servings, 240 mL each, what scaling factor is needed to scale the recipe to yield 90 servings, 350 mL each?

_______________ **28.** If a cream-of-asparagus soup recipe normally calls for 12 kg of asparagus but the chef wants to use 18 kg of asparagus, what is the scaling factor that the other ingredients need to be multiplied by?

_______________ **29.** A banquet facility where leftover food was a problem reduced waste and expenses by modifying and testing standardized recipes to ensure portion control. If their new minestrone soup recipe calls for 200 mL portions, what scaling factor should be used to prepare 180 portions if the original recipe yielded 50 portions?

_______________ **30.** To produce 5.5 kg of egg noodles, 32 large eggs are required. What is the scaling factor that the other ingredients need to be multiplied by if only 24 large eggs are available?

_______________ **31.** Instead of discarding 2 kg of fresh carrots that were accidentally frozen and are no longer crisp, the chef will use them in a vegetable stock. If the stock recipe calls for 340 g of carrots to yield 4 L, what scaling factor should be used to prepare stock from the 2 kg of carrots?

_______________ **32.** If a smoothie recipe calls for 2.5 L of mango juice but only 875 mL of mango juice are available, what is the scaling factor the other ingredients in the recipe need to be multiplied by?

_______________ **33.** A café has leftover watermelon after a catered luncheon. To ensure the watermelon is used, the café features it in a watermelon-basil lemonade using a recipe with customary measurements. If the original lemonade recipe yields 4½ cups, what scaling factor should be used to yield 4 gal. of the watermelon-basil lemonade?

_______________ **34.** A donut recipe calls for 1.4 kg of pastry flour and yields 60 donuts. If the recipe is scaled to make 200 donuts, how many kilograms of pastry flour are required?

_______________ **35.** If 1 lb of raw spaghetti noodles makes 5 c of cooked spaghetti noodles, how many pounds of raw spaghetti noodles would be needed to make 30 c?

_______________ **36.** How many liters of bolognaise sauce can be made using 2.2 kg of ground beef if the original recipe yields 2 L and calls for 0.5 kg of ground beef?

_______________ **37.** A restaurant with an on-site garden uses leftover coffee grounds as a medium for growing mushrooms. If 5½ lb of coffee grounds grow enough mushroom spores to yield 3 lb of mushrooms, how many pounds of coffee grounds are needed to yield 20 lb of mushrooms? *(Show the answer as a mixed number.)*

_______________ **38.** A chili recipe calls for 500 g of finely diced onions and normally yields 3 L. If the recipe is scaled to make 750 mL, how many grams of finely diced onions are required?

_______________ **39.** A puff pastry recipe calls for 500 g of butter and yields 1.8 kg. How many grams of butter are required to make 0.75 kg of puff pastry?

_______________ **40.** If 1 container of cherry tomatoes weighs 300 g, how many containers of cherry tomatoes are required for a recipe that calls for 6 kg of cherry tomatoes?

_______________ **41.** A jalapeño Cheddar cornbread recipe that yields 9 servings requires 115 g of butter. If the recipe is scaled to yield 198 servings, how many kilograms of butter are required?

_______________ **42.** A sweet-and-sour pork recipe calls for 4.5 kg of pork tenderloin, yielding 30 servings, 175 g each. If the recipe is scaled to yield 50 servings, 225 g each, how many kilograms of pork tenderloin are required?

____________ **43.** If 6 kg of ground bison meat yields 40 bison burger patties, 150 g each, how many kilograms of ground bison meat are needed if the recipe is scaled to yield 90 bison burger patties, 220 g each?

____________ **44.** A recipe for soft pretzels calls for 2 teaspoons of salt and yields 36 pretzels. If the recipe is scaled to yield 324 pretzels, how many tablespoons of salt are required?

____________ **45.** A crab cake recipe calls for 55 g of diced celery and yields 20 crab cakes. If the recipe is scaled to make 320 crab cakes, how many grams of diced celery are required?

____________ **46.** A gumbo recipe calls for 4 qt of cooked rice and yields 80 servings, 6 oz each. If the recipe is scaled to yield 12 servings, 5 oz each, how many cups of cooked rice are required?

______________ **47.** If a chicken enchilada recipe calls for 2 kg of shredded Cheddar cheese and yields 70 enchiladas, how many grams of shredded Cheddar cheese are needed to yield 18 enchiladas?

______________ **48.** A restaurant with seasonal demand scales recipes down during slower months to reduce waste and costs. If the restaurant's chicken marsala uses 2.7 kg of cremini mushrooms to yield 48 portions, how many grams of cremini mushrooms are needed to yield 12 portions?

______________ **49.** If a fruit tart recipe calls for 30 oz of apricot filling and yields 24 tarts, how many kilograms of apricot filling would be required to yield 240 tarts? *(Tip: 1 oz = 28.35 g.)*

______________ **50.** If a seafood bisque recipe with customary measurements calls for 1 pt of sherry and yields 4 gal., how many liters of sherry would be required to yield 12 gal. of the bisque? *(Tip: 1 L = 1.06 qt.)*

Calculating Percentages and Ratios

4

Foodservice workers use percentages to determine how much of a given food product is usable. Many food products must be cleaned and/or trimmed before they can be used in a recipe, cooked, or served. Meats are trimmed, fish are deboned, and many fruits and vegetables are peeled and seeded. In each case, only part of the food product is usable. Baker's percentages and ratios describe how ingredients are used in relation to one another and help guarantee consistent results.

Section 4-1: CALCULATING PERCENTAGES

- Explain how to change percentages to decimals and decimals to percentages.
- Calculate percentages using a percentage circle.

Section 4-2: USING YIELD PERCENTAGES (YPs)

- Explain how yield percentages (YPs) are used.
- Explain how to conduct yield tests.
- Calculate as-purchased (AP) and edible-portion (EP) amounts.
- Explain how yield percentages (YPs) are rounded.

Section 4-3: USING BAKER'S PERCENTAGES

- Explain why bakeshop recipes are called formulas.
- Calculate baker's percentages.

Section 4-4: CALCULATING RATIOS

- Explain how to convert two-ingredient ratios into fractions and percentages.
- Explain how to convert three-ingredient ratios into fractions and percentages.

Section 4-5: USING RATIOS

- Explain how ratios are used in the professional kitchen.
- Calculate ingredient amounts using ratios.

Key Terms

- percentage
- as-purchased (AP) amount
- edible-portion (EP) amount
- yield percentage (YP)
- raw yield test
- cooking-loss yield test
- baker's percentage
- ratio

Learner Resources
atplearningresources.com
access code 267628

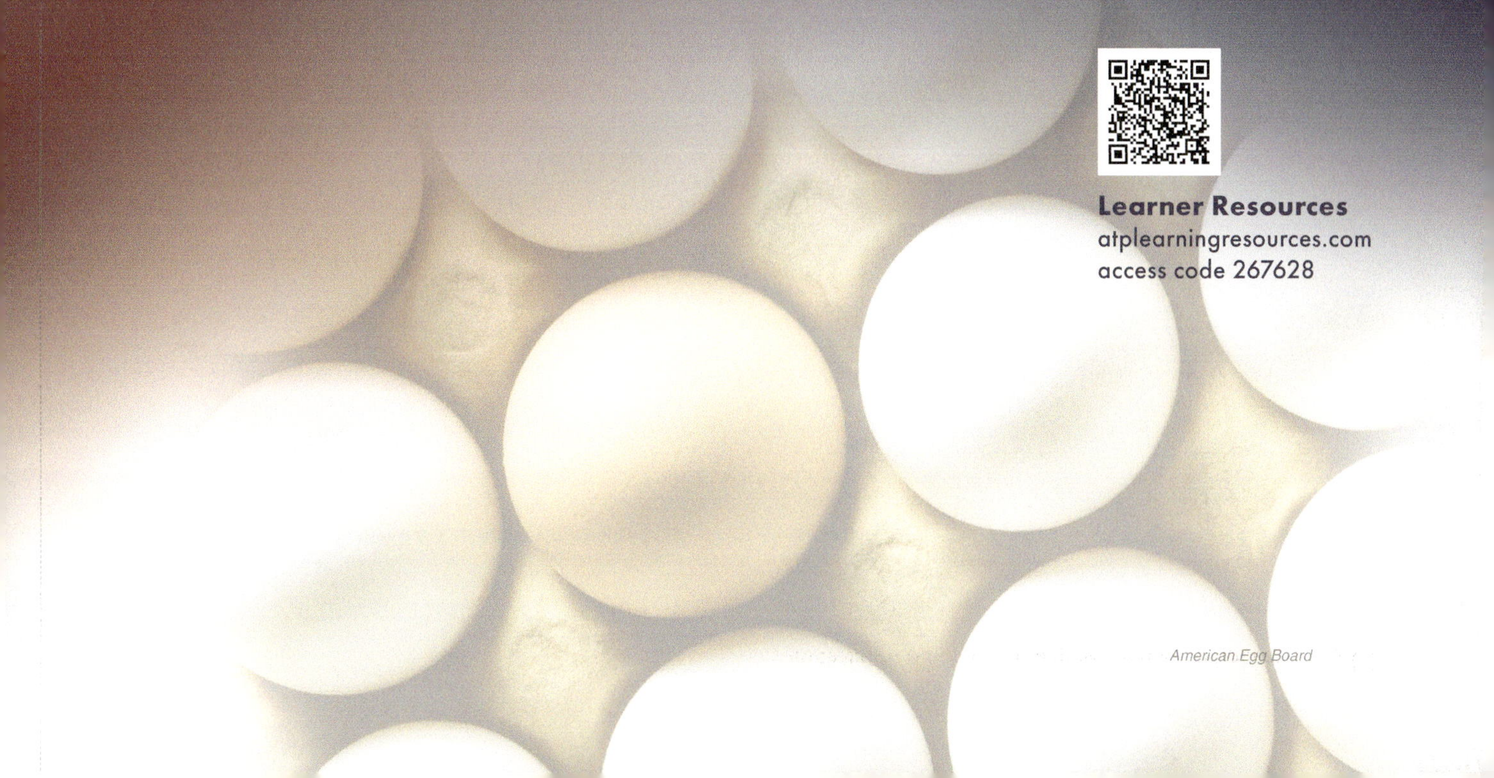

American Egg Board

Section 4-1 CALCULATING PERCENTAGES

Like fractions and decimals, percentages express parts of a whole. A *percentage* is a number that expresses part of a whole in terms of hundredths. One percent (1%) is 1 part of 100. The percent symbol (%) is used as an abbreviation for the word "percent." For example, if there are 100 jelly beans in a jar, and 40 of them are yellow and 60 of them are green, then 40 percent (40%) of the jelly beans are yellow, and 60 percent (60%) of the jelly beans are green. **See Figure 4-1.**

Percentages

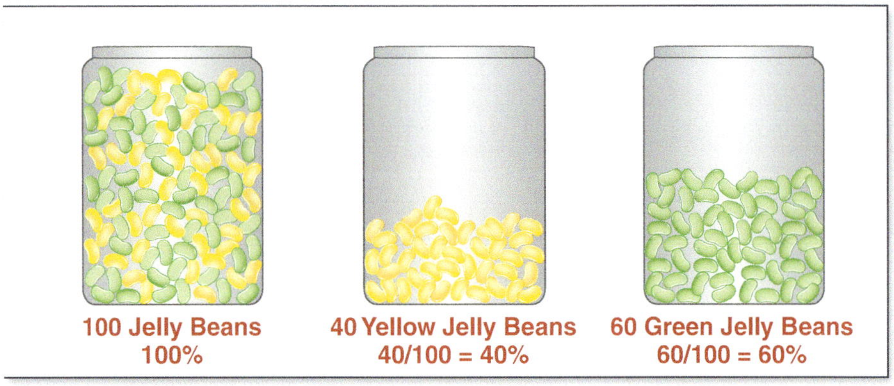

Figure 4-1. Percentages are used to express part of a whole in terms of hundredths.

An easy way to understand percentages is by using a percentage circle. **See Figure 4-2.** A percentage circle is divided into three sections. The top section of the circle contains the variable *P* that represents the part of the whole. The lower left section of the circle contains the variable *W* that represents the whole. The lower right section of the circle contains the variable % that represents the percentage.

Percentage Formulas

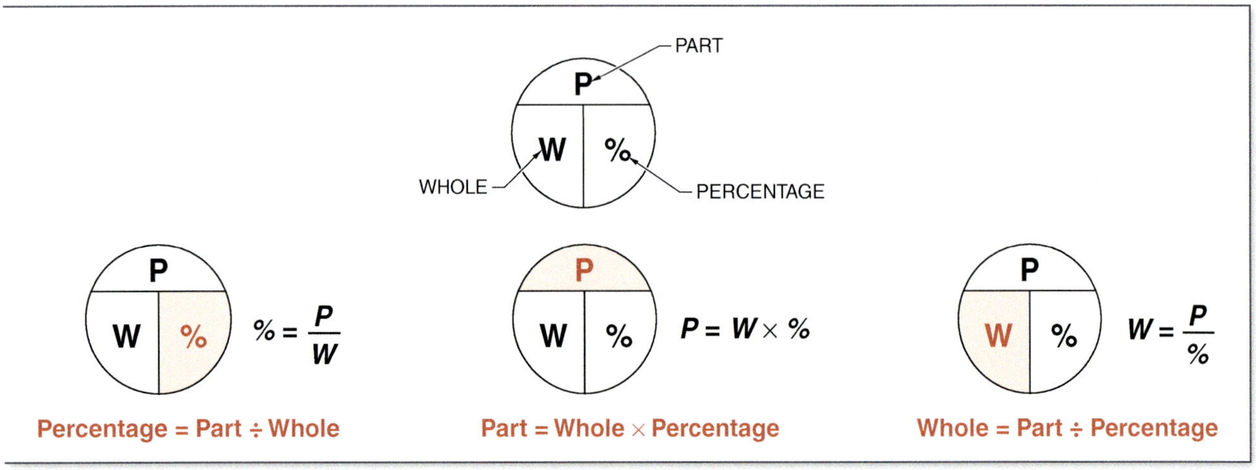

Figure 4-2. A percentage circle is a visual tool used to show how to perform basic percentage calculations.

To use a percentage circle, any variable that is unknown can be calculated by creating a formula based on where the other two variables are located in the circle. For example, if percentage (%) is the unknown variable, the circle shows the part (*P*) over the whole (*W*). This indicates that the percentage can be calculated by dividing the part by the whole.

$$\% = P \div W$$

where

% = percentage

P = part

W = whole

$$\text{Percentage} = \frac{\text{Part}}{\text{Whole}}$$

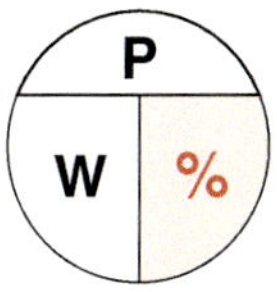

Even when there are not exactly 100 parts of something, percentages can still be calculated. For example, a jar contains 50 jelly beans. If there are 20 yellow jelly beans and 30 green jelly beans, it would still be true that 40% of the jelly beans are yellow and 60% of the jelly beans are green. This can be demonstrated using the following problem-solving steps and the formula for calculating the percentage:

Percentage Guide

In calculations using percentages, the percentage must first be changed to a decimal by dropping the percent symbol and dividing by 100, which is the same as moving the decimal two places to the left.

$$40\% = 40. = 0.40$$

To calculate the answer to a problem as a percentage, decimal answers are changed to percentages by multiplying the result by 100 and adding a percent symbol.

$$0.40 \times 100 = 40\%$$

Problem-Solving Steps

1. Calculate the percentage of jelly beans that are yellow in a jar that contains a total of 50 jelly beans if 20 jelly beans are yellow.

   $\% = P \div W$

   $\% = 20 \div 50$

   $\% = 0.40$

   % = **40% yellow jelly beans**

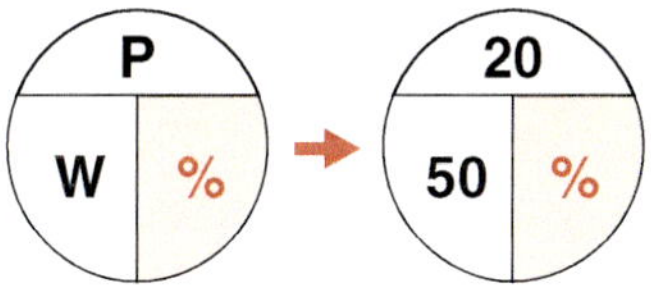

2. Calculate the percentage of jelly beans that are green in a jar that contains a total of 50 jelly beans if 30 jelly beans are green.

   $\% = P \div W$

   $\% = 30 \div 50$

   $\% = 0.60$

   % = **60% green jelly beans**

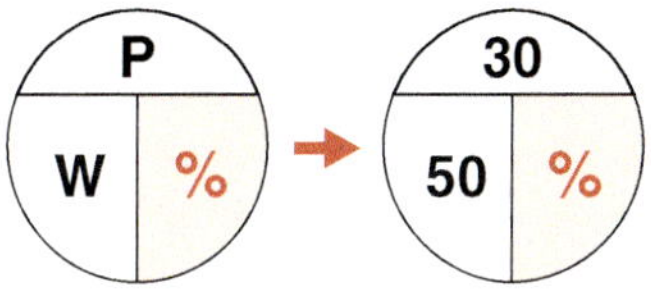

If the part (*P*) is the unknown variable, the percentage circle shows the whole (*W*) and the percentage (%) next to each other. This indicates that the whole must be multiplied by the percentage to find the part.

$$P = W \times \%$$

where

$$\text{Part} = \text{Whole} \times \text{Percentage}$$

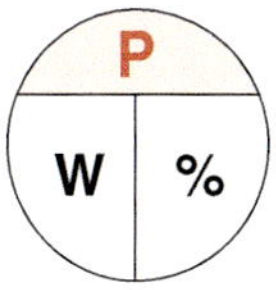

P = part

W = whole

% = percentage

The number of jelly beans that are green or yellow can be calculated by multiplying the total number of jelly beans by the percentage of each color. This can be demonstrated by using the following problem-solving steps and applying the formula for calculating the part:

Problem-Solving Steps

1. Calculate the number of yellow jelly beans in a jar that contains a total of 50 jelly beans if 40% of the jelly beans are yellow.

   $P = W \times \%$

   $P = 50 \times 40\%$

   $P = 50 \times 0.40$

   $P =$ **20 yellow jelly beans**

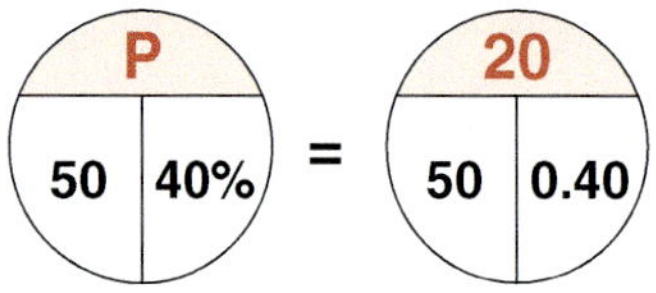

2. Calculate the number of green jelly beans in a jar that contains a total of 50 jelly beans if 60% of the jelly beans are green.

   $P = W \times \%$

   $P = 50 \times 60\%$

   $P = 50 \times 0.60$

   $P =$ **30 green jelly beans**

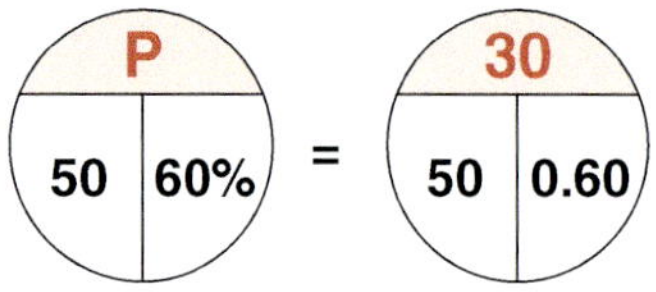

If the whole (W) is the unknown variable, the percentage circle shows the part (P) over the percentage (%). This indicates that the whole can be calculated by dividing the part by the percentage.

$W = P \div \%$

where

W = whole

P = part

% = percentage

$$\text{Whole} = \frac{\text{Part}}{\text{Percentage}}$$

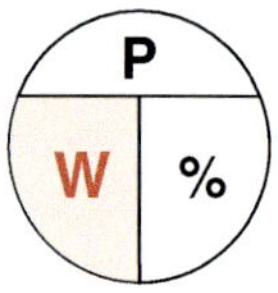

The total number of jelly beans can be calculated by dividing the number of green or yellow jelly beans by the percentage of the corresponding color of jelly beans. This can be demonstrated by using the following problem-solving steps and applying the formula for calculating the whole:

Problem-Solving Steps

1. Calculate the total number of jelly beans in a jar if 40% of the jelly beans are yellow and there are 20 yellow jelly beans in the jar.

   ***W* = P ÷ %**

   $W = 20 \div 40\%$

   $W = 20 \div 0.40$

   $W =$ **50 jelly beans**

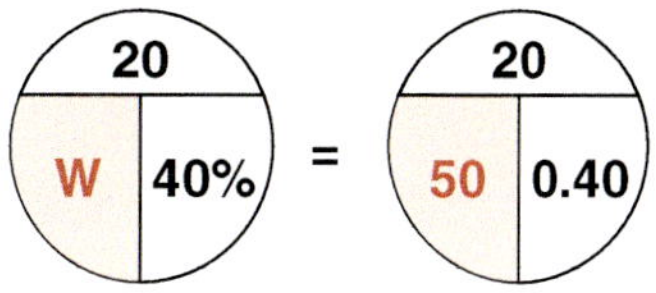

2. Calculate the total number of jelly beans in a jar if 60% of the jelly beans are green and there are 30 green jelly beans in the jar.

   ***W* = P ÷ %**

   $W = 30 \div 60\%$

   $W = 30 \div 0.60$

   $W =$ **50 jelly beans**

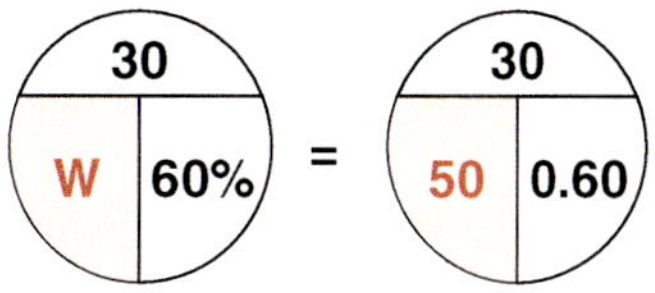

4-1 Checkpoint

1. Convert 47% to a decimal.

   ____

2. Convert 0.27 to a percentage.

   ____

3. If 18 out of 100 peppercorns are green, what percentage of the peppercorns are green?

   ____

   ____

4. If there are 18 Gala apples and 12 Fuji apples, what percentage are Fuji apples?

   ____

   ____

5. If 50 items are on a menu and 20% of them cost less than \$10, how many cost less than \$10?

   ____

   ____

6. If there are 20 oatmeal cookies on a tray and 40% of the cookies are oatmeal, how many cookies are on the tray?

   ____

   ____

Section 4-2 USING YIELD PERCENTAGES (YPs)

Foodservice operations purchase many products in forms that are different from the way the products are used. **See Figure 4-3.** For example, meats may need to be trimmed of excess fat and bone. Produce may need to be peeled and seeded. Or seafood may need to be scaled, skinned, and have the heads and fins removed. In all of these cases, unused parts are generated.

Trimming Meats

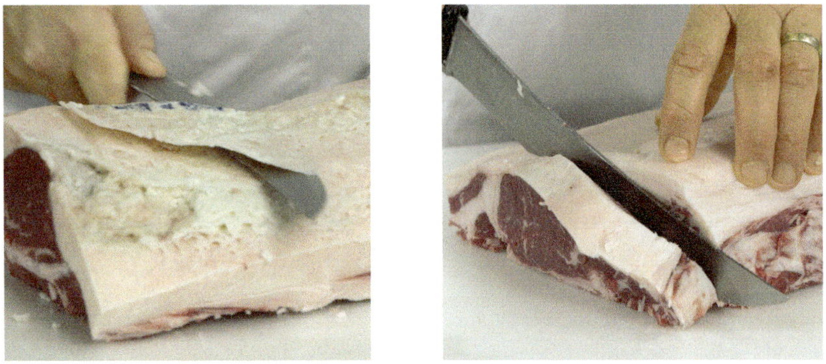

Figure 4-3. Meats are trimmed of excess fat before being used in a recipe.

The terms "as purchased (AP)" and "edible portion (EP)" are commonly used to distinguish between a food item before it is trimmed and a food item after it is trimmed. The *as-purchased (AP) amount* is the original amount of a food item as it is ordered and received. The *edible-portion (EP) amount* is the amount of a food item that remains after trimming. **See Figure 4-4.**

As Purchased (AP) vs. Edible Portion (EP)

Figure 4-4. The greens, tips, and skin of whole carrots in as-purchased (AP) form are removed prior to use, leaving the edible portion of the carrot.

To account for unused parts, foodservice workers perform calculations based on yield percentages. A *yield percentage (YP)* is the edible-portion (EP) amount of a food item divided by the as-purchased (AP) amount and is expressed as a percentage. Yield percentage (YP) helps identify how much usable product is available after processing. For items served in the same form as they are purchased, such as whole pieces of fruit or premade pastries, the yield percentage is 100%. The three formulas involving yield percentage (YP) are used for different reasons:

- **Calculating for Yield Percentages (YPs).** A yield percentage (YP) is calculated when it cannot be found for a particular food item in any reference material.
- **Calculating for As-Purchased (AP) Amounts.** An as-purchased (AP) amount is calculated when the edible-portion (EP) amount of a food item required for a recipe is known and the amount to be ordered needs to be determined.
- **Calculating for Edible-Portion (EP) Amounts.** An edible-portion (EP) amount is calculated when the as-purchased (AP) amount of a food item is already on hand and the usable amount of the food item needs to be calculated.

Calculating Yield Percentages (YPs)

A percentage circle can be modified to calculate yield percentages (YPs). The circle is modified by substituting the part (*P*) with *EP* since the edible-portion (EP) amount represents the part of the food item used in the recipe. Then, the whole (*W*) is substituted with *AP* since the as-purchased (AP) amount represents the whole item. Finally, the percentage (%) is substituted with yield percentage (*YP*). When any two of the variables are known, the third can be calculated. **See Figure 4-5.**

Yield Percentage (YP) Formulas

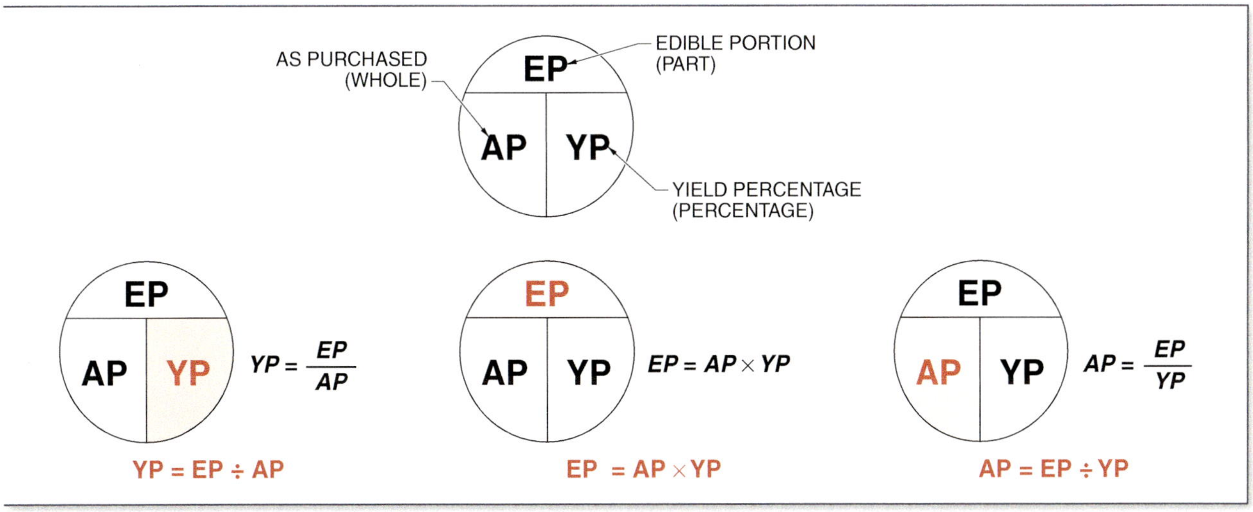

Figure 4-5. If any two variables in a yield percentage are known, the third variable can be calculated using a percentage circle.

Common examples of yield percentages (YPs) are available in various reference tables. **See Appendix.** However, if a yield percentage (YP) for a particular food item is not known and cannot be found in reference material, it can be calculated by performing a raw yield test or a cooking-loss yield test.

A *raw yield test* is a procedure used to determine the yield percentage (YP) of a food item that is trimmed prior to being used in a recipe. To perform the raw yield test, a food item is purchased and weighed to determine the as-purchased (AP) amount. The food item is then trimmed, and the edible portion is weighed to determine the edible-portion (EP) amount. The yield percentage (YP) is calculated by dividing the edible-portion (EP) amount by the as-purchased (AP) amount. For example, to calculate the yield percentage (YP) of carrots, the as-purchased (AP) amount of carrots is weighed. Then, the carrots are peeled, and the greens and tips are removed. (The trimmings can be used in a stock.) The edible-portion (EP) amount is determined by weighing the trimmed carrots. If 10 kg of carrots weigh 8.5 kg after being trimmed, the yield percentage (YP) can be calculated using the formula as follows:

$$YP = EP \div AP$$

$$\text{Yield Percentage} = \frac{\text{Edible-Portion Amount}}{\text{As-Purchased Amount}}$$

where

YP = yield percentage

EP = edible-portion amount (part)

AP = as-purchased amount (whole)

$YP = 8.5 \text{ kg} \div 10 \text{ kg}$

$YP = 0.85$

$YP = \mathbf{85\%}$

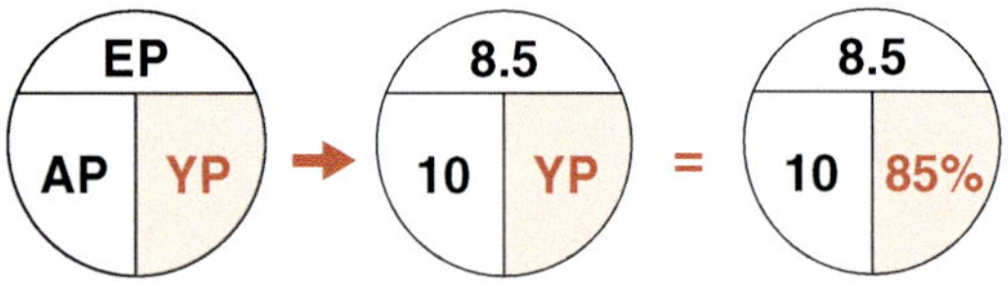

Figure 4-6. Meat can lose up to 30% of its weight as moisture is lost and fat is rendered during cooking.

The other type of yield test is called a cooking-loss yield test. A *cooking-loss yield test* is a procedure used to determine the yield percentage (YP) of a food item that loses weight during the cooking process. For example, meat loses weight as fat is rendered and moisture is lost during cooking. **See Figure 4-6.** This is commonly referred to as shrinkage. *Shrinkage* is the loss of volume and weight of a piece of food as the food cooks. The cooking-loss yield test is used when the edible portion (EP) amount is based on the amount of cooked food to be served as opposed to the as-purchased (AP) amount of raw food.

To perform the cooking-loss yield test, a food item is weighed to determine the as-purchased (AP) amount. The food item is then weighed again after being trimmed and cooked to determine the edible-portion (EP) amount. For example, a lamb chop that weighs 200 g prior to cooking might weigh 150 g after cooking. The yield percentage (YP) in this case can be calculated by using the formula as follows:

YP = EP ÷ AP

$YP = 150\text{ g} \div 200\text{ g}$

$YP = 0.75$

$YP = \mathbf{75\%}$

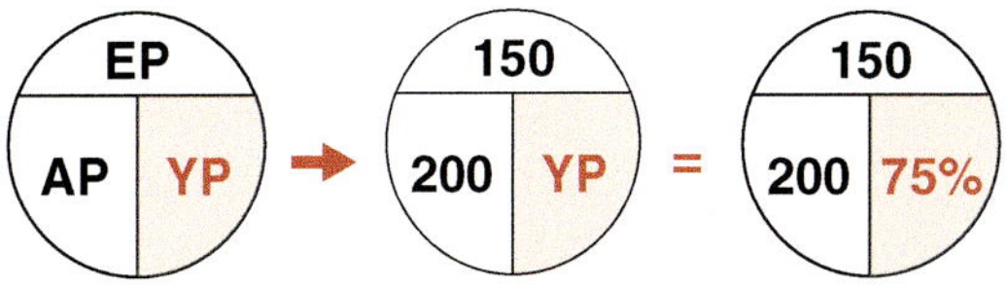

Another factor to consider when determining yield percentages (YPs) is the loss of food that can occur during service. For example, as a 10 L batch of cream soup is kept warm, 0.2 L of the soup may evaporate. Then by the end of service, 0.3 L of the soup may remain on the sides and bottom of the pot as well as on the ladle. The total shrinkage, 0.5 L, is determined by adding the amount of soup lost to evaporation and the amount of soup left in the pot and on the ladle (0.2 L + 0.3 L = 0.5 L). As a result, the edible-portion (EP) amount for the soup is 9.5 L (10 L – 0.5 L = 9.5 L). The yield percentage (YP) for the soup can be calculated by using the formula as follows:

YP = EP ÷ AP

$YP = 9.5\text{ L} \div 10\text{ L}$

$YP = 0.95$

$YP = \mathbf{95\%}$

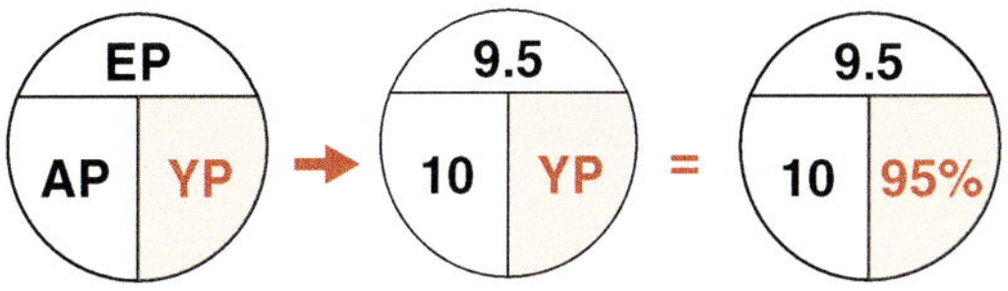

Knowing this information can help when analyzing costs. It can also help when determining menu prices.

Calculating As-Purchased (AP) Amounts

Calculating an as-purchased (AP) amount is done to determine the proper amount of an ingredient to order to make a given quantity of food. The as-purchased (AP) amount is calculated by using the following formula:

AP = EP ÷ YP

$$\text{As-Purchased Amount} = \frac{\text{Edible-Portion Amount}}{\text{Yield Percentage}}$$

where

AP = as-purchased amount (whole)

EP = edible-portion amount (part)

YP = yield percentage

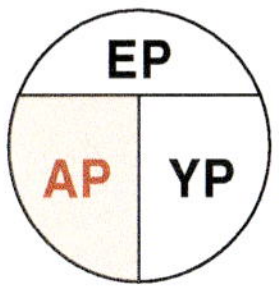

Consider a banquet for 100 people that includes grilled salmon on the menu. The recipe for the grilled salmon dish calls for a 180 g fillet of salmon per serving. The total edible-portion (EP) amount of salmon can be calculated by multiplying the amount of salmon required per person by the number of people attending the banquet (100 people × 180 g per person = 18,000 g or 18,000 g ÷ 1000 g/kg = 18 kg).

If the chef decides to order whole salmon for the banquet, the heads, fins, skin, and bones will need to be removed. **See Figure 4-7.** If the yield percentage (YP) for cutting salmon fillets from whole salmon is 60%, the chef can then calculate how much whole salmon to order. The amount of whole salmon to be ordered can be calculated by applying the formula for an as-purchased (AP) amount as follows:

$$AP = EP \div YP$$

$AP = 18 \text{ kg} \div 60\%$

$AP = 18 \text{ kg} \div 0.60$

$AP = \mathbf{30 \text{ kg}}$

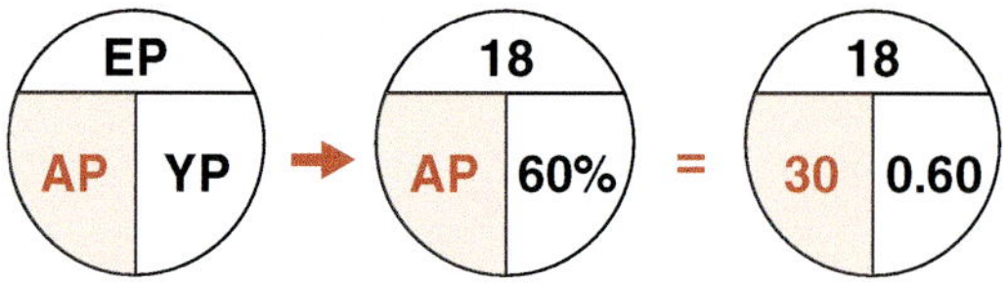

Trimming Fish

Figure 4-7. The heads, skin, and bones of whole fish are removed to produce boneless, skinless fillets.

Calculating Edible-Portion (EP) Amounts

Calculating an edible-portion (EP) amount is done to determine how much food can be prepared using an amount of an ingredient that is already on hand. The edible-portion (EP) amount can be calculated using the following formula:

$$EP = AP \times YP$$

Edible-Portion Amount = *As-Purchased Amount* × *Yield Percentage*

where

EP = edible-portion amount (part)

AP = as-purchased amount (whole)

YP = yield percentage

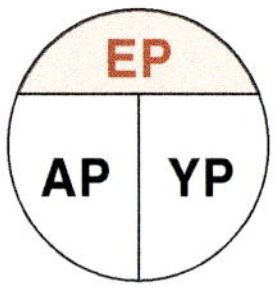

Sometimes, it is necessary to calculate how much food can be prepared from the amount of ingredients that are available. For example, a chef decides to take advantage of a special price being offered by the meat supplier and purchases 40 kg of whole beef tenderloin. The chef adds beef stroganoff to the menu and needs to calculate how many servings of the recipe can be made using the beef tenderloin.

The recipe calls for 150 g per serving of fully trimmed beef tenderloin cut into 1 in. pieces. The chef knows from experience that after trimming the fat and connective tissue from the beef tenderloin, only 75% of the tenderloin will be used. The number of servings of beef stroganoff that can be prepared is calculated using the formula for the edible-portion (EP) amount and applying the following problem-solving steps:

Problem-Solving Steps

Metric Measurements	Customary/Imperial Measurements
Chef purchases 40 kg of beef tenderloin.	Chef purchases 80 lb of beef tenderloin.
Recipe calls for 150 g of beef per serving.	Recipe calls for 6 oz of beef per serving.
Beef yield percentage is 75%.	Beef yield percentage is 75%.

Metric

1. Calculate the edible-portion (EP) amount of beef tenderloin by multiplying the as-purchased (AP) amount by the yield percentage (YP).

   EP = AP × YP

   $EP = 40\text{ kg} \times 75\%$

   $EP = 40\text{ kg} \times 0.75$

   $EP = \mathbf{30\ kg}$

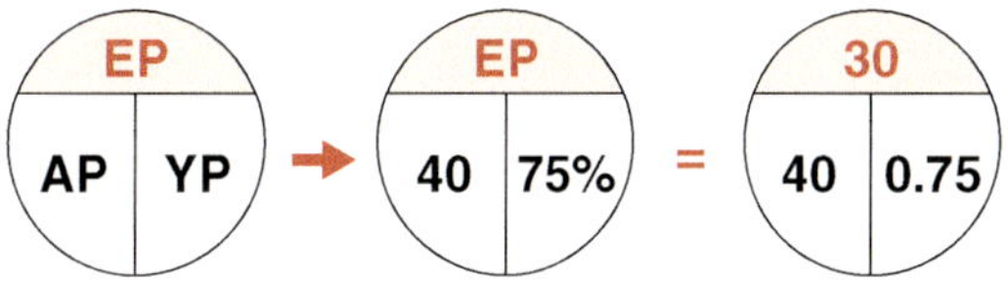

2. Calculate the number of servings of beef stroganoff that can be made using the 30 kg of trimmed beef tenderloin.

$$30\ \cancel{kg} \times \frac{1000\ \cancel{g}}{1\ \cancel{kg}} \times \frac{1\text{ serving}}{150\ \cancel{g}} = \frac{30{,}000\text{ servings}}{150} = \mathbf{200\ servings}$$

Customary/Imperial

1. Calculate the edible-portion (EP) amount of beef tenderloin by multiplying the as-purchased (AP) amount by the yield percentage (YP).

   EP = AP × YP

   $EP = 80\text{ lb} \times 75\%$

   $EP = 80\text{ lb} \times 0.75$

   $EP = \mathbf{60\ lb}$

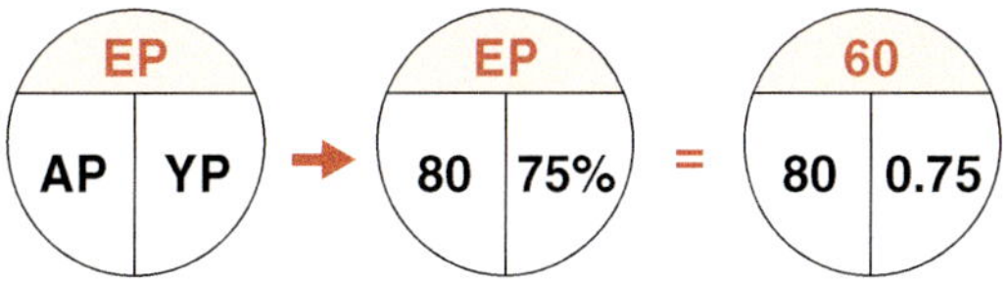

2. Calculate the number of servings of beef stroganoff that can be made using the 60 lb of trimmed beef tenderloin.

$$60\ \cancel{lb} \times \frac{16\ \cancel{oz}}{1\ \cancel{lb}} \times \frac{1\text{ serving}}{6\ \cancel{oz}} = \frac{960\text{ servings}}{6} = \mathbf{160\ servings}$$

Factors Affecting Yield Percentages (YPs)

Calculations that involve yield percentages (YPs) are performed regularly in the professional kitchen. However, special attention should be given to how the results for yield percentage (YP) calculations need to be rounded. For example, if it is determined that 30.4 kg of fish should be ordered for a banquet, this decimal result would be rounded down to 30 kg using standard math rules. However, rounding down would result in the banquet coming up short on the amount of fish needed.

For yield percentage (YP) calculations related to ordering food, the results should always be rounded up to ensure that enough food is purchased. In this case, 31.0 kg of fish should be ordered. However, if a yield percentage (YP) calculation indicates that 14.8 portions can be made from a given recipe, the result should be rounded down to 14 because the recipe will not make 15 full servings.

Employee skill levels can also affect yield percentages (YPs). Butchering meats is a skill that requires a lot of practice to master. Therefore, a trained butcher will experience a higher yield percentage (YP) when trimming meat than an entry-level cook assigned to do the same task.

Another factor affecting yield percentage (YP) is the condition and size of the initial product. For example, fruits that are unblemished will have a higher yield percentage (YP) than bruised fruits that require the removal of undesirable parts. Large potatoes have a higher yield percentage (YP) than small potatoes. More unused parts are generated by peeling many small potatoes compared to peeling fewer large potatoes.

Checkpoint 4-2

1. Explain the difference between an as-purchased (AP) amount and an edible-portion (EP) amount.

____

____

2. Define "yield percentage (YP)."

____

____

3. If 2 kg of beets generate 0.5 kg of trimmings, what is the yield percentage (YP) for the beets?

____

____

4. Describe the difference between a raw yield test and a cooking-loss yield test.

____

____

5. If a recipe calls for 170 g of grilled pork per serving, how many servings can be made from 15 kg of pork if it has a yield percentage (YP) of 85%?

____

____

6. If a recipe calls for 8 kilograms of peeled potatoes, how many kilograms of unpeeled potatoes are required if the yield percentage (YP) is 80%?

____

____

7. If a yield calculation indicates that 36.7 portions can be made from a given recipe, what should the yield calculation be rounded to in order to ensure an adequate number of servings?

____

____

Section 4-3 USING BAKER'S PERCENTAGES

Baking is based on chemical reactions among ingredients when heat is applied to them. Once a product is placed in an oven, there is no opportunity to make any changes. Therefore, bakeshop recipes are called formulas since they require precise measurements of each specific ingredient in order to ensure successful results. For example, if bread flour were substituted for cake flour, the product would have an entirely different look, texture, and flavor.

Each ingredient in a formula is often expressed as a baker's percentage to make scaling easier. A *baker's percentage* is the weight of an ingredient expressed as a percentage of the weight of the main ingredient (primary structure provider) in a formula. The baker's percentage for the main ingredient in a formula is always 100%, regardless of the amount required. The weights of the other ingredients are expressed as a percentage of the weight of the main ingredient. It is important to note that flour is often the main ingredient in cakes and breads even when the amount of flour required is not the largest ingredient amount in the recipe. This is because flour often provides the primary structure for cakes and breads.

For example, if a formula lists bread flour as its main ingredient (100%) and lists water with a baker's percentage of 60%, then no matter how much flour is used, the weight of the water will always be

Formulas

Challah Bread	
Ingredients	**Baker's Percentage**
Bread flour	100%
Salt	3%
Honey	5%
Shortening	6%
Eggs	3%
Water	60%
Yeast	5%
Total	**182%**

Figure 4-8. Baker's percentages are the weights of ingredients expressed as a percentage of the weight of the main ingredient in a formula.

60% of the weight of the flour. However, 60% of the total formula is not composed of water. It is important to remember that the sum of the baker's percentages in a formula (total baker's percentage) will always be greater than 100%. **See Figure 4-8.**

Some formulas require more than one type of flour. If the combined weights of two or more types of flour are larger than any other single ingredient in a formula, their combined weight is considered to be the main ingredient with a baker's percentage of 100%. Each type of flour is a percentage of 100%. For example, if a rye bread formula contains rye flour with a baker's percentage of 75% and all-purpose flour with a baker's percentage of 25%, the baker's percentage of the main ingredient is 100% (75% + 25% = 100%).

However, some formulas do not contain any flour. For example, dried apricots would be the main ingredient (primary structure provider) in a formula for apricot filling. In this formula, the baker's percentage for the dried apricots would be 100%. All other ingredients would be listed as a percentage of the main ingredient.

Converting Units of Measure

Each ingredient in a formula, including liquids, must be weighed using the same unit of measure. The ingredients in formulas are not measured by volume. A recipe can be changed into a formula by converting all of the ingredients to the same unit of measure. The unit of measure chosen is the most convenient measure of weight for that formula.

For example, a ciabatta bread recipe may require 2 kg of bread flour, 40 g of salt, 40 g of yeast, 160 g of olive oil, and 1.6 kg of water. To change this recipe into a formula, the ingredients must be converted to the same unit of measure (grams). First, the amount of the main ingredient that provides the structure (bread flour) is converted from 2 kg to 2000 g. Since there are 1000 grams in 1 kilogram, the number of kilograms is multiplied by 1000 (2 kg × 1000 = 2000 g). Likewise, the 1.6 kg of water are converted to 1600 g (1.6 kg × 1000 = 1600 g). The ingredients that are already listed in grams (salt, yeast, and olive oil) are not changed. **See Figure 4-9.**

If a ciabatta bread recipe is written with customary or imperial measurements, it may require 4.5 lb of bread flour, 1.5 oz of salt, 1.5 oz of yeast, 5.6 oz of olive oil, and 3.6 lb of water. In this case, the ingredients are converted to ounces to keep the units of measure the same. First, the bread flour is converted from 4.5 lb to 72 oz. Since there are 16 ounces in 1 pound, the number of pounds is multiplied by 16 (4.5 lb × 16 = 72 oz). Likewise, the 3.6 lb of water are converted to 57.6 oz (3.6 lb × 16 = 57.6 oz). Since salt, yeast, and olive oil are already listed in ounces, they are not changed.

Converting Units of Measure

Ciabatta Bread		
Ingredients	**Ingredient Weights**	**Ingredient Weights Converted to Same Unit of Measure***
Metric Measurements		
Bread flour (main ingredient)	2 kg	2 kg × 1000 g/kg = **2000 g**
Salt	40 g	**40 g**
Yeast	40 g	**40 g**
Olive oil	160 g	**160 g**
Water	1.6 kg	1.6 kg × 1000 g/kg = **1600 g**
Customary/Imperial Measurements		
Bread flour (main ingredient)	4.5 lb	4.5 lb × 16 oz/lb = **72 oz**
Salt	1.5 oz	**1.5 oz**
Yeast	1.5 oz	**1.5 oz**
Olive oil	5.6 oz	**5.6 oz**
Water	3.6 lb	3.6 lb × 16 oz/lb = **57.6 oz**

* Ingredient weights convert to grams for metric measurements and to ounces for customary/imperial measurements.

Figure 4-9. To change this recipe into a formula, the ingredients are converted to the same unit of measure, either grams for metric or ounces for customary/imperial.

Calculating Baker's Percentages

Once all of the ingredients in a formula are in the same unit of measure, the weight of each individual ingredient is divided by the weight of the main ingredient. The result is then changed to a baker's percentage using the following equation:

$$BP = (IW \div MW) \times 100$$

where

BP = ingredient baker's percentage

IW = ingredient weight

MW = main ingredient weight

$$\text{Ingredient Baker's Percentage} = \left(\frac{\text{Ingredient Weight}}{\text{Main Ingredient Weight}}\right) \times 100$$

This equation involves two mathematical operations. Division is done first because it is in parentheses. For example, the 40 g of salt is divided by the 2000 g of the main ingredient, bread flour. Then, the result is multiplied by 100 to convert it to a percentage. **See Figure 4-10.**

$$BP = (IW \div MW) \times 100$$

$$BP = (40\text{ g} \div 2000\text{ g}) \times 100$$

$$BP = \mathbf{2\%}$$

Calculating Baker's Percentages

Ciabatta Bread

Ingredients	Ingredient Weights	Baker's Percentages
Metric Measurements		
Bread flour (main ingredient)	2000 g	2000 g ÷ 2000 g = 1.0 × 100 = **100%**
Salt	40 g	40 g ÷ 2000 g = 0.02 × 100 = **2%**
Yeast	40 g	40 g ÷ 2000 g = 0.02 × 100 = **2%**
Olive oil	160 g	160 g ÷ 2000 g = 0.08 × 100 = **8%**
Water	1600 g	1600 g ÷ 2000 g = 0.8 × 100 = **80%**
Customary/Imperial Measurements		
Bread flour (main ingredient)	72 oz	72 oz ÷ 72 oz = 1.0 × 100 = **100%**
Salt	1.5 oz	1.5 oz ÷ 72 oz = 0.02 × 100 = **2%**
Yeast	1.5 oz	1.5 oz ÷ 72 oz = 0.02 × 100 = **2%**
Olive oil	5.6 oz	5.6 oz ÷ 72 oz = 0.08 × 100 = **8%**
Water	57.6 oz	57.6 oz ÷ 72 oz = 0.8 × 100 = **80%**

Figure 4-10. Once all of the ingredient weights in a formula have been converted to the same unit of measure, each ingredient weight is divided by the main ingredient weight. Then, each is multiplied by 100 to convert them to baker's percentages.

Many formulas will label the main ingredient and then list each ingredient only as a baker's percentage. In order to determine the required weight of each ingredient, the weight of the main ingredient must be calculated based on a desired yield. For example, a desired yield of 30 kg of hard-roll dough would be divided by the total baker's percentage of the formula (182%) using the following equation:

$$MW = DY \div (T\% \div 100)$$

where

MW = main ingredient weight

DY = desired yield

T% = total baker's percentage

$$\text{Main Ingredient Weight} = \frac{\text{Desired Yield}}{\left(\text{Total Baker's Percentage} \div 100\right)}$$

This equation involves two division steps. The division shown in parentheses is performed first. In this example, the total baker's percentage (182%) is divided by 100. Then, the desired yield is divided by that result to determine the weight of the main ingredient.

$$MW = DY \div (T\% \div 100)$$

$$MW = 30\text{ kg} \div (182 \div 100)$$

$$MW = 30\text{ kg} \div 1.82$$

$$MW = \mathbf{16.5\text{ kg}}$$

Once the main ingredient weight is known, the weight of each of the other ingredients can be calculated. This is done by dividing the baker's percentage of each ingredient by 100 and then multiplying the result by the main ingredient weight. **See Figure 4-11.** The weight of the remaining ingredients is calculated using the following equation:

$$IW = MW \times (BP \div 100)$$

IW = ingredient weight

MW = main ingredient weight

BP = ingredient baker's percentage

$$\text{Ingredient Weight} = \text{Main Ingredient Weight} \times \left(\frac{\text{Ingredient Baker's Percentage}}{100} \right)$$

Using Formulas

Hard-Roll Dough (Yield: 30 kg/66 lb)

Ingredients	Baker's Percentages	Ingredient Weights in Metric*	Ingredient Weights in Customary/Imperial*
Bread flour (main ingredient)	100%	16.5 kg × (100% ÷ 100) = 16.5 kg × 1.00 = **16.5 kg**	36.3 lb × (100% ÷ 100) = 36.3 lb × 1.00 = **36.3 lb**
Salt	3%	16.5 kg × (3% ÷ 100) = 16.5 kg × 0.03 = **0.5 kg**	36.3 lb × (3% ÷ 100) = 36.3 lb × 0.03 = **1.1 lb**
Sugar	5%	16.5 kg × (5% ÷ 100) = 16.5 kg × 0.05 = **0.8 kg**	36.3 lb × (5% ÷ 100) = 36.3 lb × 0.05 = **1.8 lb**
Shortening	6%	16.5 kg × (6% ÷ 100) = 16.5 kg × 0.06 = **1.0 kg**	36.3 lb × (6% ÷ 100) = 36.3 lb × 0.06 = **2.2 lb**
Egg whites	3%	16.5 kg × (3% ÷ 100) = 16.5 kg × 0.03 = **0.5 kg**	36.3 lb × (3% ÷ 100) = 36.3 lb × 0.03 = **1.1 lb**
Water	60%	16.5 kg × (60% ÷ 100) = 16.5 kg × 0.60 = **9.9 kg**	36.3 lb × (60% ÷ 100) = 36.3 lb × 0.60 = **21.8 lb**
Yeast	5%	16.5 kg × (5% ÷ 100) = 16.5 kg × 0.05 = **0.8 kg**	36.3 lb × (5% ÷ 100) = 36.3 lb × 0.05 = **1.8 lb**
	Total: 182%	**Total: 30 kg**	**Total: 66.1 lb**

*Results are rounded to the tenths place.

Figure 4-11. Ingredient weights for a formula that only lists baker's percentages can be calculated by dividing the baker's percentage for each ingredient by 100 and then multiplying the result by the main ingredient weight.

For example, if the baker's percentage for salt is 3% and the weight of the main ingredient (bread flour) is 16.5 kilograms, the weight of the salt can be calculated as follows:

$$IW = MW \times (BP \div 100)$$

$$IW = 16.5 \text{ kg} \times (3 \div 100)$$

$$IW = 16.5 \text{ kg} \times 0.03$$

$$IW = \mathbf{0.5\ kg}$$

Checkpoint 4-3

1. Define "baker's percentage."

2. What percentage is assigned to the main ingredient in a formula?

3. If a biscuit recipe calls for 2.5 kg of flour as the main ingredient and 1.5 kg of butter, what would the baker's percentage be for the butter?

4. If the main ingredient in a formula is sugar and the percentage for vanilla extract in the recipe is 2%, how many grams of vanilla extract are needed if 8 kilograms of sugar are used?

Section 4-4 CALCULATING RATIOS

Sometimes recipes are written as ratios. A *ratio* is a mathematical way to represent the relationship between two or more numbers or amounts. A ratio is expressed in terms of parts and can be shown in different ways. For example, a ratio of three parts to one part can be expressed using numbers with a colon between them (3:1) or with the word "to" between them (3 to 1).

Consider a vinaigrette that is made with a ratio of 3 parts oil to 1 part vinegar by volume. The term "parts" is used as a generic term because it does not matter what volume unit of measure is used when making the vinaigrette as long as the unit is the same for both ingredients. For example, a vinaigrette will taste the same if made with 300 mL of oil and 100 mL of vinegar or 3 L of oil and 1 L of vinegar. Likewise, the vinaigrette will taste the same if made with 3 c of oil and 1 c of vinegar or 3 qt of oil and 1 qt of vinegar.

Ratios can be converted to fractions and percentages. In the case of the vinaigrette, the ratio consists of a total of four parts (3 parts oil + 1 part vinegar). Since the oil represents three parts out of four and the vinegar represents one part out of four, a vinaigrette with this ratio can be thought of as containing ¾ oil and ¼ vinegar. By converting the fractions ¾ and ¼ to percentages, the vinaigrette can also be thought of as containing 75% oil and 25% vinegar. **See Figure 4-12.**

Converting Two-Ingredient Ratios into Fractions, Decimals, and Percentages

Vinaigrette

Ratio	Total Parts	Fractions	Decimals/ Percentages
3:1	3 + 1 = 4	¾ Oil	3 ÷ 4 = 0.75 75% Oil
		¼ Vinegar	1 ÷ 4 = 0.25 25% Vinegar

Figure 4-12. Two-ingredient ratios can easily be converted into fractions, decimals, and percentages.

An example of a ratio with three ingredients is the 2:1:1 ratio for mirepoix (a mixture of 2 parts onion, 1 part carrots, and 1 part celery used when making stock). The ratio for mirepoix contains a total of four parts where onions represent two parts of four, and carrots and celery each represent one part of four. Therefore, mirepoix is made of 50% onions and 25% each of celery and carrots. **See Figure 4-13.**

Converting Three-Ingredient Ratios into Fractions, Decimals, and Percentages

Mirepoix

Ratio	Total Parts	Fractions	Decimals/ Percentages
2:1:1	2 + 1 + 1 = 4	2/4 = ½ Onions	1 ÷ 2 = 0.50 50% Onions
		¼ Carrots	1 ÷ 4 = 0.25 25% Carrots
		¼ Celery	1 ÷ 4 = 0.25 25% Celery

Figure 4-13. Three-ingredient ratios can easily be converted into fractions, decimals, and percentages.

Checkpoint 4-4

1. Define "ratio."

____

____

2. If the ratio of sugar to shortening in a cookie recipe is 2:1, what fraction of the recipe is sugar?

____

____

3. If the ratio of flour to sugar in a cake recipe is 3:2, what percent of the recipe is flour?

____

____

Section 4-5 USING RATIOS

A ratio is similar to a baker's formula in that the ratio does not contain actual ingredient amounts. Instead, a ratio describes how the ingredients are used in relation to one another. The simplest ratio used is a ratio of 1:1 (also referred to as equal parts).

Roux (a cooked mixture of fat and flour used to thicken soups and sauces) is based on a 1:1 ratio by weight of fat to flour. This simply means that 1 kg of flour will be needed for every 1 kg of fat used to make the roux. Similarly, a roux made with 5 lb of flour will require 5 lb of fat. In a ratio of 1:1, there are two total parts. By converting the ratio to fractions, the recipe for roux becomes ½ flour and ½ fat. By converting the ratio to percentages, the recipe for roux becomes 50% flour and 50% fat.

To calculate the amount of each ingredient required to make a given amount of roux, multiply the total desired yield by the fraction associated with each ingredient. With a ratio of 1:1, it is easy to calculate that 4 kg of roux would be made from 2 kg of fat and 2 kg of flour.

Fat: $4\,\text{kg} \times \frac{1}{2} = \frac{4\,\text{kg}}{2} = \mathbf{2\,kg}$

Flour: $4\,\text{kg} \times \frac{1}{2} = \frac{4\,\text{kg}}{2} = \mathbf{2\,kg}$

It is important to know whether to use weight units or volume units when calculating ingredient amounts for a given ratio. For example, the ratio for roux is 1:1 flour to fat *by weight*. The ratio will not work with units of volume. Therefore, the roux will turn out correctly whether made with 500 g of flour and 500 g of fat or 1 lb of flour and 1 lb of fat. However, it will not turn out correctly if made with 250 mL of flour and 250 mL of fat because 250 mL of flour does not weigh the same as 250 mL of fat. Likewise, if using 1 c of flour and 1 c of fat, the roux will not turn out because 1 c of flour does not weigh the same as 1 c of fat.

When a ratio must be used in terms of weight only or volume only, the ratio will be followed by the words "by weight" or "by volume." For example, a ratio for pie dough may be three parts flour to two parts butter to one part water (3:2:1) by weight. If the desired yield of pie dough is 6 kg, how much of each ingredient would be required?

First, the ratio is converted to fractions by dividing each number in the ratio by the total number of parts (3 + 2 + 1 = 6). As a result, flour would be 3/6 (which reduces to ½), butter would be 2/6 (which reduces to ⅓), and water would be ⅙. By multiplying each fraction by the total desired amount of dough (6 kg), the recipe would require 3 kg of flour (½ × 6 = 3), 2 kg of butter (⅓ × 6 = 2), and 1 kg of water (⅙ × 6 = 1). Similarly, if the desired yield of pie dough is 12 lb, the recipe would require 6 lb of flour (½ × 12 = 6), 4 lb of butter (⅓ × 12 = 4), and 2 lb of water (⅙ × 12 = 2). **See Figure 4-14.**

Using Pie Dough Ratios

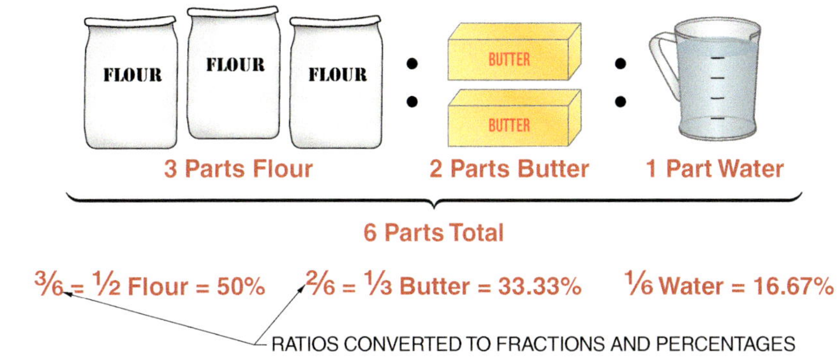

6 Kilograms* Pie Dough

Metric Measurements	
Ingredient	*Amount Required*
Flour	½ × 6 kg = 6 kg/2 = **3 kg**
Butter	⅓ × 6 kg = 6 kg/3 = **2 kg**
Water	⅙ × 6 kg = 6 kg/6 = **1 kg**

12 Pounds* Pie Dough

Customary/Imperial Measurements	
Ingredient	*Amount Required*
Flour	½ × 12 lb = 12 lb/2 = **6 lb**
Butter	⅓ × 12 lb = 12 lb/3 = **4 lb**
Water	⅙ × 12 lb = 12 lb/6 = **2 lb**

* Desired recipe yield.

Figure 4-14. When using a ratio, ingredient amounts can be calculated by multiplying the fractions of the ratio by the desired yield of the recipe.

In some cases, it may be necessary to calculate a recipe yield based on the amount of one ingredient. For example, rice pilaf is made with a ratio of 2 parts liquid to 1 part uncooked white rice by volume. If the rice is prepared using 6 L of chicken stock, how much total rice can be prepared?

In this case, the ratio has three total parts (2 + 1 = 3). The chicken stock is ⅔, and the uncooked rice is ⅓. To calculate the total amount of cooked rice that can be prepared, the amount of chicken stock is divided by the fraction of the recipe that is chicken stock.

$$6 \text{ L} \div \frac{2}{3} = 6 \text{ L} \times \frac{3}{2} = 18 \text{ L}/2 = \mathbf{9\ L}$$

Then, to calculate how much uncooked rice is required, the total amount of cooked rice is multiplied by the fraction of the recipe that is uncooked rice.

$$9 \text{ L} \times \frac{1}{3} = 9 \text{ L}/3 = \mathbf{3\ L}$$

Therefore, 9 L of cooked rice could be made from 6 L of chicken stock and 3 L of uncooked rice.

Checkpoint 4-5

1. How is a ratio similar to a baker's formula?

____

____

2. A creamy salad dressing is made with a 4:1 ratio of mayonnaise to sour cream. How many liters of salad dressing can be made from 2 liters of sour cream?

____

____

3. A cookie dough is made with a ratio of 3 parts flour to 2 parts sugar to 1 part butter. If 9 kilograms of cookie dough needs to be made, how many kilograms of sugar are required?

____

____

Math Exercises 4

Work each problem in the space provided. Write the final answer on the blank provided. Round all decimal answers to the hundredths place, and reduce all fraction answers to lowest terms.

Leaf icon indicates a math problem with a sustainability focus.

Example:

65% ____________

A restaurant has 100 tablecloths. Of those tablecloths, 35 are square, and 65 are round. What percentage of tablecloths are round?

$65 \div 100 = 0.65 = \mathbf{65\%}$

____________ **1.** A restaurant has 100 tables. Of those tables, 28 of them seat 2 people, and 72 of them seat 4 people. What percentage of the tables seat 4 people?

72 ÷ 100 = 0.72 = 72%

____________ **2.** To cut energy costs, a restaurant manager replaces 13 out of 42 incandescent lightbulbs with high-efficiency LED bulbs. What percentage of the restaurant's lighting is now high-efficiency lighting?

________________ **3.** There are 30 hors d'oeuvres on a serving tray. If 15 of the hors d'oeuvres are stuffed mushrooms, 9 are bruschetta, and 6 are grilled shrimp kabobs, what percentage of the hors d'oeuvres are grilled shrimp kabobs?

________________ **4.** The manager of a café has calculated that growing artisan lettuce on site instead of purchasing it from a purveyor saves $0.89 per entrée salad. What percentage of savings results from growing the lettuce on site if each entrée salad sells for $11.00?

________________ **5.** If 35% of the desserts on a buffet are sugar free and there are 80 desserts on the buffet, how many of the desserts are sugar free?

________________ **6.** If 40% of the pieces of cheese on a cheese platter are Cheddar and there are 50 pieces of Cheddar cheese on the platter, how many total pieces of cheese are on the platter?

________________ **7.** At a luncheon, 20% of the guests ordered a vegetarian entrée. If 45 people ordered a vegetarian entrée, what is the total number of guests attending the luncheon?

_______________ **8.** A whole catfish weighs 3.5 kg. After cleaning and filleting the fish, the unused parts weigh 1.2 kg. How heavy is the edible-portion (EP) amount of the catfish?

_______________ **9.** After trimming 2.25 kg of carrots, the edible-portion (EP) amount is 2 kg. How many grams of unused parts were generated by trimming the carrots?

_______________ **10.** After the shucking and removal of kernels from five dozen ears of corn weighing a total of 16 kg, the edible-portion (EP) amount of the corn is 5.5 kg. The husks and cobs will be donated to a local farmer to use as feed. What is the weight of the husks and cobs?

_______________ **11.** What is the edible-portion (EP) amount of 5 kg of broccoli if the yield percentage (YP) for broccoli is 56%?

_______________ **12.** What is the edible-portion (EP) amount of 12 lb of spaghetti squash if the yield percentage (YP) is 70%?

_______________ **13.** How many sandwiches can be made from 25 kg of as-purchased chuck roast if chuck roast has a yield percentage (YP) of 80% and each sandwich contains 160 g of chuck roast?

_______________ **14.** How many sandwiches can be made from 30 lb of as-purchased chuck roast if chuck roast has a yield percentage (YP) of 80% and each sandwich contains 6 oz of chuck roast?

_______________ **15.** If 8 kg of cauliflower are purchased and the edible-portion (EP) amount after trimming is 6 kg, what is the yield percentage (YP) of the cauliflower?

_______________ **16.** If 5.5 lb of peelings are generated from peeling 40 lb of potatoes, what is the yield percentage (YP) of the potatoes?

_______________ **17.** After cleaning, peeling, and deveining 5 kg of shrimp, there are 1.5 kg of unused parts. What is the yield percentage (YP) of the shrimp?

_______________ **18.** The edible-portion (EP) amount of romaine lettuce required for an event is 14 kilograms. If the yield percentage (YP) for romaine lettuce is 78%, how many kilograms of romaine lettuce should be ordered for the event? *(Round the answer to a whole number.)*

_______________ **19.** A recipe requires 8 lb of cauliflower florets. If whole cauliflower has a yield percentage (YP) of 68%, how much whole cauliflower must be purchased to make the recipe? *(Round the answer to a whole number.)*

_______________ **20.** A chef needs 4 lb of peeled and sliced apples for an apple crisp dessert. If apples have a yield percentage (YP) of 78%, how many pounds of whole apples are needed? *(Round the answer to a whole number.)*

_______________ **21.** If onions have a yield percentage (YP) of 93%, how many kilograms of onions are needed to yield an edible portion (EP) amount of 8 kilograms?

_______________ **22.** If the edible portion (EP) amount of avocados in a guacamole recipe is 7 kilograms and avocados have a yield percentage (YP) of 70%, how many kilograms of avocados need to be purchased?

________________ **23.** A prep cook debones whole turkeys to use for various recipes and saves the thighs to make ground turkey meat for burgers. The thighs yield 32% meat, while 68% is unusable bone, skin, and connective tissue. How many kilograms of turkey thighs are needed to make 9.25 kilograms of ground turkey? *(Round the answer to a whole number.)*

________________ **24.** Each of 50 guests at a banquet will be served a 225-gram portion of prime rib. If prime rib has a yield percentage (YP) of 60%, how many kilograms of prime rib must be purchased for the banquet?

________________ **25.** Each of 140 guests at a banquet will be served a 6-ounce portion of salmon. If salmon has a yield percentage (YP) of 70%, how many pounds of salmon must be purchased for the banquet?

________________ **26.** If each of 50 snack boxes are to contain hummus with 100 grams of carrot sticks and the yield percentage (YP) for carrots is 85%, how many kilograms of carrots need to be purchased for the snack boxes? *(Round the answer to a whole number.)*

_______________ **27.** If each of 70 snack boxes are to contain ranch dip with 4 ounces of celery sticks and the yield percentage (YP) for celery is 70%, how many pounds of celery need to be purchased for the snack boxes?

_______________ **28.** If cantaloupe has a yield percentage (YP) of 55%, how many pounds of edible cantaloupe are available from three cantaloupes weighing 4½ pounds, 4⅞ pounds, and 5¾ pounds?

_______________ **29.** A 3 kg melon has a yield percentage (YP) of 60% when the rind is discarded. However, to practice sustainability and reduce waste, the chef will pickle the rind. If the melon rind has a 50% yield percentage (YP), what is the weight of the edible-portion (EP) amount of the rind?

_______________ **30.** A restaurant serves 150 side dishes of skinless mashed potatoes each day. It produces two orders of mashed potatoes from each 8-ounce potato. When the skins are discarded, the potatoes have a yield percentage (YP) of 90%. However, to reduce waste and promote sales, the potato skins are instead used as an appetizer. What is the edible-portion (EP) amount of the potato skins in ounces?

_______________ **31.** After cleaning a 30 lb case of Brussels sprouts, there are 5 lb, 6 oz of unused parts. What is the yield percentage (YP) of the Brussels sprouts?

_______________ **32.** A new cook is cutting and discarding 200 g from the ends of every 900 g bunch of celery. After training, the cook learns to remove only 85 g from the ends of each celery bunch and to add them to the restaurant's compost bin. What is the yield percentage (YP) for the celery bunches after the cook's training?

_______________ **33.** If the baker's percentage for raisins in a raisin bread formula is 8% and the baker's percentage for flour is 100%, how many grams of raisins are needed if 6 kilograms of flour are used?

_______________ **34.** If the baker's percentage for milk in a pancake formula is 24% and the baker's percentage for flour is 100%, what amount of milk is needed if 8 kg of flour is used?

__________ **35.** After serving corn as the vegetable of the day, the chef uses the leftover corn to make jalapeño-corn muffins. If the baker's percentage for jalapeños in a corn muffin formula is 7% and the baker's percentage for flour is 100%, how many grams of jalapeños are needed if 5.5 kilograms of flour are used?

__________ **36.** In a bread recipe, the baker's percentage of water is 72%, salt is 1.5%, and yeast is 1.8%. How many grams of salt are needed if 18 kilograms of flour are used to prepare the bread?

__________ **37.** If the baker's percentages in a rye bread formula are 60% for bread flour, 40% for rye flour, and 4% for caraway seeds, how many grams of caraway seeds are needed if 6 kilograms of bread flour and 4 kilograms of rye flour are used?

__________ **38.** If a recipe calls for 500 g of bread flour and 10 g of salt, what would be the baker's percentage for salt if the recipe were converted to a formula with bread flour as the main ingredient?

_______________ **39.** If a cupcake recipe calls for 4 lb of cake flour and 2.5 lb of sugar, what would be the baker's percentage for sugar if the recipe were converted to a formula with cake flour as the main ingredient?

_______________ **40.** A chef purchases imperfect tomatoes for 30% less cost than perfectly shaped tomatoes to dehydrate and use on focaccia bread. If the focaccia recipe uses 3.6 kg of flour and 225 g of dehydrated tomatoes, what would be the baker's percentage for the tomatoes if the recipe were converted to a formula with flour as the main ingredient?

_______________ **41.** If a cinnamon-sugar mix is made with a 5:3 ratio of sugar to cinnamon, what percentage of the mix is sugar?

_______________ **42.** If a special sauce in a hamburger restaurant is made with a 1:1 ratio by volume of ketchup to mayonnaise, how much mayonnaise is needed to make a 6 L batch of special sauce?

______________ **43.** A restaurant uses an all-purpose seasoning mix that is made with a 7:3:2 ratio of salt to black pepper to garlic powder. What fraction of the seasoning mix is black pepper?

______________ **44.** If a salad-oil blend is made using a 4:1 ratio by volume of vegetable oil to olive oil, how much olive oil is required if 3 L of vegetable oil are used?

______________ **45.** Simple syrup is made with a 1:1 ratio of water and sugar. How many liters of simple syrup can be made from 750 milliliters of water?

______________ **46.** Simple syrup is made with a 1:1 ratio of water and sugar. How many gallons of simple syrup can be made from 3 quarts of water? *(Show the answer as a mixed fraction.)*

_______________ **47.** If a crumb topping is made with a ratio by weight of 3 parts brown sugar, 2 parts flour, and 1 part butter, how many kilograms of crumb topping can be made with 750 grams of butter?

_______________ **48.** If a crumb topping is made with a ratio by weight of 3 parts brown sugar, 2 parts flour, and 1 part butter, how many pounds of crumb topping can be made with 16 ounces of butter?

_______________ **49.** Meatballs are prepared with a ratio of 3 parts ground beef, 2 parts ground pork, and 1 part ground veal. How many kilograms of each meat is required if a total of 8 kilograms of meat is used to prepare the meatballs? *(Show the answer as a mixed number.)*

_______________ **50.** A chef purchases whole chickens because they cost less per pound than fabricated cuts and the carcasses can be used to make stock for soup. If the chef's soup consists of 9 parts chicken stock, 2 parts chicken, 1.5 parts vegetables, and 1.5 parts noodles, all by weight, how many ounces of each ingredient is needed to make 2 gallons of the soup? *(Tip: 1 gal. = 128 oz. Round the answers to whole numbers.)*

5

Calculating Costs and Menu Prices

Many costs must be monitored and managed in order to run a successful foodservice operation. Among the most significant costs are food and beverage costs. In order to calculate appropriate menu prices, the cost to prepare the menu items must be known. It is also important to know how food and beverage costs are used to help calculate menu prices and how customer perceptions influence menu pricing.

Section 5-1: IDENTIFYING AS-PURCHASED (AP) COSTS

- Explain as-purchased (AP) costs.
- Identify as-purchased (AP) costs on invoices.

Section 5-2: CALCULATING UNIT COSTS

- Calculate as-purchased (AP) unit costs.
- Calculate edible-portion (EP) unit costs.

Section 5-3: CALCULATING AS-SERVED (AS) COSTS

- Explain as-served (AS) costs.
- Calculate the as-served (AS) costs of menu items.

Section 5-4: CALCULATING FOOD AND BEVERAGE COST PERCENTAGES

- Calculate cost percentages of menu items.
- Calculate overall cost percentages of foodservice operations.

Section 5-5: CALCULATING MENU PRICES

- Calculate menu prices using the food and beverage cost percentage pricing method.
- Explain how foodservice operations use perceived value pricing.
- Calculate menu prices based on the contribution margin pricing method.

Section 5-6: USING PRICING FORMS

- Identify elements on pricing forms.
- Use pricing forms to help establish menu prices.

Key Terms

- as-purchased (AP) cost
- invoice
- unit cost
- as-purchased (AP) unit cost
- edible-portion (EP) unit cost
- as-served (AS) cost
- cost percentage
- menu-item cost percentage
- overall cost percentage
- target cost percentage
- target price
- perceived value pricing
- contribution margin
- pricing form

Learner Resources
atplearningresources.com
access code 267628

Photo Courtesy of Perdue Foodservice, Perdue Farms Incorporated

Section 5-1 IDENTIFYING AS-PURCHASED (AP) COSTS

The most fundamental food or beverage cost is referred to as the as-purchased (AP) cost. An *as-purchased (AP) cost* is the amount paid for a product in the form it was ordered and received. The as-purchased (AP) costs for food and beverage products are documented on invoices. An *invoice* is a document provided by a supplier that lists the item amounts delivered to a foodservice operation and the prices of those items.

Foodservice operations typically buy food products from suppliers in bulk quantities. Examples of bulk quantities include cases of hamburger patties, tubs of ice cream, crates of milk, and pails of pickles. If a case of 80 hamburger patties costs $30.00, the as-purchased (AP) cost is $30.00 for the entire case.

Likewise, if the invoice price of an 11.4 L tub of vanilla ice cream is $12.00, the as-purchased (AP) cost for the tub of vanilla ice cream is $12.00. **See Figure 5-1.** Beverages are also typically purchased in bulk quantities, such as 24-bottle cases of iced tea, 10-bottle cases of wine, or half barrels (kegs) of beer. As with food products, the as-purchased (AP) costs of beverage products are equal to the prices listed on the invoices from beverage suppliers.

As-Purchased (AP) Costs

DATE	PURCHASE ORDER NO. RA 05353066	PAGE NO. 1 of 1	DELIVERY DATE

SHIP TO: Acme Foods, Silver Spring Rd, West Toronto,Ontario M5H 3L5

VENDOR: Stone Cold Foods

CHARGE & INVOICE TO: Acme Foods, Silver Spring Rd, West Toronto,Ontario M5H 3L5

QUANTITY	UNIT	ITEM ID—DESCRIPTION	UNIT PRICE	ITEM TOTAL
1	Case (80 ct)	Frozen Hamburger Patties	$30.00	$30.00
1	1 Tub (11.4 L)	Signature Ice Cream	$12.00	$12.00

I certify that sufficient funds are available for this purchase.

Tax (if applicable)	
Shipping	$6.00
Total	

Signature ____ Date ____

Purchasing Manager

Title

Type of Payment: ☐ Payment Enclosed ☑ COD ☐ Credit

Figure 5-1. As-purchased (AP) costs are listed on invoices from suppliers.

Checkpoint 5-1

1. Define "as-purchased (AP) cost."

2. Where can an as-purchased (AP) cost be found?

3. What is the as-purchased (AP) cost of a 10 kg bag of rice that sells for $15.00 per bag?

4. What is the as-purchased (AP) cost of a case of 12 bottles of mineral water that sells for $18.00 per case?

Section 5-2 CALCULATING UNIT COSTS

When a product is purchased in bulk, it is often necessary to calculate a unit cost based on the as-purchased (AP) cost. A *unit cost* is the cost of a product per unit of measure. Unit costs can be based on count (bread at $2.00 per loaf), weight (ground turkey at $6.25 per kilogram or $2.85 per pound), or volume (olive oil at $8.00 per liter or $32.00 per gallon).

Calculating As-Purchased (AP) Unit Costs

Unit costs are initially calculated based on as-purchased (AP) costs. An *as-purchased (AP) unit cost* is the unit cost of a food item based on the form in which it is ordered and received. The as-purchased (AP) unit cost of an item is calculated by applying the following formula:

$$AC = AT \div NU$$

$$\text{As-Purchased Unit Cost} = \frac{\text{As-Purchased Total Cost}}{\text{Number of Units}}$$

where

AC = as-purchased unit cost

AT = as-purchased total cost

NU = number of units

For example, to calculate the as-purchased (AP) unit cost of an egg, the as-purchased (AP) cost for a case of eggs is divided by the number of eggs in the case. If the price paid for a case of eggs is $14.40 and there are 15-dozen eggs in the case, the as-purchased (AP) unit cost would be $0.08 per egg.

$$AC = AT \div NU$$

$$AC = \$14.40 \div 15 \text{ dozen}$$

$$AC = \$14.40 \div (15 \text{ dozen} \times 12 \text{ eggs/dozen})$$

$$AC = \$14.40 \div 180 \text{ eggs}$$

$$AC = \mathbf{\$0.08/egg}$$

The unit of measure used to calculate a unit cost should be based on how the product is used in recipes. Sometimes it may be helpful to calculate the unit cost of an item in more than one unit of measure. For example, some recipes may call for liters of heavy cream, and other recipes may call for milliliters of heavy cream. Likewise, some recipes may call for quarts of heavy cream, and other recipes may call for fluid ounces of heavy cream. **See Figure 5-2.**

Calculating As-Purchased (AP) Unit Costs

As-Purchased (AP) Unit Cost = As-Purchased (AP) Total Cost ÷ Number of Units

Metric Measurements		
1 Case Heavy Cream	1 L Heavy Cream	30 mL Heavy Cream
As-purchased (AP) total cost = **\$32.00** (Number of units = 12 L)	As-purchased (AP) unit cost = **\$2.67/L** (\$32.00 ÷ 12 L)	As-purchased (AP) unit cost = **\$0.08/30mL** (\$2.67/L ÷ 1000 mL/L) × 30

Customary Measurements		
1 Case Heavy Cream	1 qt Heavy Cream	1 fl oz Heavy Cream
As-purchased (AP) total cost = **\$32.00** (Number of units = 12 qt)	As-purchased (AP) unit cost = **\$2.67/qt** (\$32.00 ÷ 12 qt)	As-purchased (AP) unit cost = **\$0.08/fl oz** (\$2.67/qt ÷ 32 fl oz/qt)

Imperial Measurements		
1 Case Heavy Cream	1 qt Heavy Cream	1 fl oz Heavy Cream
As-purchased (AP) total cost = **\$32.00** (Number of units = 12 qt)	As-purchased (AP) unit cost = **\$2.67/qt** (\$32.00 ÷ 12 qt)	As-purchased (AP) unit cost = **\$0.07/fl oz** (\$2.67/qt ÷ 40 fl oz/qt)

Figure 5-2. As-purchased (AP) unit costs can be calculated based on more than one unit of measure.

Calculating Edible-Portion (EP) Unit Costs

A similar calculation is performed to determine the edible-portion (EP) unit cost based on the as-purchased (AP) unit cost. An *edible-portion (EP) unit cost* is the unit cost of a food or beverage item that includes the cost of the unused parts generated by trimming. Unless a food item has a yield percentage (YP) of 100%, the edible-portion (EP) unit cost will always be higher than the as-purchased (AP) unit cost. For example, with a mashed potato recipe that calls for 5 kg of peeled potatoes, the cost for the potatoes will be greater than the cost of 5 kg of whole potatoes. This is because more than 5 kg of whole potatoes will need to be peeled in order to yield 5 kg of peeled potatoes.

The edible-portion (EP) unit cost of a food item is calculated by applying the following formula:

$$EC = AC \div YP$$

$$\textit{Edible-Portion Unit Cost} = \frac{\textit{As-Purchased Unit Cost}}{\textit{Yield Percentage}}$$

where

EC = edible-portion unit cost (whole)

AC = as-purchased unit cost (part)

YP = yield percentage

For example, a recipe calls for peeled potatoes. The as-purchased (AP) unit cost of whole potatoes is \$1.80 per kilogram, and the yield percentage (YP) is 80%. What is the edible-portion (EP) unit cost of the peeled potatoes?

EC = AC ÷ YP

$EC = \$1.80/\text{kg} \div 80\%$

$EC = \$1.80/\text{kg} \div 0.80$

$EC = \mathbf{\$2.25/kg}$

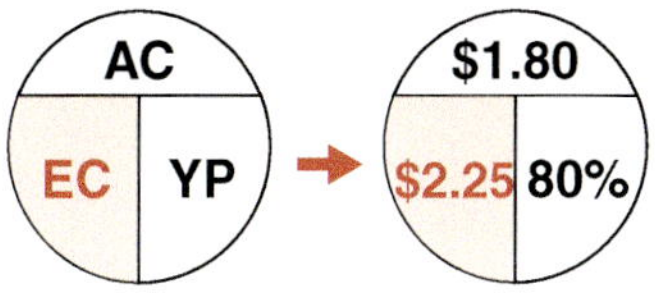

The ingredient amounts provided in a recipe are the edible-portion (EP) amounts. The total cost of an ingredient in a recipe can be calculated by multiplying the edible-portion (EP) amounts by the edible-portion (EP) unit cost for each ingredient. For example, what is the total cost of onions for a French onion soup recipe that calls for 3 kilograms of peeled and sliced onions if the as-purchased (AP) unit cost of whole onions is $0.88 per kilogram and the yield percentage (YP) is 93%? The answer can be found by applying the formula for calculating an edible-portion (EP) unit cost and using the following problem-solving steps:

Problem-Solving Steps

1. Calculate the edible-portion (EP) unit cost for whole onions.

   EC = AC ÷ YP

   $EC = \$0.88/\text{kg} \div 93\%$

   $EC = \$0.88/\text{kg} \div 0.93$

   $EC = \mathbf{\$0.95/kg}$

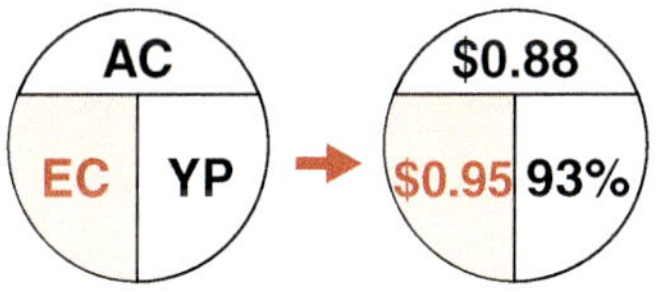

2. Then, calculate the total cost of the onions by multiplying the edible-portion (EP) amount by the edible-portion (EP) unit cost.

   $3\text{ kg} \times \$0.95/\text{kg} = \mathbf{\$2.85}$

When calculating the edible-portion (EP) unit cost of an ingredient, the unit of measure for the edible-portion (EP) amount and the as-purchased (AP) unit cost must be the same. For example, if the edible-portion (EP) amount of sugar in a cake recipe is 350 grams and the as-purchased (AP) unit cost of sugar is $1.40 per kilogram, the edible-portion (EP) amount of sugar (350 grams) will need to be converted to kilograms to keep the unit of measure the same. This conversion is done in the same manner as other conversions by multiplying the edible-portion (EP) amount by the appropriate measurement equivalent. In this case, since 1000 gram = 1 kilograms, 350 grams is calculated to be equivalent to 0.35 kilograms.

$$\frac{350\,\cancel{\text{g}}}{1} \times \frac{1\text{kg}}{1000\,\cancel{\text{g}}} = \frac{350 \times 1\text{kg}}{1000} = \frac{350\text{kg}}{1000} = \mathbf{0.35\,kg}$$

The total cost of the sugar in the recipe can then be calculated by multiplying the edible-portion (EP) amount (0.35 kilograms) by the edible-portion (EP) unit cost ($1.40 per kilogram).

$$0.35 \text{ kg} \times \$1.40/\text{kg} = \mathbf{\$0.49}$$

Likewise, since the edible-portion (EP) amount of sugar is expressed in grams (350 grams), the as-purchased (AP) unit cost of sugar ($1.40 per kilogram) can be converted to grams to keep the unit of measure the same.

$$\frac{1\cancel{\text{kg}}}{1000\text{ g}} \times \frac{\$1.40}{\cancel{\text{kg}}} = \frac{1 \times \$1.40}{1000\text{ g}} = \frac{\$1.40}{1000\text{ g}} = \mathbf{\$0.0014/g}$$

The total cost of the sugar in the recipe can then be calculated by multiplying the edible-portion (EP) amount by the edible-portion (EP) unit cost.

$$350 \text{ g} \times \$0.0014/\text{g} = \mathbf{\$0.49}$$

If a recipe uses customary or imperial measurements, and the edible-portion (EP) amount of sugar in a cake recipe is 12 ounces and the as-purchased (AP) unit cost of sugar is $0.64 per pound, the as-purchased (AP) unit cost will need to be converted to a price per ounce. Since 16 ounces = 1 pound, $0.64 per pound is calculated to be equivalent to $0.04 per ounce.

$$\frac{\$0.64}{1\cancel{\text{lb}}} \times \frac{1\cancel{\text{lb}}}{16\text{ oz}} = \frac{\$0.64 \times 1}{1 \times 16\text{ oz}} = \frac{\$0.64}{16\text{ oz}} = \mathbf{\$0.04/oz}$$

The total cost of the sugar in the recipe can then be calculated by multiplying the edible-portion (EP) amount by the edible portion (EP) unit cost.

$$12 \text{ oz} \times \$0.04/\text{oz} = \mathbf{\$0.48}$$

Checkpoint 5-2

1. Define "unit cost."

___

___

2. What is the as-purchased (AP) unit cost of coffee per kilogram if a 2.27-kilogram bag of coffee costs $36.00?

___

___

3. Explain the difference between an as-purchased (AP) unit cost and an edible-portion (EP) unit cost.

____

____

4. What is the edible-portion (EP) unit cost of bell peppers if the as-purchased (AP) unit cost is $2.40 per kilogram and the yield percent (YP) is 85%?

____

____

5. If a recipe calls for 5 kilograms of celery, what is the total cost of celery if the as-purchased (AP) unit cost of celery is $1.75 per kilogram and the yield percentage (YP) is 70%?

____

____

Section 5-3 CALCULATING AS-SERVED (AS) COSTS

Once the costs of the individual ingredients in a recipe are calculated, the costs are added to determine the total cost of the recipe. Then, as-served (AS) costs for that recipe can be calculated. An *as-served (AS) cost* is the cost of a menu item as it is served to a customer. It is important to note that an as-served (AS) cost is the total cost of the ingredients required to prepare one serving of a menu item. The exception would be a recipe with a yield equal to a single menu item, which causes the cost of the recipe to be the same as the cost of the menu item.

Consider a chicken sandwich that is offered as a stand-alone item on a menu. If the sandwich consists of a grilled chicken breast served on a bun with a slice of tomato, a slice of cheese, some lettuce, and some mayonnaise, the costs of the ingredients are added to calculate the as-served (AS) cost of the chicken sandwich. However, if the same chicken sandwich is offered on the menu as a meal that comes with fries and coleslaw, the as-served (AS) cost of that menu item is equal to the total cost of the sandwich, fries, and coleslaw. On this menu, the chicken sandwich is treated as one ingredient of the chicken sandwich meal. **See Figure 5-3.**

Calculating As-Served (AS) Costs

EQUIVALENT EDIBLE-PORTION (EP) AMOUNT × EDIBLE-PORTION (EP) UNIT COST

AS-PURCHASED (AP) UNIT COST ÷ YIELD PERCENTAGE (YP)

Chicken Sandwich

Ingredients	Edible-Portion (EP) Amount	Equivalent Edible-Portion (EP) Amount	As-Purchased (AP) Unit Cost	Yield Percentage (YP)	Edible-Portion (EP) Unit Cost	Total Cost
Chicken breast	100 g	0.1 kg	$7.20/kg	90%	$8.00	$0.80
Bun	1 each	1 each	$0.40/each	100%	$0.40	$0.40
Tomato slice	30 g	0.03 kg	$6.30/kg	90%	$7.00	$0.21
Cheese slice	1 each	1 each	$0.25/each	100%	$0.25	$0.25
Lettuce	10 g	0.01 kg	$4.00/kg	80%	$5.00	$0.05
Mayonnaise	15 g	0.015 kg	$6.00/kg	100%	$6.00	$0.09
					Total As-Served (AS) Cost:	**$1.80**

INDIVIDUAL RECIPE COST BECOMES PART OF MENU ITEM COST

Chicken Sandwich Meal

Ingredients	Edible-Portion (EP) Amount	Equivalent Edible-Portion (EP) Amount	As-Purchased (AP) Unit Cost	Yield Percentage (YP)	Edible-Portion (EP) Unit Cost	Total Cost
Chicken sandwich	1 each	1 each	$1.80/each	100%	$1.80	$1.80
French fries	100 g	0.1 kg	$8.00/kg	100%	$8.00	$0.80
Coleslaw	80 g	0.08 kg	$8.00/kg	100%	$8.00	$0.64
					Total As-Served (AS) Cost:	**$3.24**

Figure 5-3. An as-served (AS) cost is the cost of a menu item as it is served to a customer.

To calculate the as-served (AS) cost of a menu item that is prepared in large quantities and then portioned into servings, the total cost of the recipe is divided by the number of portions the recipe yields. For example, if the total cost of the ingredients to prepare 8 L of tomato soup is $15.00 and the recipe yields 32-servings, 250 mL each, the as-served (AS) cost of a serving of tomato soup would be $0.47.

$15.00 ÷ 32 servings = **$0.47/serving**

The as-served (AS) cost of a beverage menu item is calculated in exactly the same way as the as-served (AS) cost of a food menu item. For example, the as-served (AS) cost of a chocolate milkshake could include the cost of vanilla ice cream, chocolate sauce, milk, whipped cream, and a cherry. Likewise, the as-served (AS) cost of a cocktail could include the cost of soda or fruit juice, alcohol, and a garnish such as a slice of lemon or lime.

5-3 Checkpoint

1. Define "as-served (AS) cost."

2. What is the as-served (AS) cost of a taco made with $0.75 of ground beef, $0.24 of grated cheese, $0.08 of lettuce, $0.18 of tomatoes, and a $0.15 taco shell?

3. If the taco in Question 2 is served as part of a meal that comes with black beans that cost $0.45 per serving and yellow rice that costs $0.35 per serving, what is the as-served (AS) cost of the meal?

4. What is the as-served (AS) cost of a serving of tomato soup if the tomato soup recipe has a total ingredient cost of $50.00 and yields 25 servings?

Section 5-4 CALCULATING FOOD AND BEVERAGE COST PERCENTAGES

Another way of examining food and beverage costs is through the use of cost percentages. A *cost percentage* is a percentage that indicates how the cost of food or beverages relates to the menu prices and sales of a foodservice operation. There are three types of cost percentages used in the foodservice industry:

- **Menu-Item Cost Percentage.** A *menu-item cost percentage* is the as-served (AS) cost of a menu item divided by the menu price and written as a percent.
- **Overall Cost Percentage.** An *overall cost percentage* is the total amount of money a foodservice operation spends on food and beverages divided by the total food and beverage sales over a defined period of time and written as a percent.
- **Target Cost Percentage.** A *target cost percentage* is the percentage of food or beverage sales that a foodservice operation plans to spend on purchasing food or beverages.

Food cost percentages are only based on the costs of food and the sales of food. Likewise, beverage cost percentages are only based on the costs of beverages and the sales of beverages. If a menu item consists of both a food and a beverage component that is going to be offered for a single price, the menu price must be based on a combined food-and-beverage cost percentage.

Menu-Item Cost Percentages

A menu-item cost percentage is equal to the as-served (AS) cost of a menu item divided by the menu price and written as a percent. This percentage shows how the cost of the ingredients relates to the price charged for the menu item. To calculate a menu-item cost percentage, the following formula is applied:

$$\text{Menu-Item Cost Percentage} = \frac{\text{As-Served Cost}}{\text{Menu Price}}$$

$$I\% = AS \div MP$$

where

$I\%$ = menu-item cost percentage

AS = as-served cost (part)

MP = menu price (whole)

A foodservice operation earns money by charging more for the items on a menu than it costs to prepare those items. Therefore, the menu price is always higher than the as-served (AS) cost of that item. Since a menu-item cost percentage is equal to the as-served (AS) cost divided by the menu price, a menu-item cost percentage will always be less than 100%.

For example, if the menu price for the chicken sandwich shown in Figure 5-3 is \$6.95 and the as-served (AS) cost is \$1.80, the menu-item cost percentage for the chicken sandwich would be 25.9%.

$$I\% = AS \div MP$$

$$I\% = \$1.80 \div \$6.95$$

$$I\% = 0.259$$

$$I\% = \mathbf{25.9\%}$$

Likewise, if the menu price for the chicken sandwich served with fries and coleslaw is \$9.95 and the as-served (AS) cost is \$3.24, the menu-item cost percentage for the meal would be 32.6%.

$$I\% = AS \div MP$$

$$I\% = \$3.24 \div \$9.95$$

$$I\% = 0.326$$

$$I\% = \mathbf{32.6\%}$$

Overall Cost Percentages

In addition to calculating cost percentages for individual menu items, foodservice operations also calculate overall cost percentages based on total food and beverage sales. An overall cost percentage is equal to the total amount of money a foodservice operation spends on food and beverages divided by its total food and beverage sales over a defined period of time. The overall cost percentage uses the actual food and beverage costs accrued over a given time. Actual food and beverage costs account for circumstances such as spills, spoilage, imperfect portions, and theft. To calculate an overall cost percentage, the following formula is applied:

$$O\% = TC \div TS$$

$$\text{Overall Cost Percentage} = \frac{\text{Total Food and Beverage Costs}}{\text{Total Food and Beverage Sales}}$$

where

$O\%$ = overall cost percentage

TC = total food and beverage costs (part)

TS = total food and beverage sales (whole)

For example, if a restaurant spends $9,000 on food and beverages in a month and its total food and beverage sales were $36,000 for that month, then the overall cost percentage for the restaurant would be 25%.

$$O\% = TC \div TS$$

$$O\% = \$9{,}000 \div \$36{,}000$$

$$O\% = 0.25$$

$$O\% = \mathbf{25\%}$$

The other 75% of the sales ($36,000 – $9,000 = $27,000) would then be available for the foodservice operation to pay for expenses, such as payroll, rent, and utilities, and to contribute to the earnings of the owners of the operation. Lower food and beverage cost percentages translate into higher potential earnings for the owners.

Target Cost Percentages

It is common for a foodservice operation to establish a target cost percentage. A target cost percentage is the percentage of total food and beverage sales that a foodservice operation plans to spend on food or beverages. A target cost percentage can be thought of as what a foodservice operation should spend on food and beverages if portions are perfect and there are no accidental spills, spoilage, imperfect portions, or theft. Foodservice owners and managers regularly compare overall cost percentages with target cost percentages to determine if food and beverage costs are higher or lower than planned.

When the overall cost percentage of a foodservice operation is lower than the target cost percentage, the operation has earned more than planned. Likewise, if the overall cost percentage is higher than the target cost percentage, the operation has earned less than planned. It is the responsibility of management to monitor food and beverage costs and make any necessary adjustments.

Checkpoint 5-4

1. Define "cost percentage."

2. What is the menu-item cost percentage of a salad with an as-served (AS) cost of $1.75 and a menu price of $5.95? *(Round the answer to the tenths place.)*

3. What is the menu-item cost percentage of a beverage with an as-served (AS) cost of $1.24 and a menu price of $6.00? *(Round the answer to the tenths place.)*

4. What is the overall cost percentage of a restaurant that spends $400.00 a week on food and beverages when total food and beverage sales are $1,800.00? *(Round the answer to the tenths place.)*

5. Define "target cost percentage."

6. What does it mean when the overall cost percentage of a foodservice operation is lower than the target cost percentage?

Section 5-5 CALCULATING MENU PRICES

There are three primary methods used by foodservice operations to calculate menu prices. These methods include food and beverage cost percentage pricing, perceived value pricing, and contribution margin pricing. Regardless of the pricing method used, the as-served (AS) costs of the menu items must be known first.

Food and Beverage Cost Percentage Pricing

Food and beverage cost percentage pricing begins by calculating a target price for each menu item. A *target price* is the price that a foodservice operation needs to charge for a menu item in order to meet its target cost percentage. Target prices are calculated using the following formula:

$$TP = AS \div T\%$$

$$\text{Target Price} = \frac{\text{As-Served Cost}}{\text{Target Cost Percentage}}$$

where

TP = target price (whole)

AS = as-served cost (part)

$T\%$ = target cost percentage

For example, if the as-served (AS) cost of a sandwich is $1.45 and the target cost percentage is 30%, the target price would be $4.83.

$$TP = AS \div T\%$$

$TP = \$1.45 \div 30\%$

$TP = \$1.45 \div 30\%$

$TP = \mathbf{\$4.83}$

Some foodservice operations will stop at this point and set the menu price equal to the target price. However, aside from some quick-service restaurants, it is not common to see menu prices like $4.83. Most foodservice operations tend to consider a target price as a starting point and then adjust the price up or down based on how management thinks customers will perceive it.

Perceived Value Pricing

Perceived value pricing is the process of adjusting a target price based on how management thinks a customer will perceive the price. Many foodservice operations use a combination of cost percentage pricing and perceived value pricing to determine the final prices on a menu. **See Figure 5-4.**

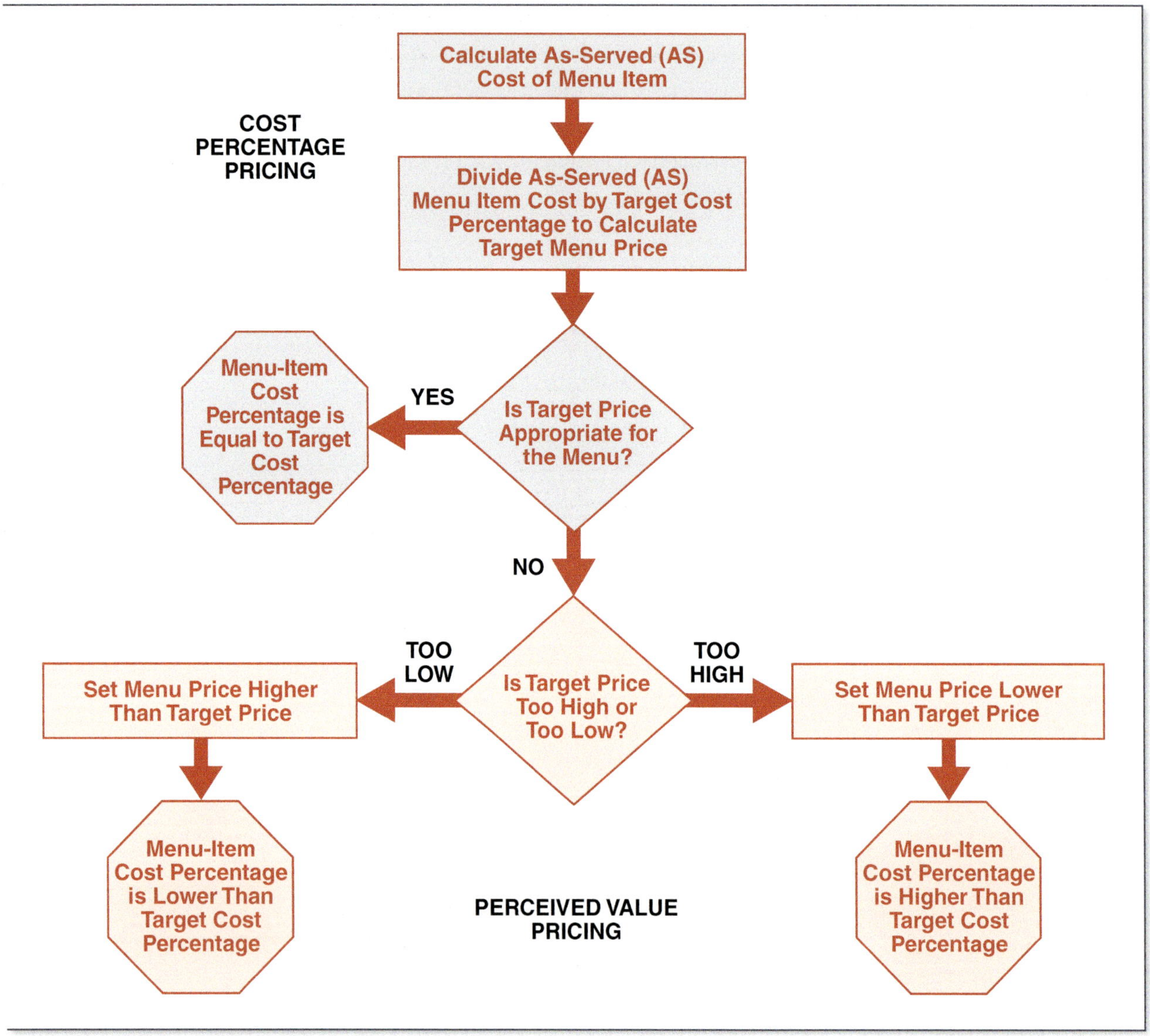

Figure 5-4. Many foodservice operations use a combination of cost percentage pricing and perceived value pricing to determine menu prices.

There are two aspects to perceived value pricing. The first involves adjusting a target price to look like a price that customers have become used to seeing on menus. For example, if a target price for a menu item is calculated to be $7.03, most foodservice operations would adjust the price to $6.95 or $7.00. Likewise, if a target price for a menu item is calculated to be $7.74, most foodservice operations would adjust the price to $7.95 or $8.00.

Therefore, the actual cost percentage for a menu item would be slightly higher or lower than the target cost percentage. For example, if the target price for a bowl of soup is calculated to be $4.67 based on an as-served (AS) cost of \$1.40 and a 30% target cost percentage, the restaurant might increase the price to \$4.95. At \$4.95, the actual cost percentage would be 28.3%, which is slightly lower than the target cost percentage of 30%.

$$I\% = AS \div MP$$

$$I\% = \$1.40 \div \$4.95$$

$$I\% = 0.283$$

$$I\% = \mathbf{28.3\%}$$

The second aspect of perceived value pricing involves adjusting a target price so that customers will view the price as reasonable relative to other items on the menu and similar items sold elsewhere. For example, a restaurant may offer an appetizer of nachos made with tortilla chips, taco meat, cheese, and tomatoes that has an as-served (AS) cost of \$1.05. If the target price is calculated based on a 28% target cost percentage, the target price would be \$3.75.

$$TP = AS \div T\%$$

$$TP = \$1.05 \div 28\%$$

$$TP = \$1.05 \div 0.28$$

$$TP = \mathbf{\$3.75}$$

If other appetizers on the restaurant menu include buffalo wings for \$8.95 and mozzarella sticks for \$5.95, customers may be willing to pay more than \$3.75 for the nachos because the perception is that nachos represent a substantial dish and should cost more than the mozzarella sticks but less than the buffalo wings. In a case like this, the restaurant is likely to increase the price of the nachos to \$6.95, which means the menu-item cost percentage for the nachos would be 15.1%.

$$I\% = AS \div MP$$

$$I\% = \$1.05 \div \$6.95$$

$$I\% = 0.151$$

$$I\% = \mathbf{15.1\%}$$

If the price was left at the target price of \$3.75, the restaurant would earn \$2.70 (\$3.75 – \$1.05 = \$2.70) on each order of nachos. With the price adjusted to \$6.95, the restaurant would earn \$5.90 (\$6.95 – \$1.05 = \$5.90) on each order of nachos. A lower menu-item cost percentage means that the foodservice operation earns more on each order of nachos that are sold. However, just because lower percentages result in higher earnings per order, it does not mean that a foodservice operation can or should base all menu prices on a lower cost percentage.

To determine the price of other items based on the same menu-item cost percentage as the nachos, the following formula is applied:

MP = AS ÷ I%

where

$$\text{Menu Item Price} = \frac{\text{As-Served Cost}}{\text{Menu-Item Cost Percentage}}$$

MP = menu item price (whole)

AS = as-served cost (part)

I% = menu-item cost percentage

For example, if the same restaurant selling the nachos prices a rib-eye steak with an as-served (AS) cost of $14.00 based on the same 15.1% cost percentage, the price of the steak would be $92.72.

MP = AS ÷ I%

MP = $14.00 ÷ 15.1%

MP = $14.00 ÷ 0.151

MP = **$92.72**

It is unlikely that customers would pay $92.72 for steak, even at a high-end restaurant. If the target cost percentage is adjusted to 28%, the price of the steak would still be relatively high at $50.00 ($14.00 ÷ 0.28 = $50.00). Depending on the type of restaurant, customers may or may not perceive that price to be high. If restaurant management thinks most customers will perceive a price of $50.00 as too high, the price may be reduced to be more in line with the perceived value of that restaurant's customers. If the final menu price set for the steak is $36.95, the cost percentage will increase to 37.9%.

I% = AS ÷ MP

I% = $14.00 ÷ $36.95

I% = 0.379

I% = **37.9%**

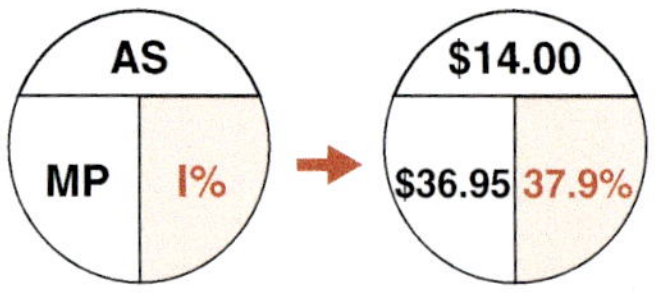

It is normal for items on a menu to have different cost percentages. As long as there is a proper balance on a menu between items with lower cost percentages and items with higher cost percentages, the foodservice operation can maintain an overall cost percentage that is close to or equal to its target cost percentage. **See Figure 5-5.**

Daily Sales Report—Lunch Target Cost Percentage = 30%						
Menu Item	**As-Served (AS) Cost**	**Menu Price**	**Menu Item Cost % (As-Served (AS) Cost ÷ Menu Price)**	**Number Sold**	**Total Cost (As-Served (AS) Cost × Number Sold)**	**Total Sales (Menu Price × Number Sold)**
Appetizers						
Bruschetta	$1.75	$5.95	29.4%	48	$84.00	$285.60
BBQ shrimp	$4.25	$11.95	35.6%	27	$114.75	$322.65
Entrées						
Fried chicken	$2.65	$12.95	20.5%	43	$113.95	$556.85
Strip steak	$9.00	$25.95	34.7%	32	$288.00	$830.40
Desserts						
Strawberry shortcake	$2.25	$5.95	37.8%	40	$90.00	$238.00
Chocolate cake	$0.50	$3.95	12.7%	30	$15.00	$118.50
Total					**$705.70**	**$2,352.00**
Overall Total Cost Percentage (Total Costs ÷ Total Sales)						**30.0%**

Figure 5-5. If the cost percentage for an individual menu item is higher or lower than the target cost percentage, the overall cost percentage can still be close to or equal to the target cost percentage.

Contribution Margin Pricing

Another method used to calculate menu prices is referred to as contribution margin pricing. A *contribution margin* is the amount added to the as-served (AS) cost of a menu item to determine a menu price. A foodservice operation calculates prices with a contribution margin to ensure that the amount of money made on each serving of food or beverage will cover expenses and still result in a profit. This type of pricing is not common in restaurants, but it is often used when calculating a price charged per person at a special event.

For example, a hotel banquet operation is planning a party for 200 people. The menu includes an entrée salad, a beverage, and a dessert for a total as-served (AS) cost of $20 per person. Therefore, the total as-served (AS) cost will be $4,000 (200 people × $20/person). The banquet manager calculates that all of the other expenses, such as labor and rental fees, amount to an additional $5,000. It is hotel policy that a party of this size must generate earnings of $2,000. Therefore, the contribution margin for this event would be $7,000 ($5,000 + $2,000).

To calculate the contribution margin on a per person basis, the banquet manager simply divides the total contribution margin by the number of people attending the event.

$7,000 ÷ 200 people = **$35/person**

This contribution margin is then added to the as-served (AS) cost per person to calculate the final menu price for the party, which in this case is $55 per person.

$20/person + $35/person = **$55/person**

Checkpoint 5-5

1. Define "target price."

2. What is the target price of an appetizer with an as-served (AS) cost of $2.30 and a target cost percentage of 26%?

3. What is the target price for bottled water that has an as-purchased (AP) unit cost of $0.34 per bottle if the target cost percentage is 22%?

4. How much money is earned from selling a dessert with an as-served (AS) cost of $2.15 and a cost percentage of 32%?

5. Define "perceived value pricing."

6. Explain what happens to the cost percentage of a menu item when the price of the menu item is increased.

____

____

7. Define "contribution margin."

____

____

8. If the total contribution margin for a catered event for 50 people is calculated to be $500.00 and the as-served (AS) cost for the event is $10.00 per person, how much should the catering department charge per person for the event?

____

____

Section 5-6 USING PRICING FORMS

A *pricing form* is a tool often used to help calculate the as-served (AS) cost of a menu item and establish a menu price. Pricing forms may vary from one foodservice operation to another. They generally contain the following elements:

- **Menu Item Name**—The name on the pricing form should match the name used on the menu.
- **Number of Portions**—This lists the number of portions that are made with the ingredients listed on the pricing form.
- **As-Served (AS) Cost per Portion**—This is calculated by dividing the total cost by the number of portions.
- **Target Cost Percentage**—This is the target cost percentage established by the foodservice operation.
- **Target Price**—This is calculated by dividing the as-served (AS) cost per portion by the target cost percentage.
- **Menu Price**—This is the price listed on the menu for a single portion of the menu item.
- **Menu-Item Cost Percentage**—This is calculated by dividing the as-served (AS) cost per portion by the menu price.

- **Ingredients**—These are the ingredients required to prepare the menu item.
- **Edible-Portion (EP) Amount**—The edible-portion (EP) amount is the amount of each ingredient (after trimming) that is required to prepare the menu item.
- **As-Purchased (AP) Unit Cost**—This is the unit cost for each ingredient listed in the same unit of measure as the edible portion (EP) amount of each ingredient.
- **Yield Percentage (YP)**—This is the yield percentage (YP) of each ingredient listed.
- **Edible-Portion (EP) Unit Cost**—This is calculated by dividing the as-purchased (AP) unit cost of each ingredient by the ingredient's yield percentage (YP).
- **Total Ingredient Cost**—The total cost for each ingredient is calculated by multiplying the edible-portion (EP) amount of each ingredient by the edible-portion (EP) unit cost of each ingredient.
- **Total Cost**—The sum of all of the individual ingredient costs.

The procedure for using a pricing form is as follows:

1. Enter the information from the standardized recipe, including the menu item name, number of portions, ingredients, and edible-portion (EP) amounts.
2. Record the as-purchased (AP) unit cost of each ingredient. If necessary, convert either the edible-portion (EP) amount or the unit cost so that the units of measure are the same.
3. Record the yield percentage (YP) for each ingredient.
4. Calculate the edible-portion (EP) unit cost of each ingredient by dividing the as-purchased (AP) unit cost of the ingredient by the yield percentage (YP) of the ingredient.
5. Calculate the total cost of each ingredient by multiplying the edible-portion (EP) amount of each ingredient by the edible-portion (EP) unit cost of each ingredient. Note that this step requires the units of measure to be the same. **See Figure 5-6.**
6. Calculate the total cost by adding the costs of each ingredient.
7. Calculate the cost per portion by dividing the total recipe cost by the number of portions.
8. Calculate the target price by dividing the as-served (AS) cost per portion by the target cost percentage.
9. Adjust the target price if desired, and record the menu price.
10. Calculate the cost percentage by dividing the cost per portion by the menu price. **See Figure 5-7.**

After a pricing form has been completed for all of the items on a menu, the foodservice operation can update the forms when the costs of ingredients change. This ensures that menu prices are adjusted as needed.

Using a Pricing Form—Steps 1–5

EDIBLE-PORTION (EP) AMOUNT × EDIBLE-PORTION (EP) UNIT COST

AS-PURCHASED (AP) UNIT COST ÷ YIELD PERCENTAGE (YP)

Menu Item Name: Pot Roast
Number of Portions: 8
As-Served (AS) Cost per Portion:
Target Cost %:
Target Price:

Menu Price:
Menu-Item Cost %:

Ingredients	Edible-Portion (EP) Amount	Equivalent Edible-Portion (EP) Amount	As-Purchased (AP) Unit Cost	Yield Percentage (YP)	Edible-Portion (EP) Unit Cost	Total Ingredient Cost
Eye of round, trimmed	2.25 kg	2.25 kg	$8.40/kg	85%	$9.88	$22.23
Vegetable oil	60 mL	0.06 L	$5.00/L	100%	$5.00	$0.30
Onions, diced	450 g	0.45 kg	$1.20/kg	93%	$1.29	$0.58
Garlic, minced	15 g	0.015 kg	$12.00/kg	85%	$14.12	$0.21
Tomato paste	175 g	0.175 kg	$8.00/kg	100%	$8.00	$1.40
Beef stock	2 L	2 L	$2.50/L	100%	$2.50	$5.00
Carrots, diced	900 g	0.9 kg	$1.40/kg	85%	$1.65	$1.49
Celery, diced	450 g	0.45 kg	$1.80/kg	70%	$2.57	$1.16
Cornstarch	85 g	0.085 kg	$2.00/kg	100%	$2.00	$0.17
Salt	15 g	0.015 kg	$2.60/kg	100%	$2.60	$0.04
Black pepper	5 g	0.005 kg	$12.00/kg	100%	$12.00	$0.06
					Total Cost:	

Figure 5-6. The cost of each ingredient in a menu item is calculated by multiplying the edible-portion (EP) amount by the edible-portion (EP) unit cost of each ingredient.

Using a Pricing Form—Steps 6–10

AS-SERVED (AS) COST PER PORTION ÷ TARGET COST PERCENTAGE

TOTAL COST ÷ NUMBER OF PORTIONS

COST PER PORTION ÷ MENU PRICE

Menu Item Name: Pot Roast
Number of Portions: 8
As-Served (AS) Cost per Portion: $4.08
Target Cost %: 30%
Target Price: $13.60

Menu Price: $13.95
Menu-Item Cost %: 29.2%

Ingredients	Edible-Portion (EP) Amount	Equivalent Edible-Portion (EP) Amount	As-Purchased (AP) Unit Cost	Yield Percentage (YP)	Edible-Portion (EP) Unit Cost	Total Ingredient Cost
Eye of round, trimmed	2.25 kg	2.25 kg	$8.40/kg	85%	$9.88	$22.23
Vegetable oil	60 mL	0.06 L	$5.00/L	100%	$5.00	$0.30
Onions, diced	450 g	0.45 kg	$1.20/kg	93%	$1.29	$0.58
Garlic, minced	15 g	0.015 kg	$12.00/kg	85%	$14.12	$0.21
Tomato paste	175 g	0.175 kg	$8.00/kg	100%	$8.00	$1.40
Beef stock	2 L	2 L	$2.50/L	100%	$2.50	$5.00
Carrots, diced	900 g	0.9 kg	$1.40/kg	85%	$1.65	$1.49
Celery, diced	450 g	0.45 kg	$1.80/kg	70%	$2.57	$1.16
Cornstarch	85 g	0.085 kg	$2.00/kg	100%	$2.00	$0.17
Salt	15 g	0.015 kg	$2.60/kg	100%	$2.60	$0.04
Black pepper	5 g	0.005 kg	$12.00/kg	100%	$12.00	$0.06
					Total Cost:	$32.64

Figure 5-7. A target price is determined before setting a menu price and calculating the menu-item cost percentage.

5-6 Checkpoint

1. Define "pricing form."

2. What are the two values that must be known in order to calculate the total ingredient cost of each ingredient of a menu item?

3. Explain the difference between the target price on a pricing form and the menu price on a pricing form.

Math Exercises 5

Work each problem in the space provided. Write the final answer on the blank provided. Round all monetary answers to the nearest cent and other decimal answers to the tenths place.

Leaf icon indicates a math problem with a sustainability focus.

Example:

$0.35/bun ________________

What is the as-purchased (AP) unit cost per hamburger bun if a 12-bun package costs $4.20?

$4.20 ÷ 12 buns = ***$0.35/bun***

________________ **1.** What is the as-purchased (AP) unit cost per kilogram of onions if a 20 kg bag of onions costs $28.00?

________________ **2.** What is the as-purchased (AP) unit cost per can of seltzer water if a 12-can case costs $4.56?

________________ **3.** What is the as-purchased (AP) unit cost per fluid ounce of chicken broth that costs $4.68 per customary gallon?

_______________ **4.** A case of eggs contains 15 dozen eggs. What is the as-purchased (AP) unit cost per egg if a case of eggs costs $18.00?

_______________ **5.** A pastry chef supports neighborhood farms and reduces fuel consumption by locally purchasing strawberries to use in strawberry shortcakes. What is the cost of the strawberries in each strawberry shortcake if the strawberries have an as-purchased (AP) cost of $7.90 per kilogram and 85 grams of them are used in each strawberry shortcake?

_______________ **6.** An omelet station uses 3 eggs to make each omelet. What is the cost for the total number of eggs in a single omelet if a case of 30 dozen eggs has an as-purchased (AP) cost of $32.40?

_______________ **7.** What is the as-purchased (AP) unit cost per ice cream cone if a 24-box case of cones costs $43.20 and there are 12 cones in each box?

______________ **8.** What is the as-purchased (AP) unit cost per fluid ounce of tomato juice that costs $12.93 for a 12-can case? *(Tip: Each can contains 46 fluid ounces.)*

______________ **9.** A chef purchases goat cheese from a local dairy to support the area's economy, reduce carbon emissions, and ensure freshness. If the goat cheese costs $24.00 per kilogram, what is the cost for the 110 grams of goat cheese used in the chef's signature salad?

______________ **10.** A restaurant pays $7.60 for 1 liter of olive oil. What is the cost of the olive oil in a vinaigrette recipe that requires 250 milliliters of olive oil?

______________ **11.** What is the edible-portion (EP) unit cost per kilogram of cantaloupe if the as-purchased (AP) unit cost is $1.29 per kilogram and the yield percentage (YP) is 56%?

______________ **12.** What is the edible-portion (EP) unit cost per kilogram of garlic if the as-purchased (AP) unit cost is $6.35 per kilogram and the yield percentage (YP) is 85%?

______________ **13.** What is the edible-portion (EP) unit cost per kilogram of a whole turkey if the as-purchased (AP) unit cost is $3.29 per kilogram and the yield percentage (YP) is 56%?

______________ **14.** What is the edible-portion (EP) unit cost per ounce of romaine lettuce if the as-purchased (AP) unit cost is $0.85 per pound and the yield percentage (YP) is 78%?

______________ **15.** A spa offers new lunch bowls with a base of cauliflower rice prepared from the center stalk of the cauliflower. Through the use of the stalk, the amount discarded from each cauliflower has gone from 40% to 8%. If cauliflower costs $3.25 a head, what is the edible-portion (EP) unit cost for the cauliflower when the stalk is used?

_______________ **16.** To increase utilization and reduce waste, a chef cuts the rinds of watermelons into julienne cuts to use in stir fries, causing the yield percentage (YP) for watermelons to change from 55% to 92%. If a 4-kilogram watermelon costs $5.52, what is the difference in the edible-portion (EP) unit cost per kilogram between a watermelon with a 55% yield percentage (YP) and one with a 92% yield percentage (YP)?

_______________ **17.** A soup recipe calls for 3.6 kilograms of peeled and diced carrots. What is the total cost of carrots in the recipe if the as-purchased (AP) unit cost of whole carrots is $0.88 per kilogram and the yield percentage (YP) is 85%?

_______________ **18.** A pasta sauce recipe calls for 400 grams of peeled, seeded, and diced tomatoes. What is the total cost of the tomatoes if the as-purchased (AP) unit cost of whole tomatoes is $2.80 per kilogram and the yield percentage (YP) is 80%?

_______________ **19.** A salsa recipe is prepared with 8 ounces of peeled and pitted mango. What is the total cost of the mango used in the salsa if the as-purchased (AP) unit cost of mango is $1.82 per pound and the yield percentage (YP) is 65%?

_______________ **20.** What is the as-served (AS) cost of a spinach salad if a single spinach salad contains $1.30 of spinach, $0.45 of tomatoes, $0.70 of bacon, and $0.64 of salad dressing?

_______________ **21.** A restaurant offers a soup-and-salad special. If the soup has an as-served (AS) cost of $0.80 per serving and the salad has an as-served (AS) cost of $1.18 per serving, what is the as-served (AS) cost of the soup-and-salad special?

_______________ **22.** The as-purchased (AP) unit cost of ground beef is $5.95 per kilogram, and the yield percentage (YP) is 85%. If a total of 180 grams of cooked ground beef are used for a three-taco meal deal, what is the as-served (AS) cost of the beef for each meal deal?

_______________ **23.** A deli runs daily specials to repurpose leftovers. Monday's special is a French dip sandwich made with leftover roast beef. What is the as-served (AS) cost of a French dip sandwich if a single sandwich comes with $2.40 of meat, $0.27 of au jus, and a bun with an as-served (AS) cost of $0.19?

_______________ **24.** A restaurant serves shrimp po-boys with a side of chips. What is the total as-served (AS) cost of the meal if the chips have an as-served (AS) cost of $0.36 and the sandwich consists of 6 ounces of shrimp at $0.13 per ounce as well as $0.11 of breading, $0.07 of frying oil, $0.17 of condiments, and a bun of $0.21?

_______________ **25.** The total cost of the ingredients in a sweet-and-sour chicken recipe is $80.55, and the recipe makes 60 portions. If the sweet-and-sour chicken is served with a side of fried rice that has an as-served (AS) cost of $0.75 per portion, what is the total as-served (AS) cost of the sweet-and-sour chicken meal?

_______________ **26.** A restaurant uses a reverse osmosis water system to reduce plastic bottle waste and decrease costs by 45%. The restaurant uses the reverse osmosis water system and the extra produce in inventory to make infused lemon-basil water. If 15 L of the infused water consist of $3.25 in lemons, $2.00 in basil, $1.10 in water, and ice of $0.10, what is the as-served (AS) cost for a 330 mL glass of the infused water?

_______________ **27.** At a carving station, 420 people were each served 180 grams of beef instead of 110 grams. What is the cost of the extra beef served if the as-served (AS) cost is $15.00 per kilogram?

_______________ **28.** A mocha ice-cream pie recipe uses ½ cup plus 1 tablespoon of fudge sauce. What is the as-served (AS) cost of the fudge sauce for a single pie if the fudge sauce costs $40.96 per customary gallon?

_______________ **29.** What is the menu-item cost percentage of an appetizer that has an as-served (AS) cost of $5.78 and a menu price of $15.95?

_______________ **30.** A chef reduces costs by using the carcass of a fabricated chicken to make stock for chicken and dumplings. What is the menu-item cost percentage for a bowl of chicken and dumplings if it has an as-served (AS) cost of $1.27 and a menu price of $4.50?

_______________ **31.** What is the menu-item cost percentage of a turkey panini that has an as-served (AS) cost of $1.86 and a menu price of $6.99?

_______________ **32.** Ham bones and trimmings are saved from a carving station and used to make soup. What is the menu-item cost percentage for a cup of the soup if it has an as-served (AS) cost of $0.93 and a menu price of $3.99?

________ **33.** What is the menu-item cost percentage of a glass of lemonade that has an as-served (AS) cost of $0.36 and a menu price of $2.95?

________ **34.** A bottle of wine has an as-purchased (AP) cost of $14.00. If the bottle of wine will fill 5 glasses, what is the menu-item cost percentage of the wine if the menu price for each glass of wine is $8.00?

________ **35.** A spa serves tea with a lemon slice for $2.50. What is the menu-item cost percentage for the tea with lemon if the tea's as-served (AS) cost is $0.72 and a bag of 15 lemons costs $7.49 with each lemon yielding 6 slices?

________ **36.** A clam chowder recipe has a total ingredient cost of $38.00 and yields 30 servings. What is the menu-item cost percentage of the clam chowder if it has a menu price of $5.00 per serving?

________ **37.** A restaurant replaced seafood items with more sustainably caught items. If a replaced item had a menu price of $19.00 and a cost percentage of 31%, and a new item has the same menu price but a cost percentage of 33%, what is the difference in their as-served (AS) costs?

______________ **38.** A café uses beets in their plant-based hot dogs and saves the leaves for a beet greens salad. The as-served (AS) costs are $1.20 for the hot dog and $2.10 for the salad. The menu prices are $3.25 for the hot dog and $8.00 for the salad. What is the menu-item cost percentage if the hot dog and the salad are offered as a meal?

______________ **39.** During the month of December, a banquet facility spent $36,578.00 on food and beverages and had total sales of $109,745.00. What was the total cost percentage for the banquet hall?

______________ **40.** On Monday, the cost of food and beverages at a café was $224.80 and total sales were $851.90. What was the total cost percentage for the café?

______________ **41.** The cost of food and beverages for one week at a pizza restaurant was $4,129.00, and the total sales for the week were $17,046.00. What was the pizza restaurant's overall cost percentage for the week?

_______________ **42.** The as-served (AS) cost of a stew is $7.40. If the bistro uses a target cost percentage of 32%, what is the target price of the stew?

_______________ **43.** If an ice-cream parlor had food-and-beverage costs of $27,416.00 for May, what was needed that month in total sales to meet their target cost percentage of 28%?

_______________ **44.** The as-purchased (AP) cost of a 24-bottle case of root beer is $22.00. If the root beer is sold by the bottle and has a target cost percentage of 30%, what is the target price for a single bottle of root beer?

_______________ **45.** What is the target price per person for a catered event with an as-served (AS) cost of $14.00 per person and a target cost percentage of 32%?

_______________ **46.** A prix fixe meal has the following as-served (AS) costs per serving: $5.50 for lobster bisque, $17.00 for beef tenderloin, and $3.76 for chocolate mousse. If the target cost percentage is 29%, what is the target price of this prix fixe meal?

_______________ **47.** The pricing form for vegetable lasagna shows a total ingredient cost of $29.30, a portion total of 12 portions, and a target cost percentage of 25%. What would be the target price for a serving of the lasagna?

_______________ **48.** The pricing form for a meal of fish and chips shows a total ingredient cost for fish of $4.90 per serving, chips at $0.80 per serving, and tartar sauce at $0.38 per serving. If the target cost percentage is 28%, what is the target price for the meal of fish and chips?

_______________ **49.** The total contribution margin of a catered event for 250 people is calculated to be $2,500.00. If the as-served (AS) cost for the event is $48.00 per person and labor expenses and rental fees total $4,000.00, how much should each person be charged for the event?

_______________ **50.** The menu for a banquet of 175 people has an as-served (AS) cost of $22.00 per person. If additional expenses total $3,500.00 and the goal is to generate earnings of $10.00 per person, how much should each person be charged for the banquet?

Calculating Revenue and Expenses

6

In order to determine whether a foodservice operation is financially successful, the amount of money coming into the operation and the amount of money leaving the operation must be known. Foodservice workers need to have a working knowledge of the tools and processes used for documenting and calculating the sale of food and beverages to customers. Likewise, foodservice workers need to understand the different types of expenses that are incurred by a foodservice operation and how those expenses relate to the operation's financial success.

Section 6-1: CALCULATING REVENUE

- Explain how a guest check is processed.
- Calculate discounts, sales taxes, guest check totals, and gratuities.
- Explain the purpose of a point-of-sale (POS) system.
- Demonstrate how to return change to a customer who pays with cash.
- Explain how daily sales revenue is calculated and recorded.

Section 6-2: CALCULATING EXPENSES

- Describe the different expense categories of a foodservice operation.
- Calculate the value of inventory.
- Calculate the cost of goods sold.
- Explain how payroll expenses are calculated.
- Explain the difference between variable and fixed expenses.

Key Terms

- revenue
- discount
- sales tax
- gratuity
- point-of-sale (POS) system
- capital expense
- cost of goods sold
- inventory
- operating expense
- payroll expense
- gross pay
- net pay
- interest
- variable expense
- fixed expense

Learner Resources
atplearningresources.com
access code 267628

Carlisle FoodService Products

Section 6-1 CALCULATING REVENUE

Determining whether a foodservice operation is financially successful starts with calculating revenue. *Revenue* is the total amount of money received by a foodservice operation from sales to customers. The process of calculating revenue begins when a customer places an order. A foodservice operation must be able to document what has been ordered by the customer, provide the customer with a total cost for that order, and properly collect and record payments.

Processing Guest Checks

One of the most common tools that a foodservice operation uses to document what is sold to a customer is a guest check, which is also referred to as "a bill." A guest check lists the items ordered by a customer, the prices to be charged for those items, and the total amount of money due. Guest checks can be written by hand or electronically generated.

In addition to the amount due for food and beverages, the guest check may also include additional charges or items, such as sales tax and service charges. It may also reflect discounts that reduce the total amount owed based on promotions offered by the foodservice operation. The processing of a guest check ends once payment has been received and the proper amount of change and a receipt for payment have been returned to the customer.

Writing Guest Checks. Servers may use handwritten guest checks to record customer orders in restaurants where customers place an order from a table or at a counter. **See Figure 6-1.** Handwritten guest checks vary, but most contain the following information:

- **General Information.** General information includes items such as the date, the table number, the number of guests at the table, and the server's identification number or name. Most guest checks include preprinted numbers so each is unique and easy to track.
- **Main Body.** The main body of the guest check is used to record the menu items ordered and the quantity and cost of each item.
- **Subtotal.** The subtotal of a guest check is the sum of all food and beverage charges.
- **Discounts.** A *discount* is a percentage or fixed amount by which the subtotal is reduced due to a promotion offered by the foodservice operation. For example, a restaurant may offer 10% off all appetizers or coupons that offer $3.00 off any large pizza.
- **Sales Taxes.** A *sales tax* is a fee that must be collected from customers based on the requirements of both the federal government and the province where the foodservice operation is located. These fees are

then paid to the government-taxing agency at a later date. In most cases, sales taxes are calculated based on a percentage of the amount charged for food and beverages minus any discounts.

- **Total.** The total on a guest check is the final amount of money due from the customer. The total is calculated by subtracting any discounts from the subtotal and then adding the sales tax.

Guest Checks

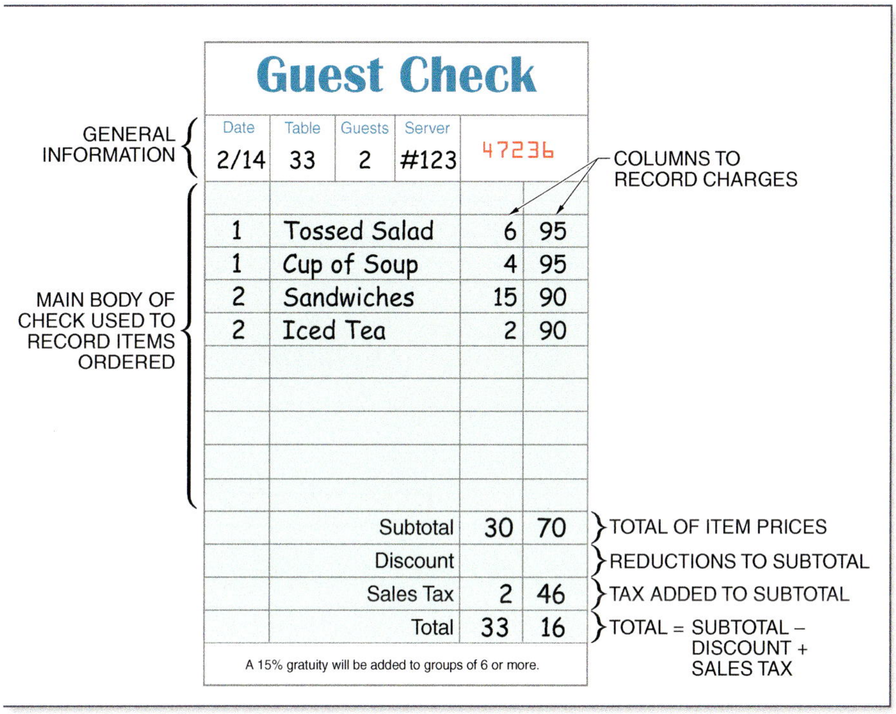

Figure 6-1. Handwritten guest checks may be used to document sales in a foodservice operation.

In order to process a handwritten guest check, certain math skills are required, such as addition, subtraction, and multiplication. The first step in processing a guest check is to fill in the general information. Next, the menu items ordered are recorded in the main body.

For example, two customers come into a pizza restaurant and are seated at Table 20. Before approaching the table, the server writes the date, table number (20), number of guests (2), and his or her name or identification number on the guest check. The server writes down additional information as the customers place their orders. The first customer orders an individual pizza with pepperoni, a house salad, and a soft drink. The second customer orders an individual pizza with sausage, green peppers, and onions; a cup of minestrone soup; and a soft drink.

After recording the order, the server may give a copy of the guest check to workers in the kitchen. Sometimes the original guest check is passed off into the kitchen and then returned to the server once the food is prepared. Before presenting the final check to the customer for payment, the server records the cost of each menu item ordered. **See Figure 6-2.** If an entry on the guest check is a single menu item, such as one house salad, the menu price is simply written in the column where the charges are recorded. If an entry includes more than one of the same menu item, such as two soft drinks, the menu price must be multiplied by the number of items ordered, and then the product is recorded in the charges column. Next, all of the charges are added to calculate the subtotal of charges for food and beverages.

Calculating Subtotals and Discounts

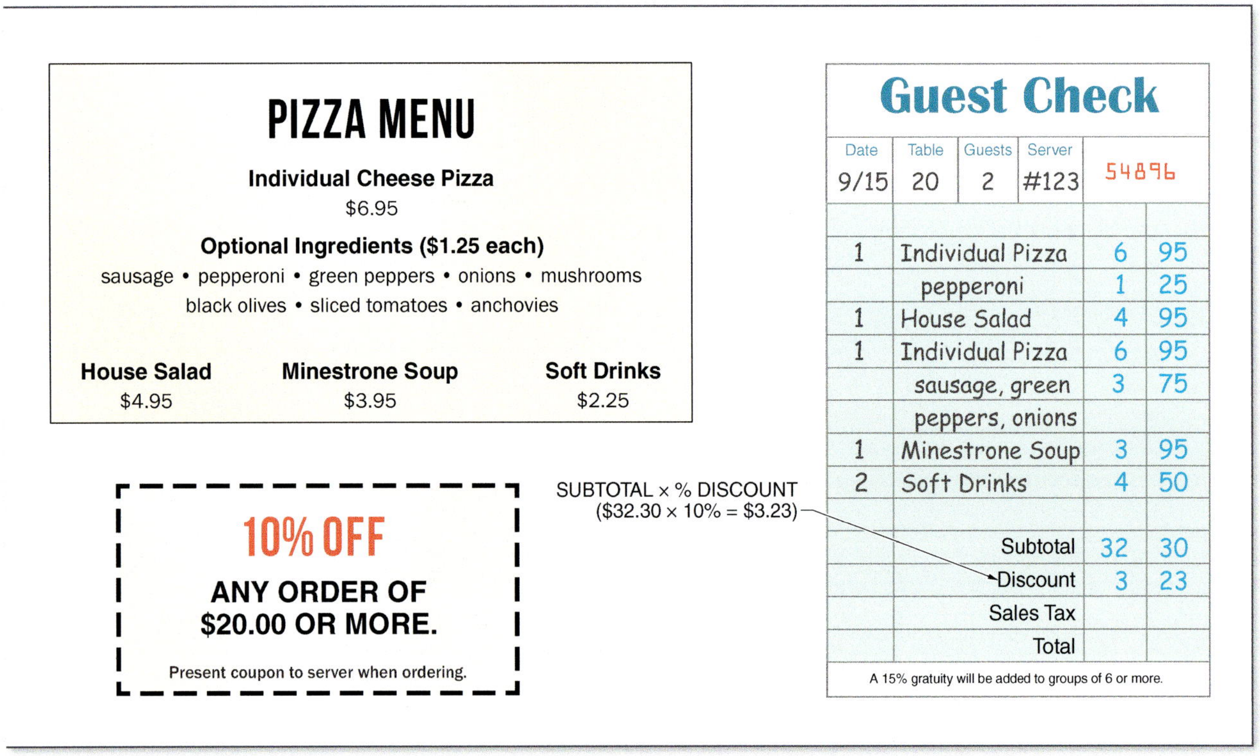

Figure 6-2. The subtotal on a guest check is the sum of the charges for all food and beverage items on an order and is sometimes reduced by a discount.

Calculating Discounts. If the foodservice operation is offering a promotion, the amount of the discount needs to be subtracted from the subtotal. For example, if a pizza restaurant offers 10% off any order of $20.00 or more, the server would multiply the subtotal by 10% and then record that amount on the guest check as the discount.

Calculating Sales Tax. The next step is to calculate the sales tax. The three types of sales taxes in Canada are the goods and services tax, the provincial sales tax, and the harmonized sales tax. The goods and services tax (GST) is a federal tax applied to most goods and services sold in Canada. The provincial sales tax (PST) is a province-specific tax and is collected separately from the GST. In many provinces, the GST is combined with the PST to create the harmonized sales tax (HST). Sales taxes generally range from 5% to 15%, depending on the province.

Because sales taxes are based on a percentage of the actual charges to the customer for food and beverages, any discount must be subtracted from the subtotal before the sales tax can be calculated. In the pizza example, the subtotal is $32.30, and the discount is $3.23. So, the actual amount being charged for food and beverages is $29.07 ($32.30 – $3.23 = $29.07). If the sales tax where the pizza restaurant is located is 5%, the tax is calculated by multiplying $29.07 by 5%. *Note:* Monetary amounts have been rounded to the nearest cent.

Sales Tax = $29.07 × 5%

Sales Tax = $29.07 × 0.05

Sales Tax = $1.4535 = **$1.45**

The total on the guest check is calculated by subtracting the discount from the subtotal and then adding the sales tax. **See Figure 6-3.**

Calculating Sales Taxes and Totals

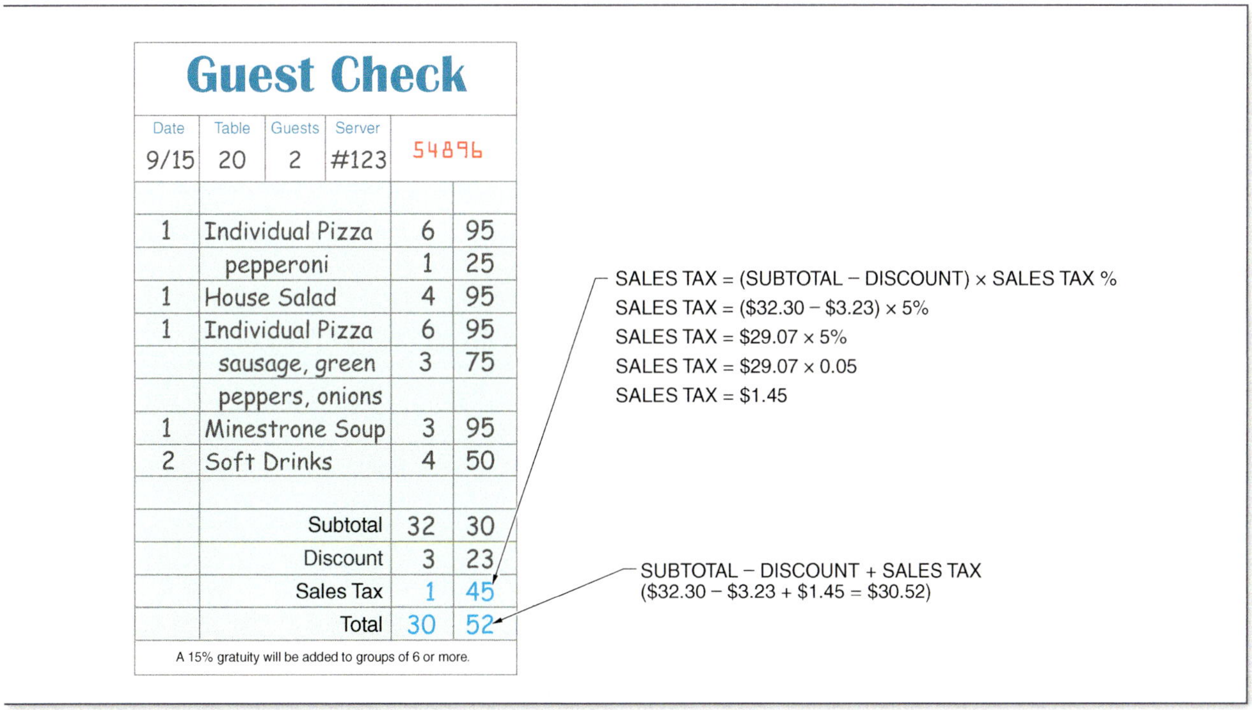

Figure 6-3. The total amount of a guest check is equal to the food and beverage subtotal minus discounts plus sales tax.

Calculating Gratuities. In a foodservice operation where a server waits on a customer, it is customary to leave a gratuity, or tip. A *gratuity* is the amount of money left by a customer to show appreciation for the services rendered. Although there are no minimum or maximum requirements when calculating gratuities, it is widely accepted that a gratuity in a full-service restaurant should be between 15% and 20% of the food and beverage subtotal on the guest check. When a customer decides to leave a gratuity after receiving the guest check, it is not necessary to consider any discounts or sales tax when calculating the gratuity. For example, a 15% gratuity on a check with a food and beverage subtotal of $45.00 would be $6.75.

$45.00 × 15% = $45.00 × 0.15 = **$6.75**

A 20% gratuity on the same check would be $9.00.

$45.00 × 20% = $45.00 × 0.20 = **$9.00**

Gratuity Guide

To calculate a 15% gratuity, multiply the food and beverage subtotal by 10%. Then, divide that result by 2 to calculate 5% of the total. Finally, add the two amounts to arrive at 15%.

For example, a 15% gratuity on a $50.00 check would be calculated as follows:

10% of $50.00 = $50.00 = $5.00

5% of $50.00 = $5.00 ÷ 2 = $2.50

15% of $50.00 =

$5.00 + $2.50 = $7.50

Based on this example, if the customer leaves a gratuity between $6.75 and $9.00, it indicates that the customer was satisfied with the level of service received. Likewise, if the gratuity left is significantly more than $9.00, it indicates that the customer was extremely satisfied with the level of service.

Although it is common for a customer to voluntarily leave a gratuity, some restaurants and most banquet facilities include a gratuity as part of the check for larger groups (typically more than six or eight people). A restaurant's gratuity policy is usually provided on the menu. A banquet facility will include the gratuity in the customer contract. When a gratuity is included by a foodservice operation, it is taxable. Therefore, it is added to the guest check before the sales tax is calculated. For example, a catered event requires a 20% gratuity on a food and beverage order of $325.00, and the event is located in an area where the sales tax rate is 15%. The total amount owed by the customer is calculated using the following problem-solving steps:

Problem-Solving Steps

1. Calculate the gratuity.

   $325.00 × 20% = $325.00 × 0.20 = **$65.00**

2. Calculate the food and beverage subtotal.

   $325.00 + $65.00 = **$390.00**

3. Calculate the sales tax.

   $390.00 × 15% = $390.00 × 0.15 = **$58.50**

4. Calculate the total due for the catered event by adding the food and beverage subtotal and sales tax.

   $390.00 + $58.50 = **$448.50**

Using Point-of-Sale Systems. Most foodservice operations use electronic point-of-sale systems to process guest checks. A *point-of-sale (POS) system* is a computerized system used to process customer orders, print guest checks, track daily operations, and generate financial reports.

Basic POS systems include a computer, a cash drawer, and a receipt printer. Most foodservice POS systems have a touch screen or handheld tablet that can be used to process food and beverage orders. **See Figure 6-4.** Orders are sent electronically to a terminal located in the kitchen or bar area, where employees prepare the order. POS systems are also used to generate and print guest checks. These systems help prevent errors due to poorly written or misplaced guest checks; lack of communication between servers and kitchen staff; and inaccurate calculations.

POS systems can increase efficiency in foodservice operations by allowing management to track daily operations more accurately. For example, POS systems have the ability to track inventory based on customer orders, which helps keep food costs down. In addition, management can track the sale of menu items to analyze which are popular and which generate the greatest profits. This information can then be used to help determine food costs and purchasing needs.

POS systems also allow management to identify the busiest periods of each shift so that employees can be scheduled appropriately. When employees arrive to work, many POS systems allow employees to clock into the system when their shift begins and clock out at the end of the shift. This data is then used to prepare paychecks.

Point-of-Sale (POS) Systems

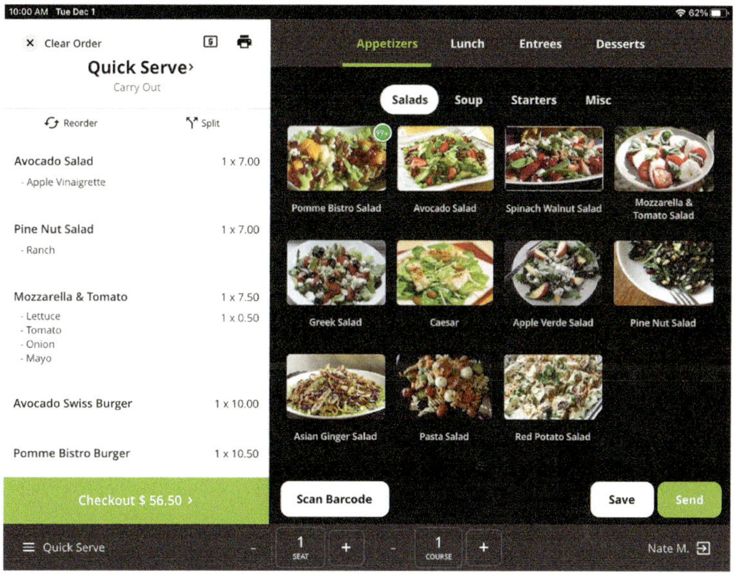

Lavu, Inc.

Figure 6-4. Most POS systems have a touch screen that can be used to process food and beverage orders.

Even though POS systems help eliminate errors by electronically performing math calculations, employees must still know how to spot a mistake. The information generated by a POS system is only as good as the information entered into it.

Collecting Payment and Returning Change. On February 4, 2013, the Royal Canadian Mint stopped producing and distributing pennies. Therefore, when a customer pays with cash, the guest check is typically rounded to the nearest 5-cent increment before change is returned to the customer. **See Figure 6-5.** For example, a check with a total of $12.02 would be rounded down to $12.00, while a guest check with a total of $12.08 would be rounded up to $12.10. The amount of change given to the customer should be equal to the difference between the amount of cash presented for payment and the total amount of the guest check. For example, if a customer uses a $20 bill to pay for a guest check with a total of $13.75, the customer should receive $6.25 in change ($20.00 – $13.75 = $6.25).

Rounding Guest Check Totals

Figure 6-5. When a customer pays with cash, the guest check is typically rounded to the nearest 5-cent increment before the change is returned to the customer.

Change should be returned to the customer in an orderly process. **See Figure 6-6.** The first step is to return any coins. In this example, the cashier would hand the customer a quarter ($0.25) and say, "Twenty-five cents makes fourteen dollars." The next step for the cashier would be to hand the customer a $1.00 bill and say "Fifteen." Then, the cashier would hand the customer a $5.00 bill and say, "And five makes twenty." The process always ends with the total amount of money originally presented by the customer for payment. This process helps ensure that the proper amount of change is returned.

In addition to cash, most foodservice operations offer customers the option of paying with a credit or debit card. Some restaurants even have their own gift cards that can be used for payment. When guests use a card for payment, the guest check total is not rounded.

Returning Change

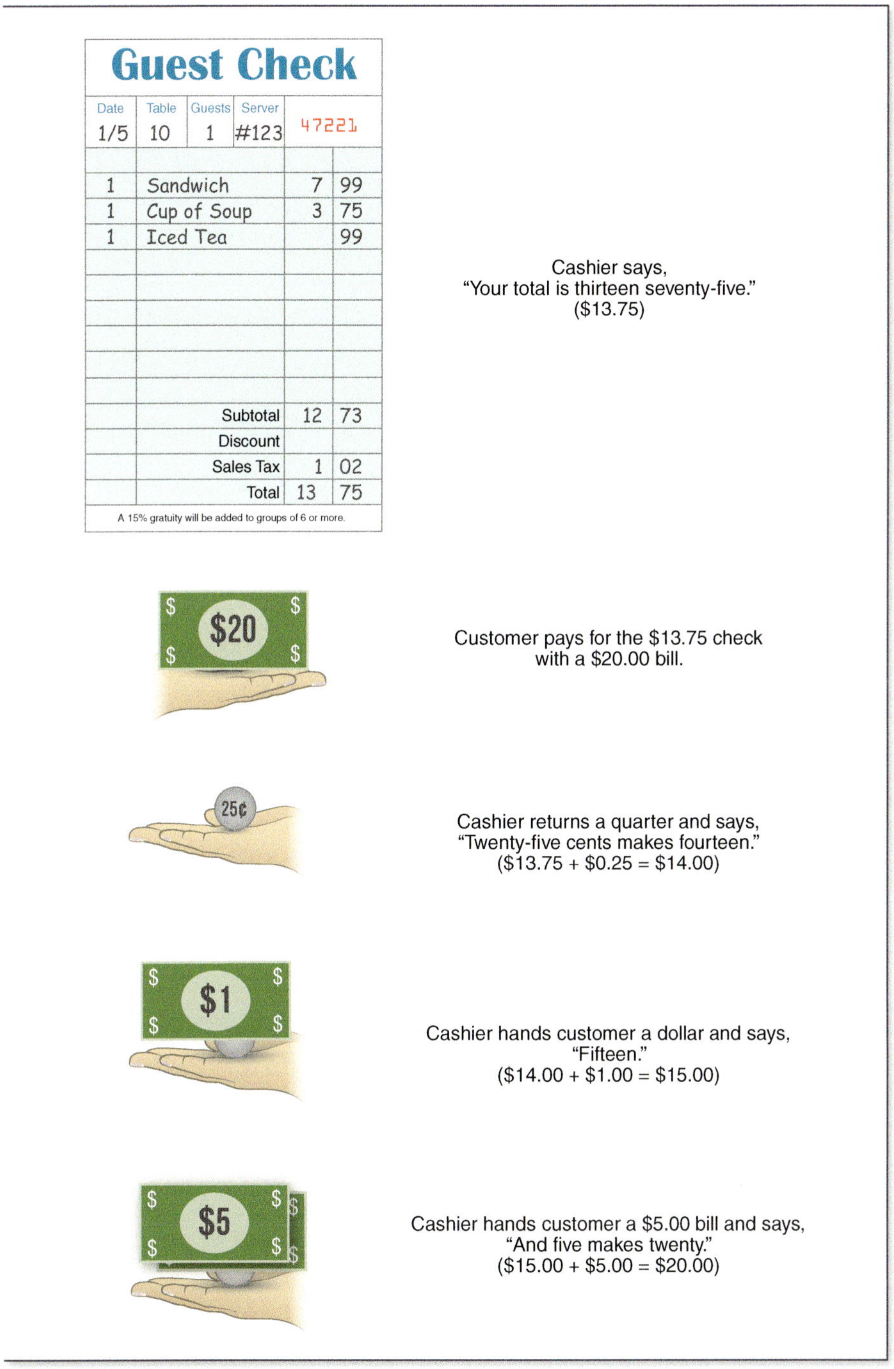

Guest Check

Date	Table	Guests	Server	47221
1/5	10	1	#123	

1	Sandwich	7	99
1	Cup of Soup	3	75
1	Iced Tea		99
	Subtotal	12	73
	Discount		
	Sales Tax	1	02
	Total	13	75

A 15% gratuity will be added to groups of 6 or more.

Figure 6-6. Returning change to a customer in an orderly fashion helps minimize the chance of mistakes.

Calculating Sales Revenue

Most foodservice operations calculate sales revenue on a daily basis. The calculations are documented using a standard form, such as a daily sales record. **See Figure 6-7.** The name of the form and the specific information recorded will vary based on the needs of the particular operation, but it will contain at least the following basic information:

- **Total Sales.** Total sales is the sum of all of the individual guest check subtotals minus all discounts. Foodservice operations that use programmable cash registers or POS systems can easily generate reports that break the total sales down into further categories, such as sales of food and sales of beverages.
- **Gross Sales.** Gross sales is the sum of the totals on all of the guest checks processed that day, which is equal to the total sales plus the total sales tax.
- **Cash at End of Day.** The total amount of cash at the end of the day is determined by physically counting all of the cash in the cash register.
- **Cash at Start of Day.** The amount of cash available at the start of the day is primarily used for returning change to customers paying with cash.

Daily Sales Records

Daily Sales Record	
Total Sales	**$ 14,536.89**
Total Food Sales	$ 11,457.60
Total Beverage Sales	$ 3,079.29
Sales Tax (15%)	$ 2,180.53
Gross Sales (*Total Sales + Sales Tax*)	**$ 16,717.42**
Cash at End of Day	$ 5,638.25
Cash at Start of Day	**$ 400.00**
Total Cash Revenue (*Cash at End of Day – Cash at Start of Day*)	**$ 5,238.25**
Total Card Revenue	**$ 11,479.17**
Credit Cards	$ 3,545.82
Debit Cards	$ 5,983.35
Gift Cards	$ 1,950.00
Total Revenue (*Total Cash Revenue + Total Card Revenue*)	**$ 16,717.42**
Over (Short) (*Total Revenue – Gross Sales*)	**$ 0.00**

Report completed by: ______________________
Signature/Date

INFORMATION FROM GUEST CHECKS, CASH REGISTER, OR POS SYSTEM REPORTS

GROSS SALES SHOULD EQUAL TOTAL REVENUE

Figure 6-7. The daily gross sales of an operation (amount charged to customers) should be equal to the total revenue (amount of money received from customers).

- **Total Cash Revenue.** Total cash revenue is the difference between the cash at the end of the day and the cash at the start of the day. This is the total amount of cash received from customers that day.
- **Total Card Revenue.** Total card revenue is the total amount of credit, debit, and gift card charges received from customers that day.
- **Total Revenue.** Total revenue is the total cash revenue added to the total card revenue. This total should also match the gross sales.
- **Over (Short).** If the total revenue is more than the gross sales, then too much money was received from customers, and this is referred to as "over." If the total revenue is less than the gross sales, then too little money was received from customers, and this is referred to as "short." The difference between the total revenue and the gross sales should be zero.

The daily sales record will indicate if the cash amount is over or short. For example, if the operation reports gross sales for the day of $2,450 and total revenue of $2,500, the report will be over by $50 because the total revenue was more than the gross sales.

$2,500 – $2,450 = **$50**

However, if the operation reports gross sales for the day of $3,575 and a total revenue of $3,550, the report will be short by $25 because the total revenue was less than the gross sales.

$3,550 – $3,575 = **–$25 or ($25) or <25>**

Note: On financial reports, negative numbers are shown inside parentheses or angle brackets. For example, "–$25" is written as "($25)" or "<$25>". Overages and shortages often occur because the wrong amount of change may have been returned to a customer or the wrong amount may have been entered when processing a card payment. Management is responsible for determining the cause of any overages or shortages and taking the appropriate corrective action.

6-1 Checkpoint

1. Define "revenue."

____

____

2. Describe the purpose of a guest check.

____

____

6-1 Checkpoint (continued)

3. What is a POS system?

____

____

4. What is the food and beverage subtotal on a guest check that contains the following order: two sandwiches for $7.95 each, one salad for $6.95, and two desserts for $4.50 each?

____

5. What would be the discount on the order in the previous question if the customers had a coupon good for 15% off their entire food and beverage order?

____

6. If the food and beverage subtotal on a guest check is $45.50 and the sales tax is 9%, what is the total of the guest check?

____

7. How much would a 15% gratuity be on a guest check with a food and beverage subtotal of $60.50?

____

8. If a customer pays with a $50.00 bill and the guest check total is $37.50, how much change should be returned to the customer?

____

9. When completing a daily sales record, if the cash at the end of the day is $1,240.50 and the cash at the start of the day is $250.25, what is the total cash revenue for the day?

____

10. On a daily sales record, if a restaurant records gross sales of $3,276.65 and a total revenue of $3,300.80, would the report be over or short and by how much?

____

Section 6-2 CALCULATING EXPENSES

In addition to calculating revenue, a foodservice operation must calculate its expenses before it can be determined whether the operation is financially successful. There are many expenses involved in building and operating a foodservice operation. These expenses fall under three general categories: capital expenses, cost of goods sold, and operating expenses. **See Figure 6-8.**

Expense Categories

Vulcan-Hart, a division of the ITW Food Equipment Group LLC

Capital Expenses

Florida Department of Citrus

Cost of Goods Sold

Charlie Trotter's

Operating Expenses

Figure 6-8. The many expenses incurred by a foodservice operation can be broken down into three general categories.

Calculating Capital Expenses

Building or improving the physical space occupied by a foodservice operation results in capital expenses. A *capital expense* is a cost to an operation for buildings, building improvements, and equipment that is expected to have a useful life longer than one year. Examples of capital expenses include buildings and signage, construction improvements made to a leased space such as new plumbing and electrical systems, major kitchen equipment such as ovens and fryers, and furniture such as tables and chairs.

For example, a business owner decides to lease an empty space in a new strip mall to open a restaurant. If the owner spends $150,000 on construction, $70,000 on equipment, and $35,000 on furniture, the total of those capital expenses would be $255,000.

$$\$150{,}000 + \$70{,}000 + \$35{,}000 = \mathbf{\$255{,}000}$$

Most capital expenses are incurred before the foodservice operation opens for business. This means that the business owner(s) must either borrow the money or already have it to pay for these expenses, since the business cannot start earning money before construction is complete and the business is operational. However, even if an existing operation needs to replace a major piece of equipment after being open for several years, the cost of the replacement equipment is still considered a capital expense.

Calculating Cost of Goods Sold

A popular saying is, "You have to spend money to make money." In accounting terms, this is the cost of goods sold. In food service, the *cost of goods sold* is the cost of the food and beverage products purchased that are ultimately sold to customers. For example, a bakery must purchase flour, sugar, eggs, milk, and butter before it can make money selling cakes and pastries. Even a can of soda—which is purchased from a beverage supplier and then resold to a customer at a higher price—is considered part of the cost of goods sold. The cost of goods sold is one of the most significant expenses of a foodservice operation.

When calculating the cost of goods sold, the value of the inventory of food and beverage products already purchased must be considered. *Inventory* is the amount of food and beverage products that have been purchased and are currently being stored for future use. For example, a case of pasta stored in a restaurant's dry storage room is considered part of the inventory until it is removed from storage and cooked for customers.

The cost of goods sold is calculated based on a specific period of time (typically a week or a month). To calculate the cost of goods sold during a specific period, the value of inventory must be determined at both the beginning and end of the period. Inventory value is determined by counting the food and beverage items in storage and multiplying the number of units of each item by their as-purchased (AP) unit costs. **See Figure 6-9.** The formula for calculating the inventory value of an individual item is as follows:

$$IV = NU \times AC$$

Inventory Value = Number of Units × As-Purchased Unit Cost

where

IV = inventory value

NU = number of units

AC = as-purchased unit cost

Calculating Inventory Value

Inventory Sheet—Pizza Restaurant

Item Type/Name	Number of Units	As-Purchased (AP) Unit Cost	Inventory Value
Dry Goods			
All-Purpose Flour	100 kg	$0.80/kg	$80.00
Dry Yeast	5 kg	$4.40/kg	$22.00
Granulated Sugar	10 kg	$1.20/kg	$12.00
Salt	20 kg	$0.50/kg	$10.00
Olive Oil	15 L	$3.85/L	$57.75
Pizza Sauce	40 L	$2.85/L	$114.00
Meats and Dairy			
Italian Sausage	12 kg	$5.10/kg	$61.20
Pepperoni	9 kg	$6.90/kg	$62.10
Mozzarella Cheese	20 kg	$5.30/kg	$106.00
Fresh Produce			
Yellow Onions	20 kg	$0.78/kg	$15.60
Green Peppers	12 kg	$3.30/kg	$39.60
Mushrooms	8 kg	$2.90/kg	$23.20
Plum Tomatoes	15 kg	$2.26/kg	$33.90
Beverages			
Cola	50 cans	$0.30/can	$15.00
Diet Cola	60 cans	$0.30/can	$18.00
Root Beer	24 bottles	$0.55/bottle	$13.20
Spring Water	38 bottles	$0.40/bottle	$15.20
		Total	$698.75

Figure 6-9. The value of an item in inventory is equal to the number of units of the item in storage multiplied by the as-purchased (AP) unit cost of the item.

For example, the inventory value of 100 kg of all-purpose flour with an as-purchased (AP) unit cost of $0.80 per kilogram is calculated as follows:

$$IV = NU \times AC$$

$$IV = 100\text{ kg} \times \$0.80/\text{kg}$$

$$IV = \mathbf{\$80.00}$$

The inventory value at the beginning of a period plus the purchases made during that period represent the total amount of food and beverages available for sale during that period. By subtracting the inventory value at the end of that period, the actual value of the products sold (the cost of goods sold) can be calculated. The formula for calculating the cost of goods sold is as follows:

$$GS = BI + IP - EI$$

where

GS = cost of goods sold

BI = beginning inventory

IP = inventory purchases

EI = ending inventory

Cost of Goods Sold = Beginning Inventory + Inventory Purchases − Ending Inventory

For example, at the beginning of January, a restaurant has a starting inventory value of $4,000. Then, a total of $25,000 in food and beverages are purchased over the course of the month. At the end of January, the restaurant has an ending inventory value of $3,000. The cost of goods sold for the month can be calculated as follows:

$$GS = BI + IP - EI$$

$$GS = \$4{,}000 + \$25{,}000 - \$3{,}000$$

$$GS = \mathbf{\$26{,}000}$$

In this example, the cost of goods sold was actually higher than the amount of food and beverages purchased during the month because the restaurant's ending inventory value was lower than its beginning inventory value. However, if the ending inventory value is higher than the beginning inventory value, the cost of goods sold would be less than the amount of food and beverages purchased during the period.

For example, in June, a cafeteria has a beginning inventory value of $15,000. A total of $80,000 in food and beverages are purchased during the month. At the end of June, the cafeteria has an ending inventory value of $20,000. The cost of goods sold for the month can be calculated as follows:

$$GS = BI + IP - EI$$

$$GS = \$15{,}000 + \$80{,}000 - \$20{,}000$$

$$GS = \mathbf{\$75{,}000}$$

When the cost of goods sold is greater than (>) the amount of food and beverages purchased, it indicates that the amount of inventory was reduced during the period. Likewise, when the cost of goods sold is less than (<) the amount of food and beverages purchased, it indicates that inventory was increased during the period. **See Figure 6-10.**

Impact of Cost of Goods Sold on Inventory

Cost of Goods Sold > Food and Beverage Purchases = Reduced Inventory

Cost of Goods Sold < Food and Beverage Purchases = Increased Inventory

Figure 6-10. Inventory is reduced when the cost of goods sold is greater than food and beverage purchases, and it is increased when the cost of goods sold is less than food and beverage purchases.

Calculating Operating Expenses

The final category of expenses for a foodservice operation is operating expenses. An *operating expense* is any ordinary and necessary cost incurred by an operation as a result of carrying out daily business activities. Basically, operating expenses are all of the other expenses incurred by an operation that are not capital expenses or part of the cost of goods sold. Some of the major operating expenses of a foodservice operation include payroll expenses, rent, interest, utilities, supplies, and insurance and licenses.

Payroll Expenses. Payroll expenses are frequently the most significant expense of a foodservice operation. A *payroll expense* is the expense of an operation that includes any money paid to an employee who performs work for the operation. Employees are paid on either a salaried basis or an hourly basis. A salaried employee, such as a manager or chef, is paid a fixed amount of money. An hourly employee, such as a line cook, server, or dishwasher, is paid an hourly wage multiplied by the number of hours worked.

Salaried employees sometimes have a contractual agreement that entitles them to extra pay if they work beyond a negotiated number of hours for a given time period. However, hourly employees are generally paid at least 1½ (1.5) times their regular hourly wage when they work more hours than the legal work amount. For example, a cook earning $15 per hour is paid an overtime wage of $22.50 per hour ($15.00 × 1.5 = $22.50). This overtime wage is commonly referred to as "time-and-a-half."

- *Gross pay*—Payroll expenses for a foodservice operation are based on the gross pay of its employees. *Gross pay* is the total amount of an employee's pay before any deductions are made. Examples of deductions include income tax, contributions to Employment Insurance (EI), and the Canada Pension Plan (CPP). The gross pay for a salaried employee is often the same for every pay period. The gross pay for an hourly employee may vary with each pay period depending on the number of hours worked.

  To calculate the gross pay of an hourly employee, regular pay is added to any overtime pay. Regular pay is equal to the number of hours worked in a legal work week (typically 40 hours per week) multiplied by the regular hourly wage. Overtime pay is equal to any hours worked over a legal work week multiplied by the overtime hourly wage. For example, the gross pay for a line cook who earns $14 per hour and works 50 hours in a 40-hour work week would be calculated as follows:

Regular Pay = 40 hr × $14.00/hr = $560.00

Overtime Pay = 10 hr × ($14.00/hr × 1.5)

= 10 hr × $21.00/hr = $210.00

Total Gross Pay = $560.00 (Regular Pay) + $210.00 (Overtime Pay)

= **$770.00**

To calculate the total payroll expenses for a foodservice operation, the gross pay of each employee is added together. **See Figure 6-11.**

Calculating Payroll Expenses

Payroll Summary Report—Week of Jan 1-7, 20XX*

Employee	Regular Hours	Overtime Hours	Pay Rate	Regular Pay	Overtime Pay	Gross Pay
Prep Cook	30	0	$15/hr	$450.00	$0.00	$450.00
Salad Cook	40	5	$15/hr	$600.00	$112.50	$712.50
Line Cook 1	40	0	$16/hr	$640.00	$0.00	$640.00
Line Cook 2	40	6	$16/hr	$640.00	$144.00	$784.00
Server 1	40	0	$14/hr	$560.00	$0.00	$560.00
Server 2	40	10	$14/hr	$560.00	$210.00	$770.00
Chef	—	—	$900/wk	$900.00	—	$900.00
General Manager	—	—	$1,100/wk	$1,100.00	—	$1,100.00
					Total	$5,916.50

*Calculations are based on a 40-hour work week.

Figure 6-11. The total payroll expenses of a foodservice operation are equal to the sum of the gross pay for all employees.

- *Net pay*—The net pay of each employee's paycheck will be less than the employee's gross pay. *Net pay* is the actual amount on an employee's paycheck and is equal to the gross pay minus payroll deductions. Taxes are one of the required deductions. The foodservice operation must therefore withhold the amount of taxes owed by the employee and then pay those taxes directly to the government on behalf of the employee. Required deductions also include EI and contributions to the CPP. **See Figure 6-12.** Other deductions commonly include contributions to private pension plans, health insurance premiums, and union dues.

Gross Pay vs. Net Pay

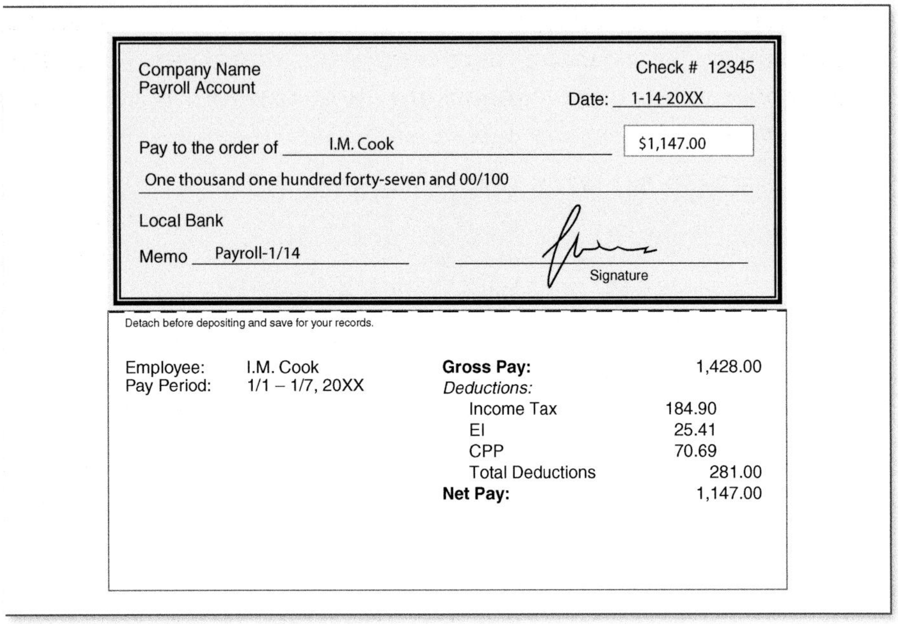

Company Name
Payroll Account

Check # 12345

Date: 1-14-20XX

Pay to the order of I.M. Cook $1,147.00

One thousand one hundred forty-seven and 00/100

Local Bank

Memo Payroll-1/14

Signature

Detach before depositing and save for your records.

Employee:	I.M. Cook	**Gross Pay:**		1,428.00
Pay Period:	1/1 – 1/7, 20XX	*Deductions:*		
		Income Tax	184.90	
		EI	25.41	
		CPP	70.69	
		Total Deductions		281.00
		Net Pay:		1,147.00

Figure 6-12. The difference between gross pay and net pay is equal to the sum of the payroll deductions.

Rent. Many foodservice operations lease space for a defined period of time and pay the owner of the building (landlord) rent. Rent is typically calculated based on a dollar amount per square meter or square foot. For example, a restaurant renting a 250 sq m space for $300/sq m would pay $75,000 in rent.

250 sq m × $300/sq m = **$75,000**

Rent is calculated on a yearly basis but is paid on a monthly basis. The monthly payment for the restaurant in this example would be $6,250.

$75,000/yr × 1 yr/ 12 months = $75,000/ 12 months = **$6,250/month**

Interest. Business owners often borrow money to get started, expand, or buy equipment. The interest paid on business loans is an expense. *Interest* is the fee charged by a bank for providing a loan to the borrower.

Utilities. Utility expenses incurred by foodservice operations can include electricity, natural gas, telephone service, and water and sewer service. Computer and media-related services such as the internet, music service, and cable or satellite television are also included.

Supplies. Supplies are all of the other items besides food and beverages that a foodservice operation purchases in the course of carrying out day-to-day operations. Supplies include items such as carryout food containers, sanitation supplies, and office supplies.

Insurance and Licenses. Foodservice operations are required to carry various types of insurance, such as liability insurance and workers compensation insurance. They are also required to pay fees for licenses to sell food. Foodservice operations that serve alcoholic beverages are required to pay additional licenses and insurance.

Miscellaneous Expenses. Minor expenses that may be applicable to a specific foodservice operation are often combined as miscellaneous operating expenses. These include expenses such as linen rentals, printing charges, and uniforms.

Variable Expenses Versus Fixed Expenses

Expenses other than capital expenses can be further categorized as variable expenses or fixed expenses. A *variable expense* is an expense that increases or decreases based on the amount of sales. A *fixed expense* is an expense that does not vary based on the amount of sales. **See Figure 6-13.**

The cost of goods sold is a perfect example of a variable expense because there is a direct relationship between the amount of food and beverages an operation sells and the amount of food and beverage ingredients that it purchases. Other variable expenses include the cost of linen rentals or certain supplies such as carryout food containers.

Rent and insurance payments are examples of fixed expenses because the same amount is paid every month regardless of the amount of sales. However, a fixed expense is not necessarily the same amount every month. For example, utilities, such as electricity and natural gas, are considered fixed expenses though the costs vary from month to month.

Variable vs. Fixed Expenses

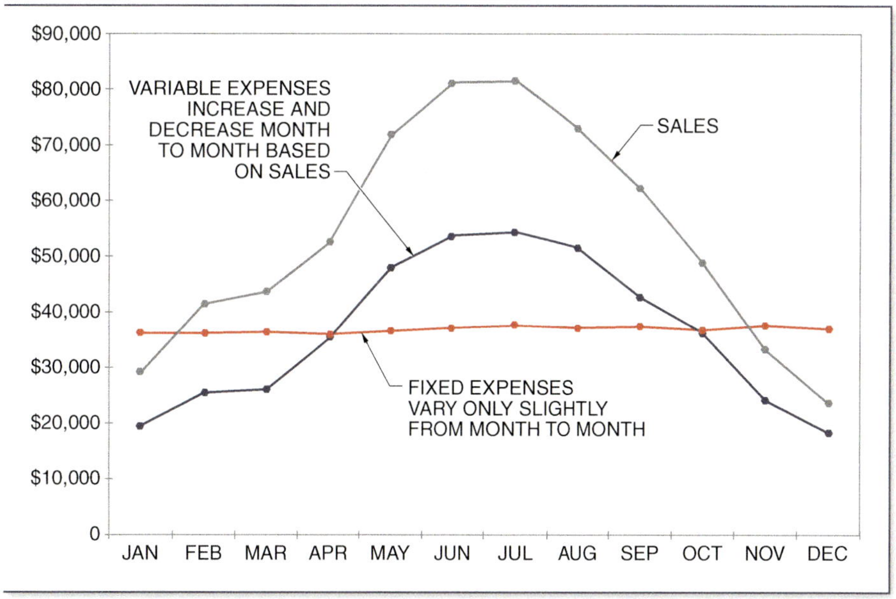

Figure 6-13. Variable expenses vary based on sales, but fixed expenses are not tied to sales.

Payroll expenses can be fixed or variable depending on how employees are paid. Generally, the payroll expenses of salaried employees are considered fixed expenses, and the payroll expenses of hourly employees are considered variable expenses. When additional food and beverages need to be prepared, which increases sales, the need for additional hourly cooks and servers increases accordingly.

Checkpoint 6-2

1. Define "capital expense."

2. Define "cost of goods sold."

3. What is the inventory value of a 25 kg case of whole chickens if the as-purchased (AP) unit cost of whole chickens is $2.30 per kilogram?

4. If a cafe has a beginning inventory value of $20,500, makes $125,000 in food and beverage purchases, and has a month-ending inventory value of $35,000, what was the cost of goods sold that month?

5. Define "operating expense."

6. Based on 40 hours per week at regular pay and time-and-a-half for overtime, what is the gross pay for the week of an hourly dishwasher who earns $15.00 per hour and works 48 hours in that week?

7. Define "net pay."

8. What is the monthly rent on a 4000 sq ft restaurant if the rent is $20/sq ft per year?

9. List three utilities that could be considered operating expenses in a foodservice operation.

10. Explain the difference between a variable expense and a fixed expense.

Math Exercises 6

Work each problem in the space provided. Write the final answer on the blank provided. Round all monetary answers to the nearest cent and other decimal answers to the tenths place.

Leaf icon indicates a math problem with a sustainability focus.

Example:

$17.55 ______________

Two customers at a sandwich shop order one beef sandwich for $7.25, one turkey sandwich for $6.75, one bag of potato chips for $0.85, and two bottled waters for $1.35 each. What is the food and beverage subtotal for this order?

$7.25 + $6.75 + $0.85 + (2 × $1.35) = ***$17.55***

______________ **1.** Two customers at a deli order one beef sandwich for $8.50, one turkey sandwich for $6.85, one bag of potato chips for $0.95, and two bottled waters for $1.30 each. What is the food and beverage subtotal for this order?

______________ **2.** One customer at an ice cream parlor orders a single scoop of vanilla ice cream. A second customer orders two scoops of chocolate ice cream, and a third customer orders three scoops of strawberry ice cream. If each scoop costs $1.45, what is the food subtotal for this order?

______________ **3.** A small popcorn is $1.60, a medium popcorn is one-and-a-half times as much as a small, and a large popcorn is twice as much as a small. Butter is an additional $0.30 for a small popcorn and an additional $0.50 for the larger sizes. A family of three orders a small popcorn with butter, a medium popcorn with no butter, and a large popcorn with butter. What is the subtotal for this order?

______________ **4.** A couple orders $95.60 in food and beverages for dinner at a Mediterranean restaurant. The restaurant offers a special promotion of 15% off any order more than $50.00. What is the discount on this order?

______________ **5.** A family goes out and orders a pizza priced at $22.50 plus $1.50 per topping. They get the pizza topped with onions, mushrooms, and pepperoni. They also have a coupon for $2.00 off any pizza. What is the total cost of the pizza, not including sales tax?

______________ **6.** A sandwich shop saves money by grinding beef trimmings for burgers. The burgers sell for $10.50, but there is a 40% discount on Mondays for burgers before toppings are added. What is the total, without sales tax, for a Monday order that includes one burger topped with mushrooms for $1.50 and one burger topped with cheese for $1.25 and bacon for $1.75?

______________ **7.** A bistro helps reduce costs and waste by offering a 10% discount to each party who brings their own to-go containers. If a customer brought to-go containers and the guest check subtotal is $59.90, what is the amount on the guest check after the discount is applied?

_______________ **8.** A group of four orders a subtotal of $115.35 of food and beverages at a restaurant. If the sales tax rate is 5%, what amount of sales tax will be charged?

_______________ **9.** A customer orders two tacos for $2.65 each and one soda for $1.15 at a quick-service restaurant. What is the total amount owed, including sales tax, for the order if the sales tax rate is 13%?

_______________ **10.** Management made changes to their restaurant, which included adding a vegetable garden and using local vendors. These changes produced higher-quality meals, allowed the restaurant to reduce menu prices by 10%, and increased sales. Before the changes and without sales tax, a typical meal cost $20.00. With the reduced menu prices and a sales tax rate of 12%, what would a typical meal now cost?

_______________ **11.** To increase efficiency and lower costs, a restaurant with an increasing number of deep-fried menu items traded in four small fryers for a larger ENERGY STAR-rated fryer priced at $14,000. What was the total cost of the new fryer if the restaurant received a 10% discount for the trade-ins and an 8.25% sales tax was applied?

________________ **12.** A couple goes out for dinner at a sit-down restaurant and orders food and beverages for $38.80. They are very happy with the service and wish to leave a 20% gratuity. How much will the gratuity be?

________________ **13.** A banquet facility charges a mandatory 18% gratuity based on the amount of food and beverages ordered for an event. If the food and beverage order totals $1,430.00, how much is the gratuity?

________________ **14.** There is a charge of $16.50 per person for a luncheon served to 60 guests. If the sales tax rate is 14% and the caterer requires an 18% gratuity, how much is the total bill for the luncheon?

________________ **15.** A party of 8 at a fondue restaurant ordered beverages totaling $84.00 and were also charged the following per person: $7.99 for cheese fondue, $4.99 per salad, $19.99 for sirloin with fondue, and $7.99 for chocolate fondue. What is the total bill if the restaurant adds a 20% gratuity and the sales tax rate is 12%?

________________ **16.** How much change should be returned to a customer who owes $75.33 and pays with a $100.00 bill? *(Tip: Guest checks are rounded with cash transactions.)*

________________ **17.** A customer owing $14.90 pays with a $20.00 bill and receives change of $5.10. How would the change be handed back to the customer in an orderly process?

________________ **18.** A customer pays $30.00 in cash for a bill of $22.75. How would the change owed to the customer be handed back in an orderly process?

________________ **19.** On a Friday night, the customers at a café ordered $658.00 in food and $210.50 in beverages. If the café gave $85.00 in discounts that night, what were the total sales?

________________ **20.** If a deli had $724.00 in food sales and $392.00 in beverage sales for the day and donated 10% of the food and beverage sales to charity, how much would be donated?

_______________ **21.** A restaurant donates 15% of its sales for the day to local growers in order to promote sustainable farming. How much does the restaurant keep if sales for the day totaled $2,462.57?

_______________ **22.** A coffee shop used an average of 1300 disposable cups per week, but this number was decreased 50% by allowing customers to use their own travel mugs. Without tax included, how much is the coffee shop now spending weekly on disposable cups if a case of 50 disposable cups costs $12.49?

_______________ **23.** Three servers work the dinner shift at a restaurant. The total of the guest checks, including sales taxes processed by each server that shift, were $356.74, $245.09, and $421.90. What was the restaurant's gross sales during that shift?

_______________ **24.** If the cash at the end of a day on a daily sales record was $980.40 and the cash at the start of the day was $165.30, what was the total cash revenue for that day?

_______________ **25.** The total cash revenue at a restaurant for the day was $1,450.23, and the card revenue was $367.08 for credit cards, $589.10 for debit cards, and $109.15 for gift cards. What was the total revenue for the day?

_______________ **26.** A restaurant started the day with $400.00 in the cash drawer. What was the total revenue for the day if there was $961.95 in the cash drawer at the end of the day and card revenue included $1,115.45 for credit cards and $749.12 for debit cards?

_______________ **27.** If an operation's total sales for the day came to $3,240.00 and the sales tax rate is 11%, what was the operation's gross sales for the day?

_______________ **28.** At the end of the day, if the total revenue of a restaurant was $2,098.50 and gross sales came to $2,075.60, would the restaurant be over or short for the day and by how much?

_______________ **29.** If a restaurant recorded a total revenue of $4,509.20 in a day and gross sales of $4,532.60, would the restaurant be over or short for the day and by how much?

______________ **30.** If a bistro's daily sales record showed gross sales of $21,699.58, total cash revenue of $5,372.40, and total card revenue of $16,377.21, would the bistro be over or short for the day and by how much?

______________ **31.** During one month, a restaurant purchased a walk-in freezer for $6,245.46. The restaurant also purchased new tables and chairs for $5,340.00, and the roof was replaced for $21,600.00. What was the total capital expense for the month?

______________ **32.** If a quick-service restaurant purchased $20,000 in food, $5,000 in supplies, a replacement deep fryer for $8,000, and an additional oven for $3,500 in the same month, what would the restaurant's total capital expenses be for that month?

______________ **33.** The attachment of a waterflow-control valve to a commercial garbage disposal decreases the amount of water used per month from 600 L to 130 L. What is the total capital expense for a corporate franchise that installs a total of 238 waterflow-control valves to the garbage disposals at their franchised restaurants if each waterflow-control valve costs $188.00?

_______________ **34.** To reduce energy costs, a cafeteria purchases an ENERGY STAR-certified griddle for $7,245.70 and an ENERGY STAR-certified convection oven for $7,930.00. The griddle has a $650.00 rebate, and the oven has a $1,000.00 rebate. What is the total capital expense for the appliances with the rebates included?

_______________ **35.** A restaurant installs awnings for $28,000 that will reduce heating and cooling expenses enough over 5 years to pay for their cost. What is the average yearly energy savings for this capital expense over 5 years?

_______________ **36.** A restaurant that is open 313 days per year eliminated paper receipts, reduced costs, and conserved natural resources by using a POS system to email receipts to their customers. If each paper receipt costs $0.015 to print and the restaurant was printing an average of 450 receipts per day, how much is saved yearly in paper costs by using the POS system?

_______________ **37.** What is the inventory value of an 18 kg case of beef tenderloin if the as-purchased (AP) unit cost of beef tenderloin is $31.90/kg?

_______________ **38.** What is the inventory value of 20 L of olive oil if the as-purchased (AP) unit cost of olive oil is $11.99/L?

_______________ **39.** What is the inventory value of the following items with their as-purchased (AP) unit costs: 5 kg of sole fillets at $9.50/kg, 5 kg of ground (minced) beef at $7.99/kg, 4 kg of pork chops at $8.49/kg, 8 kg of pork loin at $8.79/kg, and 3 kg of chicken thighs at $3.29/kg?

_______________ **40.** What is the total inventory value of the condiments used by the hot dog food truck? *(Use the chart below.)*

Inventory Sheet—Hot Dog Food Truck

Condiments	Number of Units	As-Purchased (AP) Unit Cost	Inventory Value
Ketchup Packets	380	$0.02 ea	
Mustard Packets	218	$0.02 ea	
Relish	8 bottles	$2.34/bottle	
Pickles	3 kg	$10.65/kg	
		Total	

_______________ **41.** What is the total inventory value at the end of the day for a concession stand with the following items and their as-purchased (AP) unit costs: 6 hot dogs at $0.18 each, 6 hot dog buns at $0.08 each, 8 hamburger patties at $0.21 each, 9 hamburger buns at $0.08 each, and 12 slices of cheese at $0.07 per slice?

_______________ **42.** A restaurant had 12 kg of tomatoes in inventory that were purchased at \$2.60/kg. Before all the tomatoes were used, 750 g spoiled. Based on this loss, what is the recalculated inventory value per kilogram of the usable tomatoes?

_______________ **43.** A tapas restaurant has a beginning inventory value of \$12,050 on June 1. The restaurant makes purchases of \$54,200 in food and beverages during June and has an ending inventory of \$14,025 on June 30. What was the cost of goods sold in June?

_______________ **44.** An ice cream truck has a beginning inventory of \$2,567 on July 1, makes purchases of \$6,909 during July, and has an ending inventory of \$1,945 on July 31. What was the cost of goods sold in July?

_______________ **45.** A bakery has a beginning inventory value of \$2,040 on April 1, makes purchases of \$14,500 in food and beverages during April, and has an ending inventory of \$1,960 on April 30. What was the cost of goods sold in April?

_______________ **46.** If a salaried employee earns $800.00 per week, what is the employee's gross pay for a two-week period?

_______________ **47.** If an hourly employee works 35 hours in a week and is paid $16.15 per hour, what is the employee's gross pay for the week?

_______________ **48.** What is the gross pay of a line cook who works 44 hours in a week and earns $15.30 per hour plus time-and-a-half if more than 40 hours are worked per week?

_______________ **49.** If an hourly employee works 48 hours in one week and has a regular pay rate of $18.00 per hour, what is the employee's gross pay for the week based on a 40-hour week at regular pay and time-and-a-half for overtime?

_______________ **50.** If an employee earns a gross pay of $980.50 but has payroll deductions that total $145.90, what is the employee's net pay?

Analyzing Profit and Loss

7

The quality of the food and service offered by a foodservice operation is a major factor in an operation's success. However, taking steps to ensure that an operation generates sufficient revenue while keeping expenses to a minimum is just as important. Applying the required math skills is necessary in order to analyze these business aspects of a foodservice operation. Furthermore, banquets and catered events require additional planning to ensure that all costs are identified and factored into a pricing strategy.

Section 7-1: MAKING A PROFIT

- Differentiate between profit and loss.
- Calculate percent increase of revenue and percent decrease of revenue.
- Explain how a foodservice operation can minimize expenses when planning a menu and purchasing food.
- Explain how a foodservice operation can minimize expenses when storing, preparing, and serving food.

Section 7-2: STANDARD PROFIT AND LOSS

- Calculate gross profit and net profit.
- Interpret a standard profit-and-loss statement.
- Estimate the break-even point for a foodservice operation.

Section 7-3: SPECIAL EVENT PROFIT AND LOSS

- List topics that are discussed with a customer when estimating the cost of a special event.
- Use cost percentage and contribution margin pricing methods to price special events.

Key Terms

- profit
- loss
- loss leader
- menu
- purchase specification
- par stock
- perishable food
- first in, first out (FIFO)
- portion control
- gross profit
- net profit
- standard profit-and-loss statement
- pie chart
- estimate
- break-even point

Learner Resources
atplearningresources.com
access code 267628

Daniel NYC/N. Clutton

Section 7-1 MAKING A PROFIT

Determining whether a foodservice operation is profitable is as simple as comparing revenue to expenses. A *profit* is the amount of money earned by an operation when revenue is greater than (>) expenses. The opposite of a profit is a loss. A *loss* is the amount of money lost by an operation when revenue is less than (<) expenses. These definitions translate into a fundamental math formula that applies to any business:

$$P(L) = TR - TE$$

where **Profit (Loss) = Total Revenue − Total Expenses**

$P(L)$ = profit (loss)

TR = total revenue

TE = total expenses

Although making a profit is more likely when an operation offers quality food and service, these characteristics do not guarantee financial success. An equal amount of attention must also be paid to the business aspects of running a foodservice operation. To be profitable, management and workers need to make consistent efforts to maximize revenue, minimize expenses, and maintain quality standards. **See Figure 7-1.**

Profit and Loss

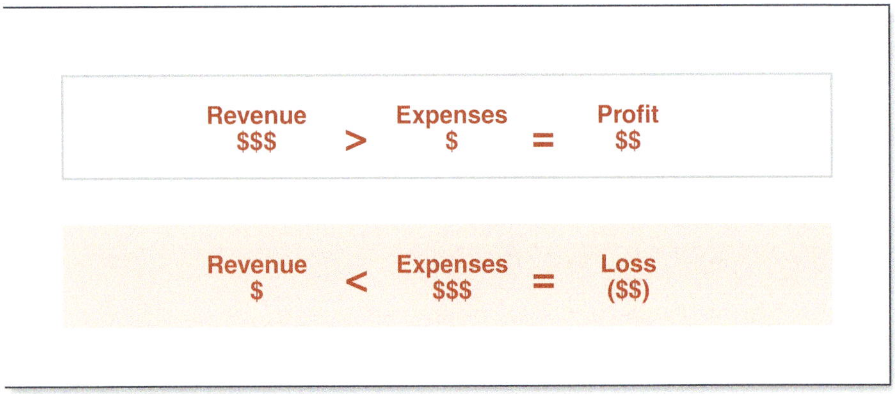

Figure 7-1. A foodservice operation earns a profit if revenue is greater than expenses but experiences a loss if revenue is less than expenses.

Maximizing Revenue

Foodservice operations strive to maximize revenue by increasing sales and profits while reducing food and labor costs. Offering quality food and service usually results in positive word-of-mouth advertising, which generates more customers and more revenue for the operation. Revenue can also be maximized by implementing creative marketing strategies and training servers to be effective salespeople.

Some foodservice operations raise prices to try to increase revenue. Raising prices is sometimes necessary to keep up with increasing expenses, but it can also result in a loss of customers.

In contrast, sometimes the price of a particular menu item is intentionally set low. The price can be set so low that the foodservice operation does not make any profit or experiences a small loss on each sale. A menu item priced in this manner is referred to as a loss leader. A *loss leader* is a menu item priced artificially low in order to attract more customers.

For example, a restaurant may advertise \$0.25 buffalo wings from 4:00 to 6:00 pm. If the buffalo wings cost \$0.30 each to prepare, the restaurant will lose \$0.05 on each wing sold. However, if the low price attracts a substantial number of customers, the profit made by selling other food and beverage items can make up for the loss on the buffalo wings.

Revenue Goals. Foodservice operations often set goals to increase revenue by a certain percent from year to year. To calculate a new revenue amount based on a percent increase, the following formula is used:

$$NR = OR \times (100\% + \%I)$$

$$\text{New Revenue} = \text{Original Revenue} \times \left(100\% + \text{Percent Increase}\right)$$

where

NR = new revenue

OR = original revenue

$\%I$ = percent increase

For example, a foodservice operation with a revenue of \$100,000 in the first year and a percent increase of 8% would have a revenue of \$108,000 in the second year.

$$NR = OR \times (100\% + \%I)$$

$$NR = \$100{,}000 \times (100\% + 8\%)$$

$$NR = \$100{,}000 \times (1.00 + 0.08)$$

$$NR = \$100{,}000 \times 1.08$$

$$NR = \mathbf{\$108{,}000}$$

If the operation's revenue increased 8% again from the second year to the third year, there would be a third-year revenue of \$116,640.

$$NR = OR \times (100\% + \%I)$$

$$NR = \$108{,}000 \times (100\% + 8\%)$$

$$NR = \$108{,}000 \times (1.00 + 0.08)$$

$$NR = \$108{,}000 \times 1.08$$

$$NR = \mathbf{\$116{,}640}$$

If the same foodservice operation is successful in increasing revenue by 8% every year for 10 years, its total revenue over 10 years would be almost $1,500,000. In contrast, if the revenue remained constant for 10 years, total revenue would only be $1,000,000. **See Figure 7-2.** Clearly, a small percent increase in revenue from year-to-year results in a significant increase over time.

Maximizing Revenue

Year of Operation	Constant Revenue	8% Revenue Increase* NR=OR × (100% + %I)
1	$100,000.00	$100,000.00
2	$100,000.00	$108,000.00
3	$100,000.00	$116,640.00
4	$100,000.00	$125,971.20
5	$100,000.00	$136,048.90
6	$100,000.00	$146,932.81
7	$100,000.00	$158,687.43
8	$100,000.00	$171,382.43
9	$100,000.00	$185,093.02
10	$100,000.00	$199,900.46
10-Year Total Revenue	$1,000,000.00	$1,448,656.25

*results rounded to the hundredths place

Figure 7-2. Foodservice operations often set goals to increase revenue by a certain percent each year.

Calculating Increases. When actual revenue amounts are known for two periods of time, the percent increase from one period to the next can be calculated. Percent increase can be calculated using the following formula:

$$\%I = (NR - OR) \div OR$$

where

$\%I$ = percent increase

NR = new revenue

OR = original revenue

$$\text{Percent Increase} = \frac{\left(\text{New Revenue} - \text{Original Revenue}\right)}{\text{Original Revenue}}$$

For example, if a foodservice operation has a first-year revenue of $450,000 and a second-year revenue of $500,000, then the percent increase from the first year to the second year would be 11.1%.

$$\%I = (NR - OR) \div OR$$

$\%I = (\$500{,}000 - \$450{,}000) \div \$450{,}000$

$\%I = \$50{,}000 \div \$450{,}000$

$\%I = 0.111$

$\%I =$ **11.1%**

Calculating Decreases. If the new revenue is less than the original revenue, the result will be a negative number. This indicates a percent decrease and is calculated with the same formula used to determine percent increase. For example, if a foodservice operation has revenue of $50,000 in June and $48,000 in July, applying the percent increase formula would result in –4.0%. This means that revenue actually decreased by 4.0% from June to July.

$$\%I = (NR - OR) \div OR$$

$$\%I = (\$48{,}000 - \$50{,}000) \div \$50{,}000$$

$$\%I = -\$2{,}000 \div \$50{,}000$$

$$\%I = -0.04$$

$$\%I = \mathbf{-4.0\% \text{ or } (4.0\%) \text{ or } <4.0\%>}$$

It is not uncommon for revenues to fluctuate from month to month. For example, many restaurants are busier during certain times of the year due to changes in seasons. However, annual revenues should increase each year if a business is to continue to be successful.

Minimizing Expenses

Maximizing revenue will contribute to higher profits, but it is equally important to minimize expenses. Calculating expenses is a straightforward process for any foodservice operation. However, controlling and minimizing expenses can be challenging. For example, power outages, equipment failures, and kitchen mishaps such as spills can increase food cost expenses by causing food to go bad or become unusable. Although these types of expenses may be difficult to control, there are many expenses that can be controlled and therefore minimized. The key to controlling and minimizing expenses is to realize that everything has value. **See Figure 7-3.**

Everything Has Value

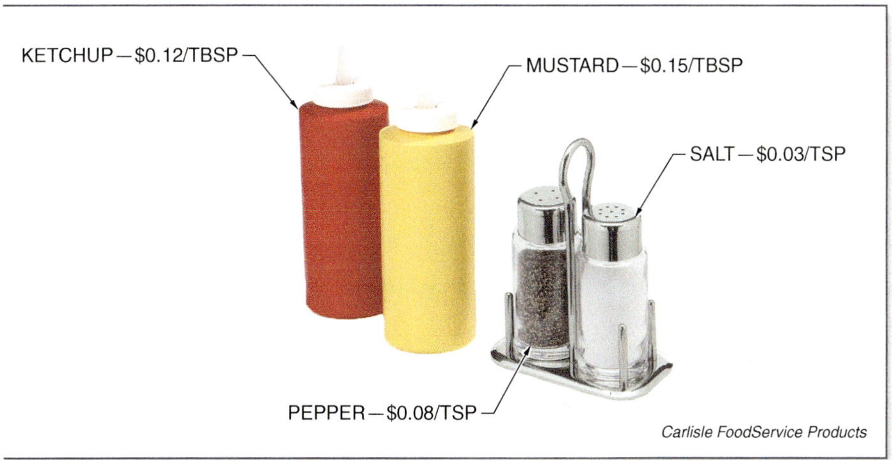

Figure 7-3. Even the most minor food products have value and are an expense to an operation.

Expenses that may seem insignificant at first can add up to substantial amounts over time. For example, when calculating the as-served (AS) cost of a cup of soup, the cost of the ingredients is considered in order to determine an appropriate price to charge customers. However, if a restaurant serves a pack of crackers with every cup of soup, the cost of the crackers must also be considered. The foodservice operation that ignores this additional cost is essentially giving the crackers away.

If a restaurant gave away a $0.05 pack of crackers to 2000 customers per week, the cost would add up to $100 per week or $5,200 per year. Losing thousands of dollars simply by overlooking the cost of a $0.05 pack of crackers can put some restaurants out of business. However, this cost can be accounted for by increasing the price of the soup $0.15 to actually make a $0.10 profit on each pack of crackers. Therefore, the owner could earn an additional profit of $10,400 per year instead of a loss of $5,200 per year. **See Figure 7-4.**

Turning a Loss into a Profit

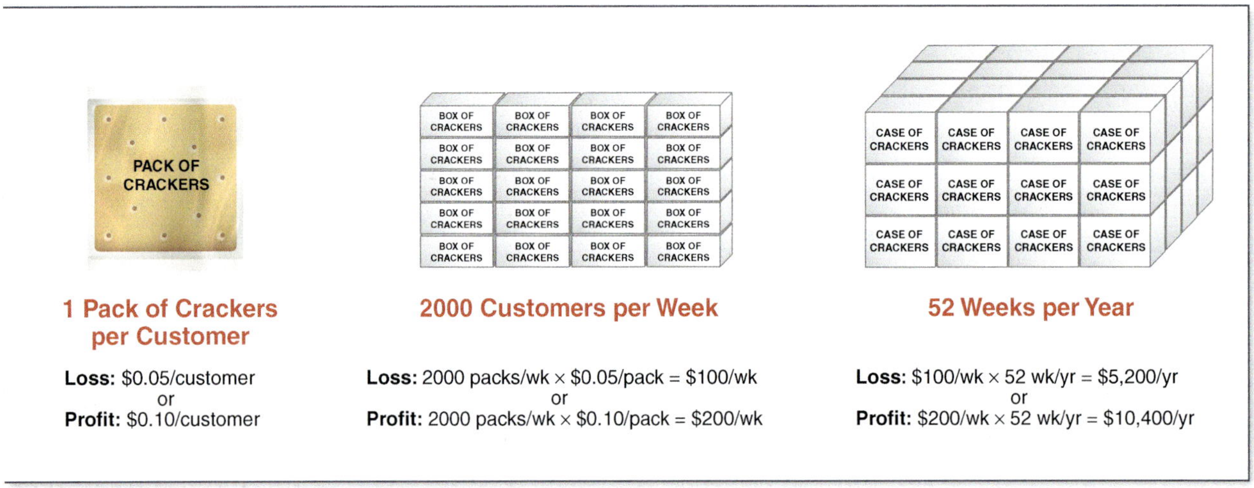

Figure 7-4. A small profit on a per-person basis can add up to a large profit over time.

Opportunities to make money or lose money are present in all aspects of a foodservice operation. The focus on earning a profit starts with the planning of the menu and continues with the purchasing, receiving, storing, preparing, and serving of the food.

Planning a Menu. A *menu* is a document that markets a foodservice operation to customers. It lists products that satisfy customers, that are profitable, and that can compete with the alternatives offered elsewhere. In addition to calculating the appropriate prices to charge for menu items, other considerations are involved when planning a profitable menu.

- *Kitchen equipment*—The kitchen must be properly equipped to efficiently prepare menu items. For example, a kitchen that is not equipped with a deep fryer should not have a large number of deep-fried items on the menu. When the appropriate equipment is not available, the operation is less efficient. This inefficiency results in higher payroll expenses.

- *Employee skill level*—The techniques used to prepare the items on a menu should be in line with the abilities of the kitchen staff. If employees lack the required skills, food products are likely to be wasted due to errors in preparation. This will cause food expenses to increase. For example, elaborate pastries should not be prepared in-house if a skilled pastry chef is not part of the kitchen staff.
- *Seasonal ingredients*—Some menu items should only be offered during certain times of the year when key ingredients are readily available at a reasonable price. For example, sweet corn is widely available at low prices during the summer. In winter, the price of corn is much higher, and the quality can be lower compared to summer corn.
- *Customer demand*—All items on a menu should be popular enough with customers that the ingredients required to prepare them are not wasted. For example, a chef may want to offer a dish featuring wild game. But if customers tend to shy away from wild game, the special ingredients would go to waste.

Purchasing Food. Purchasing involves the selection and ordering of products required to prepare and serve the items on the menu. A tool used to help ensure that the right products are purchased at the best available price is a purchase specification. A *purchase specification* is a written form listing the specific characteristics of a product that is to be purchased from a supplier. **See Figure 7-5.**

Purchase Specification—Vegetables

Item Name	Baking potatoes
Variety	Russet
Grade	CA#1
Count per Case	80
Net Weight per Case	22.7 kg
Packaging	Heavy-duty cardboard box

Photo Courtesy of the Idaho Potato Commission

Figure 7-5. A purchase specification clearly informs suppliers of a product's requirements.

Depending on the product, the information on the purchase specification may include the product's quality or grade, variety or place of origin, size, and packaging requirements. It is also common for the purchase specification to include food safety requirements, such as the temperature at which products must be transported and received.

Purchase specifications are prepared and submitted to suppliers to obtain prices. Since they provide the exact parameters that the foodservice operation requires, the operation can be assured that different suppliers are providing prices for the same products.

For example, if a chef called two different produce suppliers and asked for a price quote on apples, the suppliers might provide prices for two very different types of apples, neither of which may be exactly what the chef wants. However, if each vendor is provided with a purchase specification for Canada Extra Fancy (highest quality) red delicious apples averaging 170 grams each and packaged in 20-kilogram cardboard boxes, the chef can be assured that the prices received from each supplier are for the same product.

While a purchase specification is used to help ensure that the appropriate type and quality of product is ordered, a par stock checklist is used to help make sure that the appropriate quantity is ordered. *Par stock* is the amount of a particular product that is to be kept in inventory to ensure that an adequate supply is on hand between deliveries. Par stock values should be set high enough to ensure that the operation does not run out of a product. However, the values should be low enough to avoid disposing of products because they were left in storage too long.

Receiving Food. Another opportunity to help control costs is when food is received from suppliers. All products should be checked upon arrival to ensure that the product received matches the purchase specification. Products should be weighed or counted to make sure that the amount or quantity received is the same as that on the invoice. **See Figure 7-6.**

Receiving Food

Detecto, A Division of Cardinal Scale Manufacturing Co.

Figure 7-6. Food products should be checked for quality upon receipt. It is also important to verify that the correct amounts were received and correct prices charged.

Special attention should be paid to perishable foods to make sure they are in good condition and at the proper temperature when received. *Perishable food* is food that has a short shelf life and is subject to spoilage and decay. Perishable foods include dairy products, produce, and fresh meats and fish. These items should be purchased frequently and in the smallest quantities possible.

Nonperishable items have a longer shelf life and generally can be kept for six months to a year. These items are ideally stored between 10°C and 15°C (50°F and 59°F) in their original packaging. Nonperishable items include canned goods, tea bags, and jars of olives. Since these products have a long shelf life, they can be purchased in bulk.

Storing Food. Storing foods properly is essential for controlling costs. Immediately after items have been received and checked-in, they should be placed into inventory following the first-in, first out inventory process.

First-in, first-out (FIFO) is the process of dating new items as they are placed into inventory while rotating older items to the front of inventory and new items behind. FIFO helps ensure that the oldest items are used first. **See Figure 7-7.**

Preparing Food. Many foods are trimmed or broken down before being served or used in a recipe. Sometimes the parts trimmed from products, such as meats and vegetables, can be used in other recipes, such as stocks or soups, instead of being disposed of as waste. Likewise, high-quality leftovers can potentially be used to prepare other dishes. For example, leftover roasted chicken can be diced for resale as chicken salad.

Serving Food. In addition to following a standardized recipe, one of the most important ways foodservice workers can help minimize expenses is to serve food using the proper portion-control techniques. *Portion control* is the process of ensuring that a specific amount of food or beverage is served for a given price. This is accomplished by using portion-control equipment such as ladles, portion-controlled scoops, scales, and slicers. When the quantity of food served is more than the amount the menu price was based upon, food expenses increase, and profit is reduced. **See Figure 7-8.**

First-In, First-Out (FIFO) Inventory Process

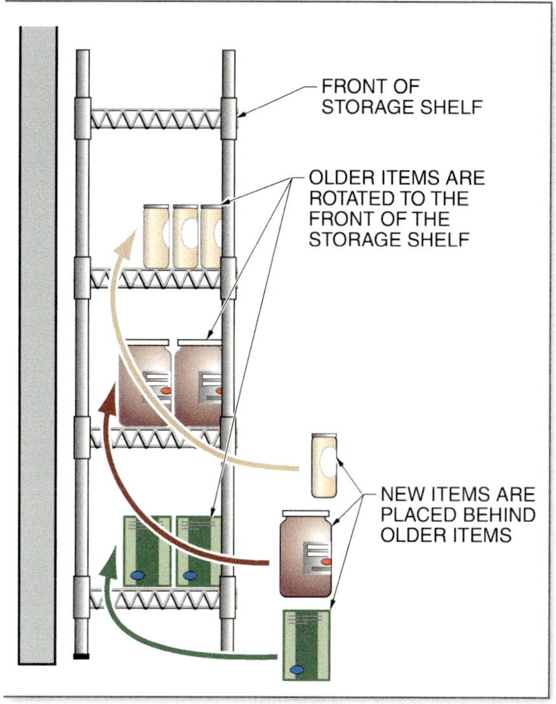

Figure 7-7. The FIFO inventory process ensures that older products are used before newer products.

Portion-Control Equipment

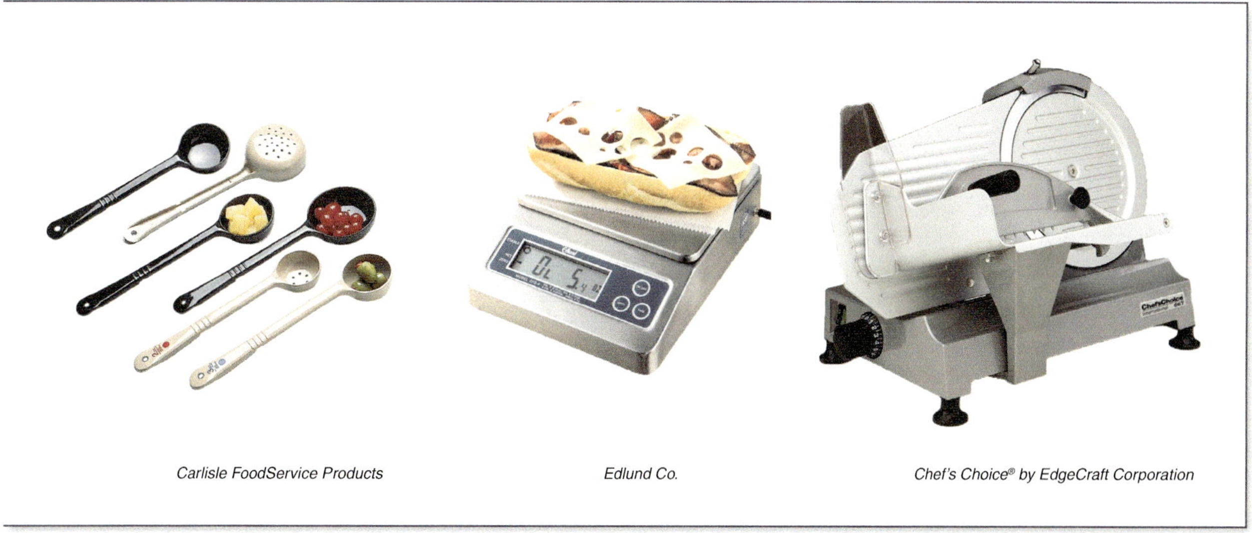

Figure 7-8. Portion-control equipment is used to ensure that a consistent amount of food is served to each customer.

Checkpoint 7-1

1. Explain the difference between a profit and a loss.

2. If a foodservice operation has a first-year revenue of $250,000 that increases by 9% from the first year to the second year, what is the amount of revenue in the second year?

3. If a restaurant had revenue of $30,000 in September and $33,000 in October, what was the percent increase in revenue from September to October?

4. If a catering company had revenue of $22,000 in January and $21,000 in February, what was the percent decrease in revenue from January to February?

5. List four considerations that should be accounted for when planning a menu.

6. What is a purchase specification?

7. Why should food products be weighed or counted when they are received?

8. Explain the FIFO inventory process.

9. Define "portion control."

Section 7-2 STANDARD PROFIT AND LOSS

Although every foodservice operation is somewhat unique, the methods for calculating and estimating profits and losses are fairly standard. Foodservice operations, from sandwich shops to fine-dining restaurants, have revenues based on the sales of food and beverages. They also have expenses that can be categorized as either fixed or variable based on the amount of those sales.

Gross Profit Versus Net Profit

There are two categories of profit associated with any foodservice operation: gross profit and net profit. *Gross profit* is the calculated difference between a foodservice operation's total revenue and the cost of goods sold. *Net profit* is the calculated difference between a foodservice operation's gross profit and its operating expenses.

Calculating Gross Profit. Gross profit can be thought of as the amount of money that is made by a foodservice operation as a result of charging more money for the food items served than the amount spent producing those items. The formula for calculating gross profit is as follows:

$$GP = TR - GS$$

Gross Profit = Total Revenue − Cost of Goods Sold

where

GP = gross profit

TR = total revenue

GS = cost of goods sold

For example, if a restaurant had a total revenue of $31,000 in a month and the cost of goods sold was $10,500, then the gross profit would be $20,500.

$$GP = TR - GS$$

$$GP = \$31{,}000 - \$10{,}500$$

$$GP = \mathbf{\$20{,}500}$$

Calculating Net Profit. Net profit can be thought of as the amount of money left over after the gross profit is used to pay for all the operating expenses incurred by the operation. The formula for calculating net profit is as follows:

$$NP = GP - OE$$

Net Profit = Gross Profit − Operating Expenses

where

NP = net profit

GP = gross profit

OE = operating expenses

If the restaurant with a gross profit of \$20,500 had \$18,250 in operating expenses, then there would be a net profit of \$2,250.

NP = GP – OE

NP = \$20,500 – \$18,250

NP = **\$2,250**

However, if the same restaurant had \$21,500 in operating expenses, the restaurant would have a net profit of –\$1,000, which is a loss of \$1,000.

NP = GP – OE

NP = \$20,500 – \$21,500

NP = **–\$1,000 or (\$1,000) or <\$1,000>**

A loss is not uncommon at certain times. It is especially common in the first several months of a new operation when employees are new and management works to get things operating smoothly.

Standard Profit-and-Loss Statements

The relationship between gross profit and net profit is clearly shown on a standard profit-and-loss statement. A *standard profit-and-loss statement* is a form that shows the revenue, expenses, and resulting gross profit and net profit (or loss) over a specific period of time. The purpose of a standard profit-and-loss statement is to provide management with an indication of the financial status of the foodservice operation.

A standard profit-and-loss statement can be prepared at a summary level or a detailed level depending on the complexity required and the needs of the foodservice operation. **See Figure 7-9.** The net profit is the last entry on the statement and is referred to as "the bottom line."

Standard profit-and-loss statements often show expenses and net profit in terms of a percent of revenue as well as actual dollar amounts. Any expense can be expressed as a percent of revenue by dividing the amount of the expense by the total revenue. For example, if the utility expenses for a restaurant totaled \$1,125 in a month and total revenue was \$34,900, utility expenses for the month would be 3.2% of revenue.

\$1,125 ÷ \$34,900 = 0.032 = **3.2%**

Likewise, if the restaurant's net profit for the month was \$3,707, then the net profit as a percent of revenue would be 10.6%.

\$3,707 ÷ \$34,900 = 0.106 = **10.6%**

Standard Profit and Loss Statement Summary

Total Revenue	**$ 34,908.59**
Cost of Goods Sold	**$ 10,432.90**
Gross Profit	**$ 24,475.69**
Operating Expenses	**$ 20,768.25**
Net Profit	**$ 3707.44**

Standard Profit and Loss Statement Detailed

	Dollar Amount	*Percent of Revenue*
Total Revenue	**$ 34,908.59**	
Total Food Sales	$ 27,801.23	
Total Beverage Sales	$ 7107.36	
Cost of Goods Sold	**$ 10,432.90**	29.9%
Total Food Costs	$ 7794.38	
Total Beverage Costs	$ 2638.52	
Gross Profit	**$ 24,475.69**	
Operating Expenses	**$ 20,768.25**	
Payroll Expenses	$ 13,010.15	37.3%
Utilities	$ 1124.67	3.2%
Rent	$ 2800.00	8.0%
Interest	$ 325.19	1.0%
Insurance	$ 1050.75	3.0%
Licenses	$ 356.80	1.0%
Kitchen Supplies	$ 803.21	2.3%
Advertising	$ 1047.26	3.0%
Miscellaneous	$ 250.22	0.7%
Net Profit	**$ 3707.44**	**10.6%**

Figure 7-9. A standard profit-and-loss statement can be prepared at a summary level or a detailed level.

One way of illustrating expenses and net profit as percentages of revenue is through a pie chart. A *pie chart* is a circle that is divided into pieces where each piece represents a percentage of the whole circle (or pie). The sizes of the pieces are proportional to the percent of the whole pie that each piece represents. For example, if payroll expenses are 37.3% of revenue and rent is 8.0% of revenue, the piece of pie associated with payroll expenses will be over four times larger than the piece representing rent. **See Figure 7-10.**

Expenses and Net Profit in Pie Chart Form

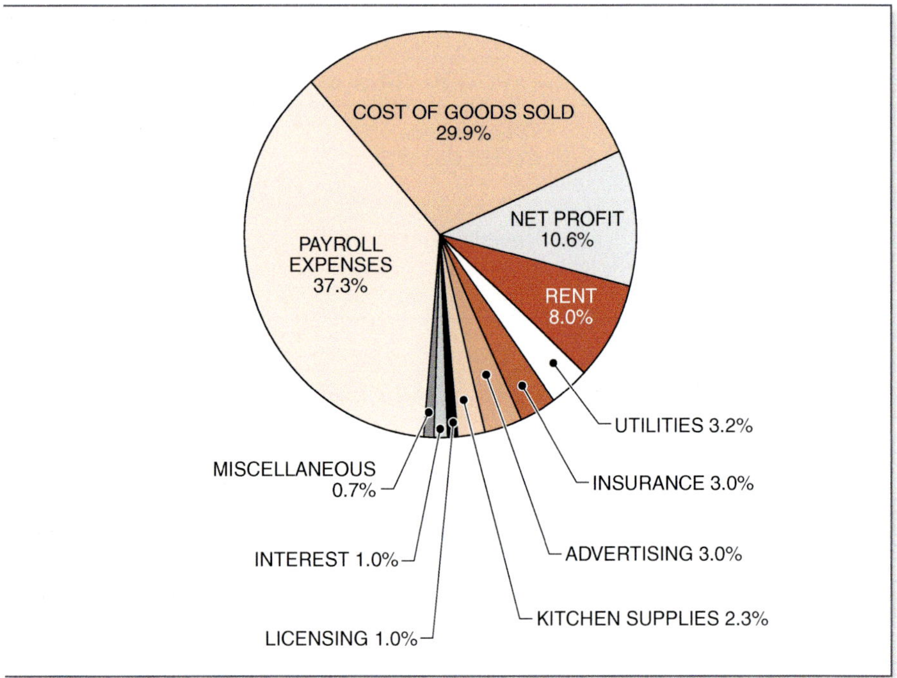

Figure 7-10. Operating expenses and net profit can also be expressed as a percent of revenue and illustrated in a pie chart.

Reviewing financial information as percentages instead of dollar values can often be more meaningful. When the percentage associated with a particular expense item changes significantly from one month to another, management should take a close look at that expense to determine the reason for the change. Sometimes those changes can be good. For example, if the cost of garbage services as a percent of revenue decreases, it could indicate that employees are recycling better.

However, changes could also indicate a problem. For example, if the cost of kitchen supplies as a percent of revenue increases significantly, it could indicate that supplies are being wasted. Likewise, the way in which the net profit percentage varies is an indication of how well the operation is doing overall.

Estimating Profit and Loss

Creating a standard profit-and-loss statement is straightforward for a foodservice operation that is up and running. However, it is common to estimate the profit and loss of a foodservice operation before it is operational to help determine whether it will be profitable.

An *estimate* is a calculation made using approximate numbers based on research, experience, and best judgment. Since actual numbers for revenue and expenses are not available, certain assumptions need to be made when preparing an estimate.

A good starting point when creating a profit-and-loss estimate is to perform a break-even analysis to calculate the break-even point of an operation. A *break-even point* is the minimum amount of revenue a foodservice operation must earn before it can make a profit. The formula for calculating the break-even point for a foodservice operation is as follows:

$$BE = FE \div (100\% - VE\%)$$

$$\text{Break-Even Point} = \frac{\text{Fixed Expenses}}{(100\% - \text{Variable Expense Percentage})}$$

where

BE = break-even point

FE = fixed expenses

$VE\%$ = variable expense percentage

For example, a chef considering opening a restaurant conducts some research and estimates that the fixed expenses for rent, utilities, and management-staff payroll will be a total of $24,000 per month. Based on restaurants offering similar food and service, the chef estimates that variable expenses will be about 45% of sales. The break-even point for the new restaurant would be estimated as follows:

$$BE = FE \div (100\% - VE\%)$$

$BE = \$24{,}000/\text{month} \div (100\% - 45\%)$

$BE = \$24{,}000/\text{month} \div (1.00 - 0.45)$

$BE = \$24{,}000/\text{month} \div 0.55$

$BE = \mathbf{\$43{,}636/month}$

This means that if the restaurant's revenue is more than $43,636 per month, the restaurant will make a profit. However, if the restaurant's revenue is less than $43,636 per month, it will experience a loss. **See Figure 7-11.**

Break-Even Point Analysis*

Total Revenue	$30,000	$40,000	$43,636	$50,000	$60,000
Fixed Expenses	$24,000	$24,000	$24,000	$24,000	$24,000
Variable Expenses (45% of Revenue)	$13,500	$18,000	$19,636	$22,500	$27,000
Profit (Loss)	($7500)	($2000)	$0	$3500	$9000
	Loss ←		Break Even Point	→	Profit

* based on fixed expenses of $24,000/month and variable expense percent of 45%

Figure 7-11. A break-even point analysis is a technique used to help analyze the profitability of a new foodservice operation.

New Restaurant Estimate. The break-even analysis can help determine the likelihood of a restaurant being profitable. For example, the chef opening the new restaurant has estimated that the restaurant is large enough to serve 100 customers per day (approximately 3000 customers per month). The chef can divide the break-even point by the estimated number of customers to calculate how much each person would be required to spend to generate the required revenue.

$$\$43{,}636/\cancel{\text{month}} \div 3000\ \text{customers}/\cancel{\text{month}} = \mathbf{\$14.54/customer}$$

The chef can then decide if $14.54 is a reasonable amount to expect each customer to spend per visit by comparing that amount to the menu prices. For example, the average price for a main course on the menu is between $14.00 and $15.00, and the chef expects that most customers will order a beverage as well as an appetizer or dessert. Therefore, it would be reasonable to assume that the average customer would spend more than the $14.54 required to make a profit.

In contrast, if the concept for the restaurant was different and it was estimated that a customer would only spend an average of $9.00, the chef would likely decide that a profit could not be made. The chef could then consider other options, such as altering the menu or looking for another location with lower fixed expenses.

Second Location Estimate. Calculating a break-even point is a good place to start when evaluating the profitability of a completely new restaurant. However, estimates for expanding an existing operation are performed differently. For example, the owner of a breakfast restaurant is considering opening a second location. The new location will offer the same menu but will be a little larger than the existing location. Since the owner is already established, some of the information from the existing restaurant can be used to evaluate whether the second location will be profitable.

If the menu is going to be the same, the amount each customer spends should be similar. The most significant changes to consider would likely be changes in fixed costs and the number of customers. *Note:* A larger location will typically have higher rent, but it will also have room for more seats.

To estimate the profitability of the second location, the owner needs to first estimate the revenue and the expenses. Estimating the revenue is straightforward. The owner expects the average customer to spend $9.80 (the same as the existing location) and has estimated that the new location will serve 4000 customers per month. Therefore, the estimated revenue would be $39,200 per month.

$$4000\ \cancel{\text{customers}}/\text{month} \times \$9.80/\cancel{\text{customer}} = \mathbf{\$39{,}200/month}$$

The total monthly expenses would be equal to the monthly fixed expenses plus the monthly variable expenses. This owner has already calculated the monthly fixed expenses to be \$19,000. The monthly variable expenses are estimated by multiplying the estimated monthly total revenue by the variable expense percentage. The variable expense percentage at the existing restaurant is 40% and is expected to be the same at the new location. The total monthly expenses are estimated using the following formula:

$$TE = FE + (TR \times VE\%)$$

$$\text{Total Expenses} = \text{Fixed Expenses} + \left(\text{Total Revenue} \times \text{Variable Expense Percentage}\right)$$

where

TE = total expenses

FE = fixed expenses

TR = total revenue

VE% = variable expense percentage

Therefore, the total expenses for the second location are estimated as follows:

$$TE = FE + (TR \times VE\%)$$

$$TE = \$19{,}000/\text{month} + (\$39{,}200/\text{month} \times 40\%)$$

$$TE = \$19{,}000/\text{month} + (\$39{,}200/\text{month} \times 0.40)$$

$$TE = \$19{,}000/\text{month} + \$15{,}680/\text{month}$$

$$TE = \mathbf{\$34{,}680/month}$$

Finally, the monthly profit can be estimated based on the estimated total revenue of \$39,200 per month and total expenses of \$34,680 per month.

$$P(L) = TR - TE$$

$$\text{Profit (Loss)} = \text{Total Revenue} - \text{Total Expenses}$$

$$P(L) = \$39{,}200/\text{month} - \$34{,}680/\text{month}$$

$$P(L) = \mathbf{\$4{,}520/month}$$

Based on this estimate, the owner of the breakfast restaurant can decide whether earning an additional \$4,520 profit per month justifies opening a second location. Since estimates are based on assumptions, there is no guarantee that actual results will match the estimate.

Many new restaurants fail within the first year of operation. However, a new venture is more likely to be successful when estimates are prepared using sound assumptions based on research.

7-2 Checkpoint

1. Describe the difference between gross profit and net profit.

2. What is the gross profit of a deli with total revenue of $28,500 and cost of goods sold of $9,450?

3. What is the net profit of a bakery with a gross profit of $11,090 and operating expenses of $8,075?

4. What is a standard profit-and-loss statement?

5. If a foodservice operation has payroll expenses of $9,700 in a month when the total revenue was $32,000, how much were payroll expenses as a percent of revenue?

6. In the following pie chart, which expense is the largest part of total expenses?

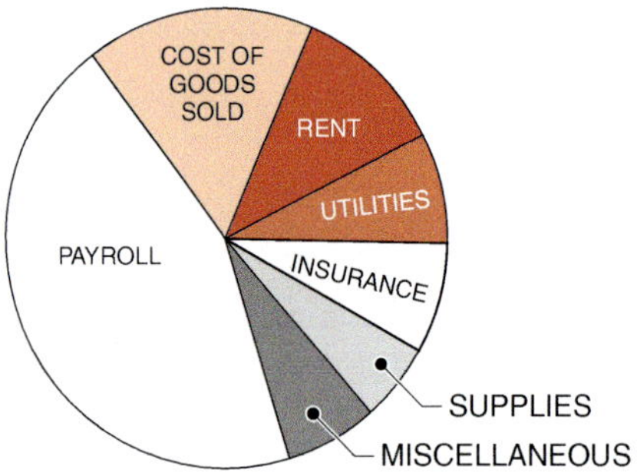

7. What is an estimate?

8. What is the break-even point of a foodservice operation with fixed expenses of $15,000 per month and a variable expense percentage of 38%? *(Round the answer to whole dollars.)*

9. What is the estimated total expense of a foodservice operation with fixed expenses of $22,000 per month, a total revenue of $52,000, and a variable expense percentage of 42%?

Section 7-3 SPECIAL EVENT PROFIT AND LOSS

Standard calculations for profit and loss are similar for most ongoing foodservice operations. However, additional items must be considered when planning and setting prices for special events, such as banquets and catered events, to ensure the operations are profitable.

Planning Special Events

In addition to freestanding banquet facilities, many restaurants also have rooms designated for small banquets. Both types of operations accommodate groups of people planning to gather for a special event. Banquet facilities may have multiple rooms that can each accommodate several hundred to more than 1000 people. Restaurant banquet rooms typically accommodate smaller groups ranging from 20 to 50 people.

Another term used for "banquet" is "on-site catering" because food is prepared at the same location where it is served. In contrast, off-site catering occurs when food is prepared in a professional kitchen and then transported to a separate location before being served. **See Figure 7-12.**

On-Site vs. Off-Site Catering

On-Site Catering

Food prepared and served at banquet hall or restaurant

Off-Site Catering

Food prepared in professional kitchen and transported to another location

Figure 7-12. Off-site catering differs from banquets (on-site catering) because the food is prepared in one location and transported to another.

The menu and services vary for both banquets and catered events depending on the specific needs of the customer. Therefore, a banquet or catering manager is usually responsible for determining the specific price for each event. To calculate a price that will ensure a profit, the manager will need to discuss the following subjects with the customer.

Number of People. The number of people attending the event must be known to determine how much food to order and prepare; how much space will be required; and the number of staff needed to prepare and serve the food. Most special event prices are determined on a per-person basis.

Type of Seating. The manager needs to know if all guests will be seated at the event and, if so, the number of people seated at each table. Seating arrangements need to be considered to determine how much room will be needed for the event. For example, a wedding for 100 guests with 10 guests seated at each table will require less space than if guests are seated 6 to a table. Some events, such as cocktail parties, will not have seating for each guest and would require even less space per person.

Menu. The food items that will be served need to be determined in order to calculate the cost of food to be purchased. It is also important to know if guests will be served the same menu items or if they will be given a choice. If the guests are given a choice, the manager needs to know prior to the event. When decisions are made ahead of time, the exact amount of each item to be prepared is known, which helps keep food expenses to a minimum.

Style of Food Service. The style of service must be known to determine how much staff will be needed to serve at the event. For example, more servers will be needed if guests are served plated courses while seated at tables than if guests serve themselves from a buffet. Food costs can be higher for a buffet because portions cannot be easily controlled when guests serve themselves, and food is often wasted.

Style of Beverage Service. The manager needs to know if beverages will be brought to guests seated at tables or served from a bar. If a bar is used, the manager needs to know if the beverages are to be included in the per-person price of the event (an open bar) or if the guests will be paying for their own beverages (a cash bar).

Rentals. If the banquet facility or caterer does not have all the equipment needed to execute the event, virtually anything can be rented from a rental company. Commonly rented items include tents, tables, chairs, flatware, glassware, linens, chafing dishes, and serving platters. **See Figure 7-13.**

Entertainment. Many events include entertainment such as bands, musicians, or disc jockeys. Entertainment providers are frequently hired directly by the customer, but the banquet hall or caterer may also make the arrangements. In such cases, the cost of entertainment is built into the total price of the event.

Special Event Rental Items

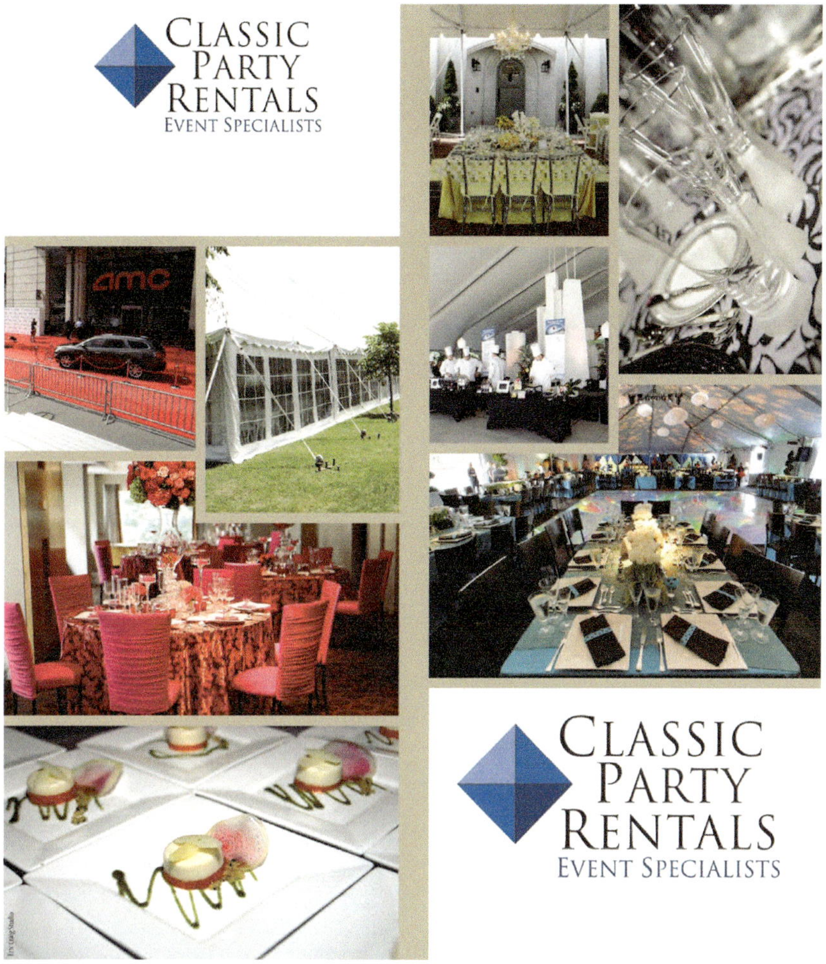

Classic Party Rentals

Figure 7-13. Many foodservice items used for special events are available for rent.

Transportation. For off-site catered events, the method of transporting the food to the service location needs to be determined. Many caterers have their own delivery vehicles. In other circumstances, vehicles may need to be rented, delivery services may need to be hired, or customers may pick up the food and transport it themselves. Insulated containers are used to keep food at safe holding temperatures during transport. **See Figure 7-14.**

Deposits and Method of Payment. Since many events are planned well in advance, it is common to require the customer to pay a deposit. A *deposit* is an amount of money paid by a customer as a down payment or pledge for a special event to be held at a later date.

Insulated Containers

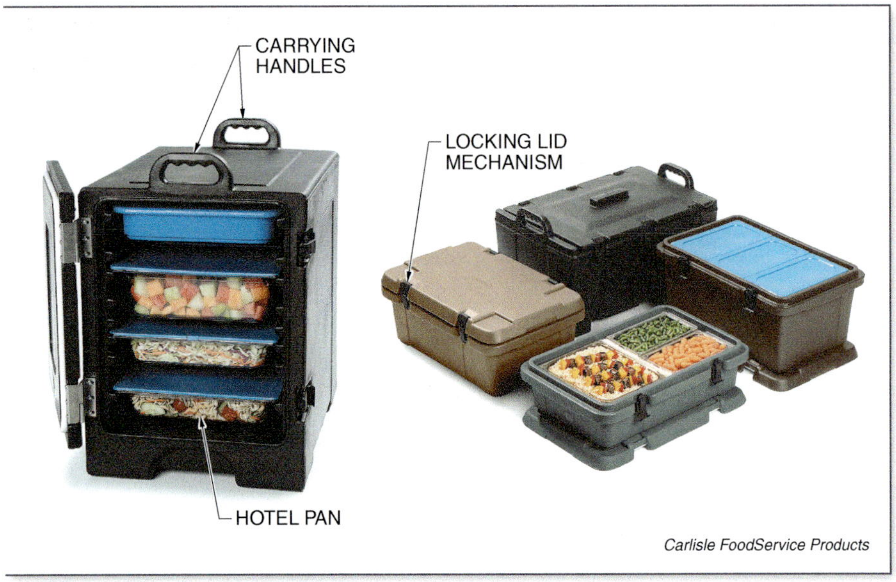

Figure 7-14. Caterers use insulated containers to keep food at proper temperatures during transport.

The deposit is usually based on a percentage of the estimated cost of the event. The manager and customer must have a clear understanding of whether the deposit can be refunded if the event is cancelled and how the remaining balance will be paid. These details are usually documented in a contract that is signed by both the manager and the customer.

Calculating Special Event Profit and Loss

Once the details of an event have been planned, the manager can determine an appropriate price to charge for the event to ensure a profit. This process is similar to determining the prices charged on a restaurant menu. Prices can be based on a target cost percentage or a contribution margin as discussed in "Chapter 5: Calculating Costs and Menu Prices."

Target cost percentage pricing is most appropriate for small special events that are limited to the serving of food and beverages in a traditional atmosphere (e.g., dinner for a group of people in the party room of a restaurant). For large special events, especially when temporary staff needs to be hired or outside equipment is rented, contribution margin pricing is more appropriate.

Banquet Profit and Loss. For example, a restaurant has a banquet room that can accommodate a group of up to 50 people. A customer wants to hold a birthday party that includes dinner for 50 people with a cash bar. The customer selects a menu and does not have any requests that require items to be rented or outside staff to be hired.

The as-served (AS) cost of the menu selected is \$8.90 per person, and the restaurant has a target cost percentage of 28%. The target price for the food and beverages would be calculated using the following formula:

TP = AS ÷ T%

$$\text{Target Price} = \frac{\text{As-Served Cost}}{\text{Target Cost Percentage}}$$

TP = \$8.90/person ÷ 28%

TP = \$8.90/person ÷ 0.28

TP = **\$31.79/person**

The restaurant manager would likely adjust this price to \$31.95 per person. The restaurant also has a policy that parties of more than 8 people are charged a 20% gratuity. Furthermore, the sales tax rate is 15% for that location. The total revenue generated could then be calculated using the following problem-solving steps:

Problem-Solving Steps

1. Calculate the food and beverage charges based on 50 people at \$31.95/person.
   \$31.95/person × 50 people = **\$1,597.50**
2. Calculate the gratuity.
   \$1,597.50 × 20% = \$1,597.50 × 0.20 = **\$319.50**
3. Calculate the food and beverage subtotal.
   \$1,597.50 + \$319.50 = **\$1,917.00**
4. Calculate the sales tax.
   \$1,917.00 × 15% = \$1,917.00 × 0.15 = **\$287.55**
5. Calculate the total due (revenue) for the party by adding the food and beverage subtotal and sales tax.
   \$1,917.00 + \$287.55 = **\$2,204.55**

To estimate the gross profit from the party, the cost of goods sold must be calculated. The cost of goods sold is equal to the as-served (AS) cost of the food and beverages since inventory is not maintained for a one-time event. Therefore, the cost of goods sold in this example is equal to the as-served (AS) cost of food per person multiplied by the number of people.

\$8.90/person × 50 people = **\$445.00**

Then, the gross profit can be calculated as follows:

GP = TR − GS

Gross Profit = Total Revenue − Cost of Goods Sold

GP = \$2,204.55 − \$445.00

GP = **\$1,759.55**

It is difficult to determine a net profit from a single event like a party because operating costs, such as utilities, apply to the operation as a whole and not to a specific event. However, if the net profit for the restaurant in this example is typically 9% of total revenue based on profit-and-loss statements, the party would generate an estimated net profit of $198.41

$$\$2{,}204.55 \times 9\% = \$2{,}204.55 \times 0.09 = \mathbf{\$198.41}$$

Catered Event Profit and Loss. If a caterer is asked to provide a price for a dinner party for 50 people under a tent at a location, such as a home, the caterer is likely to price the event using the contribution margin method. If the same menu that was used at the restaurant birthday party is prepared, it can be assumed that the as-served (AS) cost of the food will be about the same.

However, the caterer will have other costs to add that did not apply to the restaurant event. **See Figure 7-15.** For example, the tent, tables, chairs, linens, flatware, and glassware will need to be rented, and temporary staff may need to be hired.

Catering Estimate

Estimate

Event Type: Dinner Party
Date: June 1
Customer Name: J. Smith

Location: Customer's Home
Menu: Salad, baked chicken, roasted vegetables, coconut cake

Item	Cost per Unit	Number of Units	Total Cost
Food	$8.90/person	50 people	$445.00
Rental Items			
Tent	$200.00	1	$200.00
Tables	$8.50 each	10	$85.00
Chairs	$1.00 each	50	$50.00
Flatware (3 pieces per person)	$0.25 each	150	$37.50
Glassware (2 pieces per person)	$0.30 each	100	$30.00
Plates (2 pieces per person)	$0.50 each	100	$50.00
Linens—Tablecloths	$2.30 each	5	$11.50
Linens—Napkins	$0.20 each	50	$10.00
Payroll Expenses—Employees			
Sous Chef to oversee event	$18.00/hr	4 hrs	$72.00
Cooks to prepare food	$15.00/hr	8 hrs	$120.00
Servers (3 @ 4 hours each)	$15.00/hr	12 hrs	$180.00
		Total Cost	**$1,291.00**

Figure 7-15. A catering estimate is used to help calculate all of the costs associated with a special event.

If the caterer determines that the total cost to cater the dinner party for 50 people will be $1,291.00 and their policy is to charge a contribution margin based on $10.00 per person, the target price for the party would be $35.82 per person.

Target Price (TP) = ($1,291.00 ÷ 50 people) + $10.00/person

Target Price (TP) = $25.82/person + 10.00/person

Target Price (TP) = **$35.82/person**

If the caterer adjusts this price to $35.95 per person, adds a 20% gratuity, and includes a sales tax rate of 15%, the total revenue generated would be calculated using the following problem-solving steps:

Problem-Solving Steps

1. Calculate the food and beverage charges based on 50 people at $35.95/person.
   $35.95/person × 50 people = **$1,797.50**
2. Calculate the gratuity.
   $1,797.50 × 20% = $1,797.50 × 0.20 = **$359.50**
3. Calculate the food and beverage subtotal.
   $1,797.50 + $359.50 = **$2,157.00**
4. Calculate the sales tax.
   $2,157.00 × 15% = $2,157.00 × 0.15 = **$323.55**
5. Calculate the total due (revenue) for the party by adding the food and beverage subtotal and sales tax.
   $2,157.00 + $323.55 = **$2,480.55**

As in the banquet example, the cost of goods sold is simply equal to the cost of the food ingredients ($445.00). The gross profit generated by this party is calculated using the following formula:

GP = TR − GS

Gross Profit = Total Revenue − Cost of Goods Sold

GP = $2,480.55 − $445.00

GP = **$2,035.55**

It is very difficult to calculate a net profit for this particular event as well as for a banquet. However, if the net profit is typically 12% of total revenue according to the caterer's profit-and-loss statements, the event would generate an estimated net profit of $297.67.

$2,480.55 × 12% = $2,480.55 × 0.12 = **$297.67**

The key to ensuring that a profit is earned from any special event starts with thorough planning. All costs associated with the event must be considered before providing the customer with a final price that will result in a profit.

Checkpoint 7-3

1. When determining the price for a special event, why is it necessary to know the number of people attending?

___

___

2. List four things a caterer may need to rent for a special event.

___

___

3. When is it more appropriate to use contribution margin pricing for an event rather than target cost percentage pricing?

___

___

4. If the as-served (AS) cost of a menu for a banquet is $7.50 per person, what is the target price for the event if the target cost percentage is 30%?

___

___

5. If the price of a special event is $25.00 per person and 80 people attend, what is the total revenue generated if a 15% gratuity and an 11% sales tax are added to the price?

___

___

6. What is the gross profit of a banquet with a total revenue of $4,050 and a cost of goods sold of $1,025?

___

___

7. If the as-served (AS) cost of a menu for a party is $12.00 and the caterer adds a contribution margin of $9.00 per person, what is the total price if 40 people attend the party?

___

___

8. What is the gross profit of a catered event for 200 people if the revenue is $12,500 and the as-served (AS) cost of the menu is $20 per person?

___

___

9. What is the estimated net profit if the total revenue of an event is $5,000 and the average net profit as a percent of total revenue is 8%?

___

___

Math Exercises 7

Work each problem in the space provided. Write the final answer on the blank provided. Round all monetary answers to the nearest cent and other decimal answers to the tenths place.

Leaf icon indicates a math problem with a sustainability focus.

Example:

$172,800 ________________ What is the second-year revenue of a foodservice operation if its first-year revenue was $160,000 and revenue increased by 8% from the first year to the second year?

$160,000 × (100% + 8%) =

$160,000 × (1.00 + 0.08) =

$160,000 × 1.08 = ***$172,800***

________________ **1.** What is the second-year revenue of a foodservice operation if its first-year revenue was $280,000 and revenue increased by 10% from the first year to the second year?

________________ **2.** A restaurant has a first-year revenue of $240,000. The revenue increased by 6% from the first year to the second year and then increased by 6% again from the second year to the third year. What is the restaurant's third-year revenue?

________________ **3.** A cafeteria has a first-year revenue of $350,000. Revenue increased by 4% from the first year to the second year and then increased by 8% from the second year to the third year. What is the total revenue of the cafeteria over all three years?

______________ **4.** The average Saturday revenue for a steakhouse is 319% of the average weekday revenue. If the average weekday revenue for the steakhouse is $1,987, what is the average Saturday revenue for the steakhouse?

______________ **5.** A deli had revenue of $12,000 in May and $15,000 in June. What was the percent increase in revenue from May to June?

______________ **6.** A coffee shop had revenue of $8,400 in August and $8,988 in September. What was the percent increase in revenue from August to September?

______________ **7.** A restaurant increased its sustainable menu items by adding more plant-based items. Before the changes, the average monthly revenue was $5,800. But with the new menu changes, the average monthly revenue is now $6,032. What is the percent increase in average monthly revenue?

______________ **8.** A juice bar had revenue of $8,000 in October and $6,500 in November. What was the percent decrease in revenue from October to November?

______________ **9.** A food truck had revenue of $22,000 in July and $19,500 in August. What was the percent decrease in revenue from July to August?

______________ **10.** A pastry shop had revenue of $12,165 in December, but the revenue for January dropped to $11,460. What was the percent decrease in revenue from December to January?

______________ **11.** Twelve small restaurants in a town formed a purchasing cohort to get better pricing based on volume purchasing. One of the restaurants found that purchasing expenses had averaged $11,250 prior to forming the cohort and are now averaging $10,237. What is the percent decrease in purchasing expenses for this restaurant? *(Tip: Replace revenue [R] with expense [E] in the formula for calculating percent decrease.)*

______________ **12.** A coffee shop uses eco-friendly, biodegradable paper straws that cost $0.025 each. To reduce the expense of the paper straws and cut down on waste, a new policy was enacted requiring employees to ask customers if they needed a straw. If the coffee shop went from using 1,000 straws per week to 785 straws per week as a result of the new policy, how much less is spent on straws per year?

_______________ **13.** A restaurant gives one fortune cookie to 1,500 customers per week at a cost of $0.04 per cookie. What is the total cost to the restaurant in one year for the fortune cookies?

_______________ **14.** A school district has 16 cafeterias that are open 240 days per year. Each cafeteria uses 9 gallons of clean, leftover water from their steam tables to mop the floor on the days they are open. If the village charges $12.50 per 1000 gallons of water, how much money is the school district saving each year by reusing the water from steam tables?

_______________ **15.** A survey revealed that leftover food on customer plates was going into the trash due to the restaurant's large portion sizes. As a result, portion sizes were decreased by 10%, which led to a 6% annual reduction in food cost expenses and waste. What is the annual reduction in food cost expenses if annual food cost expenses were $725,000 prior to decreasing portion sizes?

_______________ **16.** At a banquet for 300 people, a line cook serves 170 g of sautéed spinach instead of 115 g to each customer. What is the cost of the extra spinach that was served if the as-served (AS) cost of the spinach is $0.01/g?

_______________ **17.** A restaurant installed motion detectors in all walk-in units, dining rooms, storage rooms, and restrooms in order to turn lights off and to regulate temperature when a person is not detected. If monthly electric costs had been $1,875 but have decreased by 37% since the installation of the motion detectors, what are the new monthly electric costs?

_______________ **18.** By shutting down deep-fat fryers during slow periods, a restaurant reduces monthly utility costs by $40 per fryer. If a restaurant applies this energy-saving technique to 7 fryers over the course of 12 years, how much will they save in utility expenses?

_______________ **19.** What is the gross profit of a foodservice operation that has total revenue of $3,600 when the cost of goods sold was $750?

_______________ **20.** What is the gross profit of a foodservice operation that has a total food revenue of $3,000 and a total beverage revenue of $1,000 when its cost of goods sold was $800?

_______________ **21.** What is the gross profit for a party of 120 guests if each guest pays $22.75 and the cost of goods sold was $958.00?

_______________ **22.** What is the gross profit if the total revenue for a banquet of 180 guests is $6,243.00 and the cost of goods sold is $17.50 per person?

_______________ **23.** What is the net profit of a sandwich shop that has a gross profit of $4,200 when its operating expenses were $3,300?

_______________ **24.** What is the net profit of a restaurant with a total revenue of $57,000, a cost of goods sold of $15,000, and operating expenses of $36,000?

_______________ **25.** An event generated a gross profit of $34,980. What was the net profit for the event if expenses included $11,200 in labor costs, $2,300 in food costs, and $1,670 in miscellaneous costs?

_______________ **26.** A restaurant with a utility expense of $1,500 a month has a total revenue of $24,000. What is the utility expense expressed as a percentage of revenue?

_______________ **27.** A cafeteria has a net profit of $12,000 a month and a total revenue of $140,000. What is the net profit of the cafeteria expressed as a percentage of revenue?

_______________ **28.** A food truck has total quarterly revenue of $45,960. The quarterly payroll expenses are $13,278, and the quarterly cost of goods sold is $12,000. What is the combined cost of payroll expenses and cost of goods sold expressed as a percentage of revenue for the quarter?

_______________ **29.** A restaurant had total annual expenses of $42,167.59. Of those expenses, utilities were $2,165.00. If the restaurant purchased low-flow aerators for their sinks, they would save $495.00 each year in utility costs. If the total annual expenses remained the same, what would be the new cost of utilities expressed as a percentage of total expenses?

_______________ **30.** A pie chart used for a standard profit-and-loss statement shows the cost of goods sold was 32.3% of the total revenue. What was the total revenue if the cost of goods sold was $15,126.09?

_______________ **31.** What is the break-even point of a restaurant with fixed expenses of $18,000 and a variable expense percentage of 32%?

_______________ **32.** What is the break-even point of a banquet hall with fixed expenses of $40,000 and a variable expense percentage of 38%?

_______________ **33.** A cafeteria replaced a traditional commercial ice maker with an ENERGY STAR-rated model, causing fixed expenses to go from $27,000 to $24,000. What is the maximum amount the variable expense percentage can be with the ENERGY STAR-rated ice maker if the break-even point is $75,000? *(Tip: The formula BE = FE ÷ [100% – VE%] can be rewritten as VE% = 100% – [FE ÷ BE].)*

_______________ **34.** The break-even point for a new restaurant is estimated to be $52,000 per month, and the owner estimates that each customer will spend $18 per visit. How many customers must visit the restaurant per month in order for the restaurant to break even?

_______________ **35.** The break-even point for a brasserie is $29,700 per month, and the manager estimates that each customer will spend $13.50 per visit. How many customers must visit per month for the brasserie to break even?

_______________ **36.** If an average of 3,600 customers visits a restaurant each month, what does each customer need to spend for the restaurant to have a monthly break-even point of $62,000?

_______________ **37.** A restaurant where customers order seafood 11% of the time revises its menu to include only sustainable seafood options in an effort to increase revenue and profits. If there are 4,500 total orders over the course of a month and the goal is to double the percentage of seafood orders, how many orders need to be seafood?

__________ **38.** What are the total estimated expenses of a foodservice operation with fixed expenses of $24,000, a total revenue of $100,000, and a variable expense percentage of 42%?

__________ **39.** What are the total estimated expenses of a bar and grill with fixed expenses of $28,000, a total revenue of $65,000, and a variable expense percentage of 38%?

__________ **40.** Using the target cost percentage pricing method, what is the target price per person for a banquet with an as-served (AS) cost of food and beverages of $12 per person and a target cost percentage of 30%?

__________ **41.** What is the total amount of revenue generated from a banquet for 30 people with a price of $22.95 per person, a 15% mandatory gratuity, and 12% sales tax?

__________ **42.** What is the gross profit of a banquet with a total revenue of $4,300 and a total cost of food and beverages of $950?

_______________ **43.** What is the estimated net profit of a banquet with a total revenue of $5,200 and an average net profit percentage of 9%?

_______________ **44.** What is the estimated net profit of an event for 60 people with a total revenue of $35.95 per person and an average net profit percentage of 10%?

_______________ **45.** What is the net profit per person for an event attended by 361 people if the total revenue is $25,930.63 and the only expense accounted for is the as-served (AS) menu cost of $15.73 per person?

_______________ **46.** The total cost to cater a party for 80 people is calculated to be $1,300.00, and the caterer adds a contribution margin of $12.50 per person. What is the target price per person for the party?

_______________ **47.** The cost to cater a wedding for 100 people includes $1,200.00 for food, $800.00 for beverages, $900.00 for rental items, and $800.00 for labor. What is the target price per person for the party if a contribution margin of $14.25 per person is added to the catering cost?

______________ **48.** A reception held in a hotel ballroom for 150 guests costs $45.00 per person for food and $17.50 per person for beverages. If the hotel adds a contribution margin of $1,800.00, what is the target price per person?

______________ **49.** The price charged for a catered party of 50 people is $25.95 per person, and the caterer charges a 20% gratuity and 5% sales tax. What is the gross profit from the party if the cost of goods sold was $450.00?

______________ **50.** What is the estimated net profit of a catered event if the total revenue from the event is $14,000 and the caterer's average net profit is 11% of revenue?

Checkpoint Answers

1 Measuring in the Professional Kitchen

Checkpoint 1-1

1. Cooks use standard units of measure to promote consistency in foods.

2. The metric system uses grams to measure weight, liters to measure volume, hours and minutes to measure time, degrees Celsius to measure temperature, and meters to measure distance.

3. The customary and imperial systems use pounds and ounces to measure weight; gallons, quarts, pints, cups, gills (imperial only), fluid ounces, tablespoons, and teaspoons to measure volume; hours and minutes to measure time; degrees Fahrenheit to measure temperature; and feet and inches to measure distance.

Checkpoint 1-2

1. A recipe may call for 2 large eggs (count), 250 g of flour (weight), or 100 mL of milk (volume). A guest might be served a meal consisting of a half dozen (6) oysters (count), an 8 oz steak (weight), and 250 mL of soup (volume).

2. A scale must be tared prior to adding ingredients to consider the weight of the container when measuring its contents.

3. The proper procedure for measuring dry ingredients in a dry measuring cup is to spoon the ingredient into the cup, initially overfilling it, and then leveling to remove the excess.

4. A #32 portion-controlled scoop holds 1 fl oz/scoop (32 fl oz ÷ 32 scoops = 1 fl oz/scoop).

5. Weight measurements are considered to be more accurate than volume measurements because a volume measurement can be affected by the technique used to fill the measuring tool.

6. Eight ingredients that have densities close to water include alcohol, juices, vinegar, oil, milk, butter, eggs, and granulated sugar.

7. Three types of kitchen timers include hanging timers, countertop timers, and digital timers.

8. Temperature is measured in the professional kitchen with a thermometer using either metric units of degrees Celsius (°C) or customary/imperial units of degrees Fahrenheit (°F).

9. A steam table that holds two full hotel pans can also hold twelve ⅙ pans.

Checkpoint 1-3

1. A measurement equivalent is an amount in one unit of measure that is equal to another unit of measure.

2. The equivalent of 6000 g in kilograms is 6 kg (1000 g = 1 kg; 6000 ÷ 1000 = 6 kg).

3. The equivalent of 8 L in milliliters is 8000 mL (1000 mL = 1L; 8 × 1000 = 8000 mL).

4. The customary/imperial weight measurement equivalent that every cook should know is 16 oz = 1 lb.

5. There are 32 fl oz in a customary quart compared to 40 fl oz in an imperial quart.

6. Every cook should memorize the following customary volume measurement equivalents: 4 qt = 1 gal.; 2 pt = 1 qt; 2 c = 1 pt; 8 fl oz = 1 c; 2 tbsp = 1 fl oz; and 3 tsp = 1 tbsp.

7. To change from a larger to a smaller unit of measure, multiply the number in the original measurement by the number of smaller units that make up the larger unit. To change from a smaller to a larger unit, divide the number in the original measurement by the number of smaller units that make up the larger unit.

8. The number of inches equal to 1 ft is 12 in.

2 Calculating Measurements

Checkpoint 2-1

1. 3000 g (1 kg = 1000 g; 2 × 1000 = 2000 g; and 2000 g + 250 g + 750 g = 3000 g)
2. 435 mL (1 L = 1000 mL; 1000 mL – 565 mL = 435 mL)
3. 14 c (4 pt = 8 c; 8 c + 6 c = 14 c)
4. 1 qt (2 pt = 1 qt; 2 qt – 1 qt = 1 qt)
5. 24 L (4 L × 6 = 24 L)

Checkpoint 2-2

1. A fraction is a part of a whole.
2. The numerator is above the fraction bar, and the denominator is below the fraction bar.
3. A mixed number is a combination of a whole number and a fraction.
4. $8\frac{1}{3}$ (25 ÷ 3 = 8 remainder 1)
5. $\frac{21}{8}$ (the numerator = [2 × 8] + 5 = 16 + 5 = 21, and the denominator stays the same)
6. $\frac{3}{4}$ (both the numerator and denominator have a factor of 3)
7. 25 c ($12\frac{1}{2} = \frac{25}{2}$, $\frac{25}{2} \times \frac{2}{1} = \frac{50}{2}$, and 50 ÷ 2 = 25)
8. 29 portions ($9\frac{2}{3} = \frac{29}{3}$, and $\frac{29}{3} \div \frac{1}{3} = \frac{29}{3} \times \frac{3}{1} = 29$)

Checkpoint 2-3

1. A decimal is a number that represents part of a whole and can be expressed as a fraction with a denominator that is a power of 10.
2. $\frac{3}{8}$ ($\frac{375}{1000} \div \frac{125}{125} = \frac{3}{8}$)
3. 0.67 (2 ÷ 3 = 0.6666)
4. Rounding is the process of replacing a number with another number of similar value.
5. A decimal rounded to the hundredths place.
6. Twelve and fifty-six hundredths.
7. 6.2
8. 34.658
9. 10.5 kg (3.9 kg + 3.4 kg + 3.2 kg = 10.5 kg)
10. 0.6 kg (6.2 kg – 5.6 kg = 0.6 kg)
11. 45.36 c (12.96 c per can × 3.5 cans = 45.36 c)
12. 25 portions (62.5 ÷ 2.5 = 25)

Checkpoint 2-4

1. Area is the size of a two-dimensional (flat) surface.
2. Stovetop B (90 cm × 66 cm = 5940 sq cm and 98 cm × 62 cm = 6076 cu cm)
3. The radius of a circle is equal to one-half of the circle's diameter.
4. 153.86 in^2 [r = 14 ÷ 2 = 7, and A = 3.14 × (7 in.)^2 = 3.14 × 49 in^2 = 153.86 in^2]
5. Capacity is the volume that can be placed inside an empty three-dimensional object.
6. 50 cu m (5 m × 4 m × 2.5 m = 50 cu m)
7. 8 L (3.14 × [12 cm]^2 × 18 cm = 8138.88 cm^3 and 8138.88 ÷ 1000 = 8.1 L = 8 L)
8. 4 equal pieces (360 ÷ 90 = 4)

Checkpoint 2-5

1. An average is the sum of a set of numbers divided by how many numbers there are in the set.
2. A median is the middle value within a set of numbers that are arranged in numerical order.
3. Mode is the value that appears most frequently within a set of numbers.
4. 17 (188 ÷ 11 = 17.09 = 17 rounded to the nearest whole number)
5. 17 (half the numbers [12, 14, 16, 16, and 16] are less than 17 and half the numbers [18, 18, 19, 20, and 22] are greater than 17)
6. 16 (16 is the most common number, which appears three times in the set of numbers)

3 Converting Measurements and Scaling Recipes

Checkpoint 3-1

1. Cancelling is the process of crossing out and eliminating matching units in the numerators and denominators of fractions in a calculation.

2. 4250 g

$$\left(\frac{4.25\,\cancel{\text{kg}}}{1}\times\frac{1000\text{ g}}{1\,\cancel{\text{kg}}}=\frac{4.25\times 1000\text{ g}}{1\times 1}=\frac{4250\text{ g}}{1}=4250\text{ g}\right)$$

3. 1.5 qt

$$\left(\frac{6\,\cancel{\text{c}}}{1}\times\frac{1\text{qt}}{4\,\cancel{\text{c}}}=\frac{6\times 1\text{qt}}{1\times 4}=\frac{6\text{ qt}}{4}=6\text{ qt}\div 4=1.5\text{ qt}\right)$$

4. 2.4 L

$$\left(\frac{10\,\cancel{\text{c}}}{1}\times\frac{1\,\cancel{\text{qt}}}{4\,\cancel{\text{c}}}\times\frac{0.95\text{ L}}{1\,\cancel{\text{qt}}}=\frac{10\times 1\times 0.95\text{ L}}{1\times 4\times 1}=\frac{9.5\text{ L}}{4}=9.5\text{ L}\div 4=2.4\text{ L}\right)$$

5. 220°C

$$°C=\frac{(425-32)}{1.8}=\frac{393}{1.8}=218.3°C=220°C$$

6. The volume-to-weight equivalent for chopped pecans will be higher than the equivalent for whole pecans because the chopped pecans will fill a volume measurement tool more compactly.

7. Estimating calculations before using a kitchen calculator helps identify errors that may be made by inputting an incorrect number or unit of measure or by using an incorrect key on the calculator keypad.

Checkpoint 3-2

1. Most standardized recipes include the following elements: recipe's name, yield, portion size, ingredients and procedures, cooking temperature, cooking time, and nutrition information.

2. 4.8 L (20 × 240 mL = 4800 mL and 4800 mL ÷ 1000 = 4.8 L)

3. 4 (2 L × 1000 = 2000 mL and 2000 mL ÷ 500 mL = 4)

4. 0.66 (20 × 170 g = 3400 g; 10 × 225 g = 2250 g; and 2250 g ÷ 3400 g = 0.66)

5. 1.25 (5 ÷ 4 = 1.25)

6. 1.36 kg (85 g × 16 = 1360 g and 1360 ÷ 1000 = 1.36 kg)

7. 1.5 or 1½ cups

4 Calculating Percentages and Ratios

Checkpoint 4-1

1. 0.47 (47 ÷ 100 = 0.47)

2. 27% (0.27 × 100 = 27%)

3. 18% (18 ÷ 100 = 0.18 = 18%)

4. 40% (18 + 12 = 30 and 12 ÷ 30 = 0.40 = 40%)

5. 10 (50 × 20% = 50 × 0.20 = 10)

6. 50 (20 ÷ 40% = 20 ÷ 0.40 = 50)

Checkpoint 4-2

1. An as-purchased (AP) amount is the original amount of a food item as ordered and received. An edible-portion (EP) amount is the amount of a food item that remains after trimming.

2. Yield percentage (YP) is the edible-portion (EP) amount of a food item divided by the as-purchased (AP) amount and is expressed as a percentage.

3. 75% (2 kg − 0.5 kg = 1.5 kg and 1.5 kg ÷ 2.0 kg = 0.75 = 75%)

4. A raw yield test is a procedure used to determine the yield percentage (YP) of a food item that is trimmed prior to being used in a recipe. A cooking-loss yield test is a procedure used to determine the yield percentage (YP) of a food item that loses weight during the cooking process.

5. 75 servings of grilled pork [15 × 1000 g = 15,000 g, 15,000 g × 85% = 15,000 g × 0.85 = 12,750 g, and 12,750 g/1 × 1 serving/170 g = 12,750 servings/170 = 75 servings]

6. 10 kg of unpeeled potatoes (8 kg ÷ 80% = 8 lb ÷ 0.80 = 10 kg)

7. The recipe should be rounded down to 36 portions to ensure an adequate number of servings.

Checkpoint 4-3

1. A baker's percentage is the weight of an ingredient expressed as a percentage of the weight of the main ingredient in a formula.

2. The percent assigned to a main ingredient in a formula is 100%.

3. 60% (1.5 kg ÷ 2.5 kg = 0.6 × 100 = 60%)

4. 160 g [8 kg × (2 ÷ 100) = 8 kg × 0.02 = 0.16 kg and 0.16 kg × 1000 g/kg = 160 g]

Checkpoint 4-4

1. A ratio is a mathematical way to represent the relationship between two or more numbers or amounts.

2. ⅔

3. 60% (3 + 2 = 5 and ⅗ = 0.60 = 60%)

Checkpoint 4-5

1. A ratio is similar to a baker's formula in that the ratio does not contain actual ingredient amounts.

2. 10 L of salad dressing (4 + 1 = 5, and 2 L ÷ ⅕ = 10 L)

3. 3 kg of sugar (3 + 2 + 1 = 6, 2/6 = ⅓, and ⅓ × 9 kg = 3 kg)

5 Calculating Costs and Menu Prices

Checkpoint 5-1

1. An as-purchased (AP) cost is the amount paid for a product in the form it was ordered and received.
2. An as-purchased (AP) cost can be found on the invoice from a supplier.
3. $15.00
4. $18.00

Checkpoint 5-2

1. A unit cost is the cost of a product per unit of measure.
2. $15.86/kg ($36.00 ÷ 2.27 kg = $15.86/kg)
3. The as-purchased (AP) unit cost of a product is based on the form in which it is ordered and received. The edible-portion (EP) unit cost of a product reflects the cost of the product including the cost of the unused parts generated by trimming it.
4. $2.82/kg ($2.40 ÷ 0.85 = $2.82)
5. $12.50 ($1.75/kg ÷ 0.7 = $2.50/kg, and $2.50/kg × 5 kg = $12.50)

Checkpoint 5-3

1. An as-served cost is the cost of a menu item as it is served to a customer.
2. $1.40 ($0.75 + $0.24 + $0.08 + $0.18 + $0.15 = $1.40)
3. $2.20 ($1.40 + $0.45 + $0.35 = $2.20)
4. $2.00/serving ($50.00 ÷ 25 servings = $2.00/serving)

Checkpoint 5-4

1. A cost percentage is a percentage that indicates how the cost of food and beverages relates to the menu prices and sales of a foodservice operation.
2. 29.4% ($1.75 ÷ $5.95 = 0.294 = 29.4%)
3. 20.7% ($1.24 ÷ $6.00 = 0.207 = 20.7%)
4. 22.2 % ($400.00 ÷ $1,800.00 = 0.222 = 22.2%)
5. A target cost percentage is the percentage of food or beverage sales that a foodservice operation plans to spend on purchasing food or beverages.
6. When the overall cost percentage of a foodservice operation is lower than the target cost percentage, the operation has earned more than planned.

Checkpoint 5-5

1. A target price is the price that a foodservice operation needs to charge for a menu item in order to meet its target cost percentage.
2. $8.85 ($2.30 ÷ 0.26 = $8.85)
3. $1.55 ($0.34 ÷ 0.22 = $1.55)
4. $4.57 ($2.15 ÷ 0.32 = $6.72, and $6.72 − $2.15 = $4.57)
5. Perceived value pricing is the process of adjusting a target menu price based on how management thinks a customer will perceive the price.
6. The cost percentage of a menu item decreases when the price of the menu item increases.
7. A contribution margin is the amount added to the as-served cost of a menu item to determine a menu price.
8. $20.00/person ($500.00 ÷ 50 people = $10.00/person, and $10.00/person + $10.00/person = $20.00/person)

5 Calculating Costs and Menu Prices (*continued*)

Checkpoint 5-6

1. A pricing form is a tool used to help calculate the as-served cost of a menu item and establish a menu price.

2. To calculate the total cost of each ingredient in a menu item, the edible-portion (EP) amount and the edible-portion (EP) unit cost of the ingredient must be known.

3. A target price is the price calculated based on a target cost percentage. The menu price is the final price provided on the menu.

6 Calculating Revenue and Expenses

Checkpoint 6-1

1. Revenue is the total amount of money received by a foodservice operation from sales to customers.

2. A guest check lists the items ordered by a customer, the prices charged for those items, and the total amount of money due.

3. A POS system is a computerized system used to process customer orders, print guest checks, track daily operations, and generate financial reports.

4. $31.85 ([2 × $7.95] + $6.95 + [2 × $4.50] = $31.85)

5. $4.78 ($31.85 × 15% = $31.85 × 0.15 = $4.78)

6. $49.60 ($45.50 × 9% = $45.50 × 0.09 = $4.10, and $45.50 + $4.10 = $49.60)

7. $9.08 ($60.50 × 15% = $60.50 × 0.15 = $9.08)

8. $12.50 ($50.00 – $37.50 = $12.50)

9. $990.25 ($1,240.50 – $250.25 = $990.25)

10. Over $24.15 ($3,300.80 – $3,276.65 = $24.15)

Checkpoint 6-2

1. A capital expense is a cost to an operation for buildings, building improvements, and equipment that is expected to have a useful life longer than one year.

2. The cost of goods sold is the cost of the food and beverage products purchased that are ultimately sold to customers.

3. $57.50 (25 kg × $2.30/kg = $57.50)

4. $110,500 ($20,500 + $125,000 – $35,000 = $110,500)

5. An operating expense is any ordinary and necessary cost incurred by an operation as a result of carrying out day-to-day operations.

6. \$780 (40 hr × \$15.00/hr = \$600, 8 hr × [\$15.00/hr × 1.5] = 8 hr × \$22.50 = \$180, and \$600 + \$180 = \$780)

7. Net pay is the actual amount on an employee's paycheck and is equal to the gross pay minus payroll deductions.

8. \$6,666.67 per month (4000 sq ft × \$20/sq ft = \$80,000, and \$80,000/yr × 1 yr/12 months = \$6,666.67/month)

9. Any of the following are considered operating expenses: payroll expenses, rent, interest, utilities, supplies, and insurance and licenses.

10. A variable expense varies based on the sales of an operation, and a fixed expense does not vary based on sales.

7 Analyzing Profit and Loss

Checkpoint 7-1

1. A profit occurs when total revenue is more than total expenses, and a loss occurs when total revenue is less than total expenses.

2. \$272,500 (\$250,000 × [1 + 9%] = \$250,000 × 1.09 = \$272,500)

3. 10% ([\$33,000 – \$30,000] ÷ \$30,000 = \$3,000 ÷ \$30,000 = 0.10 = 10%)

4. –4.5% ([\$21,000 – \$22,000] ÷ \$22,000 = –\$1,000 ÷ \$22,000 = –0.045 = –4.5%)

5. The following should be considered when planning a menu: kitchen equipment, employee skill level, seasonal ingredients, and customer demand.

6. A purchase specification is a written form listing the specific characteristics of a product that is to be purchased from a supplier.

7. Food products should be weighed or counted when received to verify that the amount or quantity is the same as that on the invoice.

8. FIFO is the process of dating new items as they are placed into inventory while rotating older items to the front of inventory and new items behind.

9. Portion control is the process of ensuring that a specific amount of food or beverage is served for a given price.

7 Analyzing Profit and Loss (continued)

Checkpoint 7-2

1. Gross profit is the calculated difference between total revenue and the cost of goods sold. Net profit is the calculated difference between the gross profit and the operating expenses of a foodservice operation.

2. $19,050 ($28,500 – $9,450 = $19,050)

3. $3,015 ($11,090 – $8,075 = $3,015)

4. A standard profit-and-loss statement is a form that shows the revenue, expenses, and resulting gross and net profit (or loss) over a specific period of time.

5. 30.3 % ($9,700 ÷ $32,000 = 0.303 = 30.3%)

6. Payroll is the largest part of total expenses.

7. An estimate is a calculation made using approximate numbers based on research, experience, and best judgment.

8. $24,194 ($15,000 ÷ [100% – 38%] = $15,000 ÷ [1–0.38] = $15,000 ÷ 0.62 = $24,194)

9. $43,840 ($22,000 + [$52,000 × 42%] = $22,000 + [$52,000 × 0.42] = $22,000 + $21,840 = $43,840)

Checkpoint 7-3

1. The number of people attending a special event must be known in order to determine how much food to order and prepare, how much space will be required, and the number of staff needed to prepare and serve the food.

2. The following are items commonly rented for catered events: tents, tables, chairs, flatware, glassware, linens, chafing dishes, and serving platters.

3. Contribution margin pricing is appropriate when temporary staff needs to be hired or equipment needs to be rented.

4. $25.00 per person ($7.50 per person ÷ 30% = $7.50 per person ÷ 0.3 = $25.00 per person)

5. $2,553 ($25.00 per person × 80 people = $2,000; $2,000 × 15% = $2,000 × 0.15 = $300; $2,000 + $300 = $2,300; $2,300 × 11% = $2,300 × 0.11 = $253; and $2,300 + $253 = $2,553)

6. $3,025 ($4,050 – $1,025 = $3,025)

7. $840.00 ($12.00 per person + $9.00 per person = $21.00 per person; and $21.00 per person × 40 people = $840.00)

8. $8,500 ($12,500 – [$20.00 per person × 200 people] = $12,500 – $4,000 = $8,500)

9. $400 ($5,000 × 8% = $5,000 × 0.08 = $400)

Appendix

Math Formulas

Reference Tables

Forms

Math Formulas

Area of a Square or Rectangle

To calculate the area of a two-dimensional square or rectangular object or space:

Area = Length × Width

$$A = L \times W$$

where

A = area
L = length
W = width

Volume of a Rectangular Solid

To calculate the volume or capacity of a three-dimensional rectangular object or space:

Volume = Length × Width × Height

$$V = L \times W \times H$$

where

V = volume
L = length
W = width
H = height (or depth)

Area of a Circle

To calculate the area of a circle or circular object:

Area = 3.14 × Radius²

$$A = \pi \times r^2$$

where

A = area
π = 3.14 (constant number)
r = radius

Volume of a Cylinder

To calculate the volume or capacity of a cylindrical object:

Volume = 3.14 × Radius² × Height

$$V = \pi \times r^2 \times H$$

where

V = volume
π = 3.14 (constant number)
r = radius of the base
H = height

Scaling Factor Based on Yield or Product Availability

To calculate the scaling factor when increasing or decreasing a recipe yield:

$$\text{Scaling Factor} = \frac{\text{Desired Yield}}{\text{Original Yield}}$$

$$SF = DY \div OY$$

where

SF = scaling factor
DY = desired yield
OY = original yield

New Ingredient Amounts in Scaled Recipes

To calculate the new amount of each ingredient to use when preparing a scaled recipe:

$$\text{New Amount} = \text{Original Amount} \times \text{Scaling Factor}$$

$$NA = OA \times SF$$

where

NA = new amount
OA = original amount
SF = scaling factor

Percentage—Given the Part and the Whole

To calculate the percentage that represents a part of a whole:

$$\text{Percentage} = \frac{\text{Part}}{\text{Whole}}$$

$$\% = P \div W$$

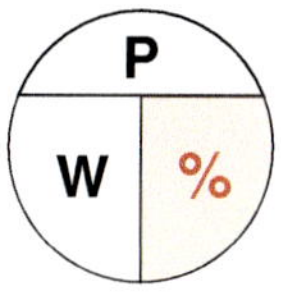

where

% = percentage
P = part
W = whole

The Part—Given the Whole and the Percentage

To calculate the part when the whole and the percentage are known:

$$\text{Part} = \text{Whole} \times \text{Percentage}$$

$$P = W \times \%$$

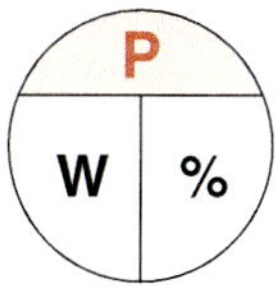

where

P = part
W = whole
% = percentage

The Whole—Given the Percentage and the Part

To calculate the value of the whole when the percentage and the part are known:

$$\text{Whole} = \frac{\text{Part}}{\text{Percentage}}$$

$$W = P \div \%$$

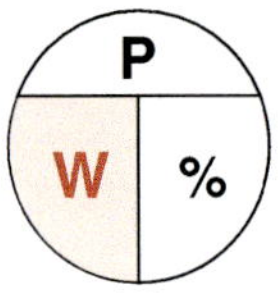

where
W = whole
P = part
% = percentage

As-Purchased Amount

To calculate how much of an ingredient in its as-purchased form is required:

$$\text{As-Purchased Amount} = \frac{\text{Edible-Portion Amount}}{\text{Yield Percentage}}$$

$$AP = EP \div YP$$

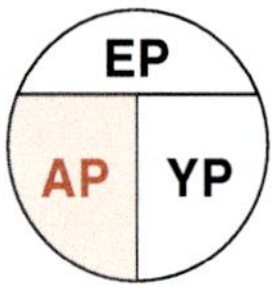

where
AP = as-purchased amount (whole)
EP = edible-portion amount (part)
YP = yield percentage

Yield Percentage

To calculate the yield percentage of a food item that is trimmed prior to being used:

$$\text{Yield Percentage} = \frac{\text{Edible-Portion Amount}}{\text{As-Purchased Amount}}$$

$$YP = EP \div AP$$

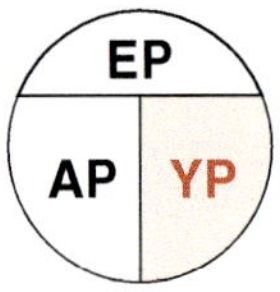

where
YP = yield percentage
EP = edible-portion amount (part)
AP = as-purchased amount (whole)

Edible-Portion Amount

To calculate the amount of edible food that can be obtained from its as-purchased form:

$$\text{Edible-Portion Amount} = \text{As-Purchased Amount} \times \text{Yield Percentage}$$

$$EP = AP \times YP$$

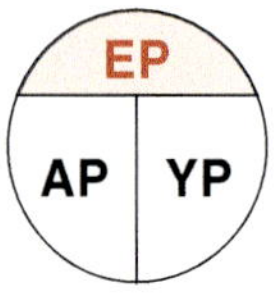

where
EP = edible-portion amount (part)
AP = as-purchased amount (whole)
YP = yield percentage

Baker's Percentage

To calculate the weight of the main ingredient in a formula as a percentage:

$$\text{Ingredient Baker's Percentage} = \left(\frac{\text{Ingredient Weight}}{\text{Main Ingredient Weight}}\right) \times 100$$

$$BP = (IW \div MW) \times 100$$

where

BP = ingredient baker's percentage

IW = ingredient weight

MW = main ingredient weight

Additional Ingredient Weights in a Formula

To calculate the weight of the other ingredients in a formula when the weight of the main ingredient is known:

$$\text{Ingredient Weight} = \text{Main Ingredient Weight} \times \left(\frac{\text{Ingredient Baker's Percentage}}{100}\right)$$

$$IW = MW \times (BP \div 100)$$

where

IW = ingredient weight

MW = main ingredient weight

BP = ingredient baker's percentage

Main Ingredient Weight in a Formula

To calculate the weight of the main ingredient in a formula based on a desired yield:

$$\text{Main Ingredient Weight} = \frac{\text{Desired Yield}}{\left(\text{Total Baker's Percentage} \div 100\right)}$$

$$MW = DY \div (T\% \div 100)$$

where

MW = main ingredient weight

DY = desired yield

T% = total baker's percentage

As-Purchased Unit Cost

To calculate the as-purchased unit cost of a food or beverage item.

$$\text{As-Purchased Unit Cost} = \frac{\text{As-Purchased Total Cost}}{\text{Number of Units}}$$

$$AC = AT \div NU$$

where

AC = as-purchased unit cost

AT = as-purchased total cost

NU = number of units

Edible-Portion Unit Cost

To calculate the edible-portion unit cost of a food item:

$$\text{Edible-Portion Unit Cost} = \frac{\text{As-Purchased Unit Cost}}{\text{Yield Percentage}}$$

$$EC = AC \div YP$$

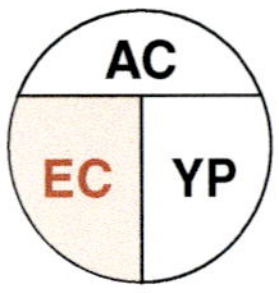

where

EC = edible-portion unit cost (whole)

AC = as-purchased unit cost (part)

YP = yield percentage

Overall Cost Percentage

To calculate the cost percentage that relates a foodservice operation's total food and beverage costs to its total sales:

$$\text{Overall Cost Percentage} = \frac{\text{Total Food and Beverage Costs}}{\text{Total Food and Beverage Sales}}$$

$$O\% = TC \div TS$$

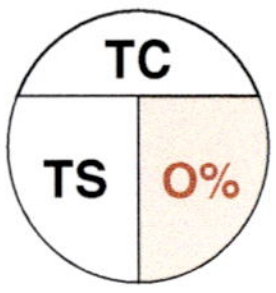

where

O% = overall cost percentage

TC = total food and beverage costs (part)

TS = total food and beverage sales (whole)

Menu-Item Cost Percentage

To calculate the cost percentage that relates the ingredient costs to the price charged for a menu item:

$$\text{Menu-Item Cost Percentage} = \frac{\text{As-Served Cost}}{\text{Menu Price}}$$

$$I\% = AS \div MP$$

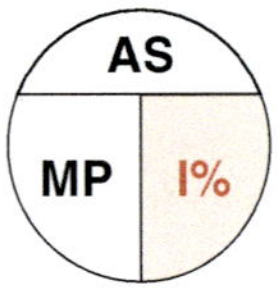

where

I% = menu-item cost percentage

AS = as-served cost (part)

MP = menu price (whole)

Food and Beverage Target Price

To calculate the menu price of a food item based on a target food cost percentage:

$$\text{Target Price} = \frac{\text{As-Served Cost}}{\text{Target Cost Percentage}}$$

$$TP = AS \div T\%$$

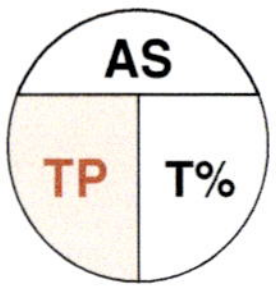

where

TP = target price (whole)

AS = as-served cost (part)

T% = target cost percentage

Menu Item Price

To calculate the price of a menu item when the as-served cost and the menu-item cost percentage are known:

$$\textit{Menu Item Price} = \frac{\textit{As-Served Cost}}{\textit{Menu-Item Cost Percentage}}$$

$$MP = AS \div I\%$$

where

MP = menu item price (whole)

AS = as-served cost (part)

$I\%$ = menu-item cost percentage

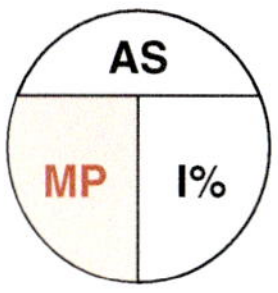

Cost of Goods Sold

To calculate the cost of goods sold over a specific period of time:

$$\textit{Cost of Goods Sold} = \textit{Beginning Inventory} + \textit{Inventory Purchases} - \textit{Ending Inventory}$$

$$GS = BI + IP - EI$$

where

GS = cost of goods sold

BI = beginning inventory

IP = inventory purchases

EI = ending inventory

Inventory Value

To calculate the dollar value of a product in inventory:

$$\textit{Inventory Value} = \textit{Number of Units} \times \textit{As-Purchased Unit Cost}$$

$$IV = NU \times AC$$

where

IV = inventory value

NU = number of units

AC = as-purchased unit cost

Profit (Loss)

To calculate profit or loss based on total revenue and total expenses over a specific period of time:

$$\textit{Profit (Loss)} = \textit{Total Revenue} - \textit{Total Expenses}$$

$$P(L) = TR - TE$$

where

$P(L)$ = profit (loss)

TR = total revenue

TE = total expenses

Revenue Based on a Percent Increase

To calculate the new revenue when the original revenue is increased by a specific percent:

$$\text{New Revenue} = \text{Original Revenue} \times \left(100\% + \text{Percent Increase}\right)$$

$$NR = OR \times (100\% + \%I)$$

where

NR = new revenue

OR = original revenue

%I = percent increase

Percent Increase

To calculate a percent increase based on original revenue and new revenue:

$$\text{Percent Increase} = \frac{\left(\text{New Revenue} - \text{Original Revenue}\right)}{\text{Original Revenue}}$$

$$\%I = (NR - OR) \div OR$$

where

%I = percent increase

NR = new revenue

OR = original revenue

Gross Profit

To calculate the profit earned by a foodservice operation:

$$\text{Gross Profit} = \text{Total Revenue} - \text{Cost of Goods Sold}$$

$$GP = TR - GS$$

where

GP = gross profit

TR = total revenue

GS = cost of goods sold

Net Profit

To calculate net profit after taking operating expenses into account:

$$\text{Net Profit} = \text{Gross Profit} - \text{Operating Expenses}$$

$$NP = GP - OE$$

where

NP = net profit

GP = gross profit

OE = operating expenses

Break-Even Point

To estimate the minimum amount of revenue a foodservice operation must generate before the operation can make a profit:

$$\text{Break-Even Point} = \frac{\text{Fixed Expenses}}{\left(100\% - \text{Variable Expense Percentage}\right)}$$

$$BE = FE \div (100\% - VE\%)$$

where

BE = break-even point

FE = fixed expenses

VE% = variable expense percentage

Estimating Total Expenses

To estimate total expenses based on fixed expenses and the estimated variable expense percentage:

$$\text{Total Expenses} = \text{Fixed Expenses} + \left(\text{Total Revenue} \times \text{Variable Expense Percentage}\right)$$

$$TE = FE + (TR \times VE\%)$$

where

TE = total expenses

FE = fixed expenses

TR = total revenue

VE% = variable expense percentage

Reference Tables

Common Foodservice Units of Measure

Metric Units of Measure		
Measurement Type	**Unit**	**Abbreviation**
Weight (mass)	gram	g
Volume	liter	L
Temperature	degrees Celsius	°C
Distance	meter	m

Customary and Imperial Units of Measure		
Measurement Type	**Unit**	**Abbreviation**
Weight	pound	lb or #
	ounce	oz
Volume	gallon	gal.
	quart	qt
	pint	pt
	cup	c
	gill (imperial)	—
	fluid ounce	fl oz
	tablespoon	tbsp
	teaspoon	tsp
Temperature	degrees Fahrenheit	°F
Distance	foot	ft
	inch	in.

Metric Unit Equivalents

Prefix	Meaning	Weight	Volume	Length
kilo-	1000	**kilo**gram (kg) = 1000 g	**kilo**liter (kL) = 1000 L	**kilo**meter (km) = 1000 m
hecto-	100	**hecto**gram (hg) = 100 g	**hecto**liter (hL) = 100 L	**hecto**meter (hm) = 100 m
deca-	10	**deca**gram (dag) = 10 g	**deca**liter (daL) = 10 L	**deca**meter (dam) = 10 m
basic unit	1	gram (g)	liter (L)	meter (m)
deci-	1/10 or 0.1	**deci**gram (dg) = 0.1 g	**deci**liter (dL) = 0.1 L	**deci**meter (dm) = 0.1 m
centi-	1/100 or 0.01	**centi**gram (cg) = 0.01 g	**centi**liter (cL) = 0.01 L	**centi**meter (cm) = 0.01 m
milli-	1/1000 or 0.001	**milli**gram (mg) = 0.001 g	**milli**liter (mL) = 0.001 L	**milli**meter (mm) = 0.001 m

Customary and Imperial Volume Equivalents

Customary Volume Equivalents

Gallon		Quarts		Pints		Cups		Fluid Ounces		Tablespoons		Teaspoons
1	=	4	=	8	=	16	=	128	=	256	=	768
		1	=	2	=	4	=	32	=	64	=	192
				1	=	2	=	16	=	32	=	92
						1	=	8	=	16	=	48
								1	=	2	=	6
										1	=	3

Imperial Volume Equivalents

Gallon		Quarts		Pints		Cups		Fluid Ounces		Tablespoons		Teaspoons
1	=	4	=	8	=	16	=	160	=	320	=	960
		1	=	2	=	4	=	40	=	80	=	240
				1	=	2	=	20	=	40	=	120
						1	=	10	=	20	=	60
								1	=	2	=	6
										1	=	3

Metric and Customary/Imperial Equivalents

Weight

Metric and Customary or Imperial Equivalents

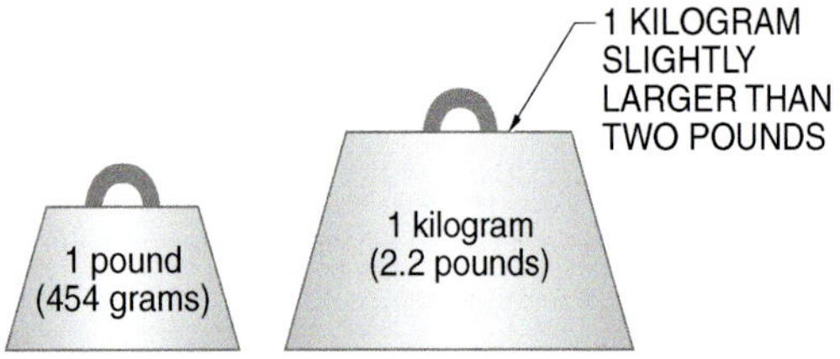

1 pound	=	0.454 kilograms
1 pound	=	454 grams
1 ounce	=	28.35 grams
1 kilogram	=	2.2 pounds

Volume

Metric and Customary Equivalents			Metric and Imperial Equivalents		
1 gallon	=	3.79 liters	1 gallon	=	4.55 liters
1 quart	=	0.95 liters	1 quart	=	1.14 liters
1 pint	=	473.18 milliliters	1 pint	=	568.26 milliliters
1 cup	=	236.59 milliliters	1 gill	=	142.07 milliliters
1 fluid ounce	=	29.57 milliliters	1 fluid ounce	=	28.41 milliliters
1 teaspoon	=	4.93 milliliters	1 teaspoon	=	5.92 milliliters
1 liter	=	1.06 quarts	1 liter	=	0.88 quart
1 liter	=	33.8 fluid ounces	1 liter	=	35.2 fluid ounces

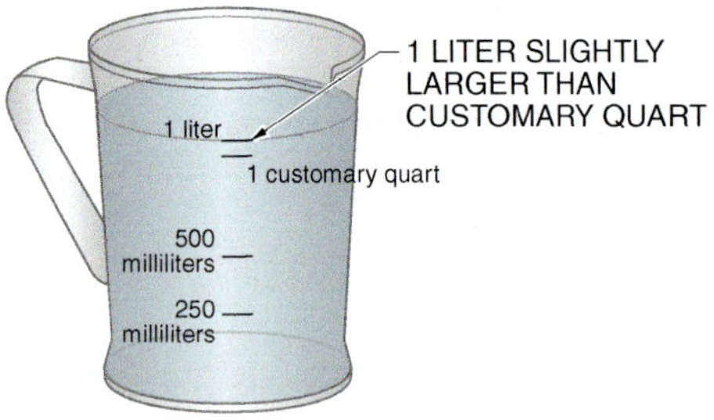

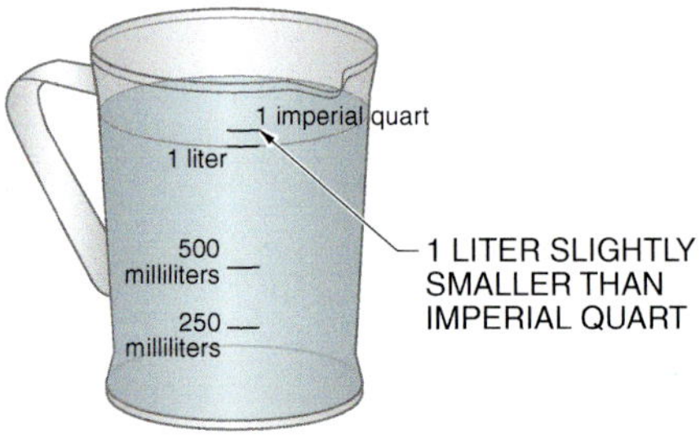

Soft Equivalents

Customary Measurement	Metric Measurement
¼ teaspoon	1 milliliter
½ teaspoon	2 milliliters
1 teaspoon	5 milliliters
1 tablespoon	15 milliliters
1 fluid ounce	30 milliliters
1 cup	250 milliliters
1 pint	500 milliliters
1 quart	1 liter
1 gallon	4 liters

Customary and Imperial Volume Measurement Differences

Unit of Measure	Customary Measurement	Imperial Measurement
Fluid ounce	1 fl oz (29.57 mL)	1 fl oz (28.41 mL)
Gill	–	5 fl oz
Cup	8 fl oz	10 fl oz (not commonly used)
Pint	16 fl oz	20 fl oz
Quart	32 fl oz	40 fl oz
Gallon	128 fl oz	160 fl oz

Metric and Customary/Imperial Conversion Factors

When Instructions Show:	Divide by the Conversion Factor:	To Get:	When Instructions Show:	Multiply by the Conversion Factor:	To Get:
Metric and Customary Volume Conversion Factors					
milliliters	4.93	teaspoons	teaspoons	4.93	milliliters
milliliters	14.79	tablespoons	tablespoons	14.79	milliliters
milliliters	29.57	fluid ounces	fluid ounces	29.57	milliliters
milliliters	236.59	cups	cups	236.59	milliliters
liters	0.236	cups	cups	0.236	liters
liters	0.473	pints	pints	0.473	liters
liters	0.95	quarts	quarts	0.95	liters
liters	3.79	gallons	gallons	3.79	liters
Metric and Imperial Volume Conversion Factors					
milliliters	5.92	teaspoons	teaspoons	5.92	milliliters
milliliters	17.76	tablespoons	tablespoons	17.76	milliliters
milliliters	28.41	fluid ounces	fluid ounces	28.41	milliliters
milliliters	142.07	gills	gills	142.07	milliliters
liters	0.568	pints	pints	0.568	liters
liters	1.14	quarts	quarts	1.14	liters
liters	4.55	gallons	gallons	4.55	liters
Metric and Customary/Imperial Weight Conversion Factors					
grams	28.35	ounces	ounces	28.35	grams
grams	454	pounds	pounds	454	grams
kilograms*	0.454	pounds	pounds*	0.454	kilograms
Metric and Customary/Imperial Distance Conversion Factors†					
millimeters	25.4	inches	inches	25.4	millimeters
centimeters	2.54	inches	inches	2.54	centimeters
Metric and Customary/Imperial Temperature Conversion Factors					
degrees Celsius	multiply by 1.8 and add 32	degrees Fahrenheit	degrees Fahrenheit	subtract 32 and divide by 1.8	degrees Celsius

*Since 1 kg = 2.2 lb, another way to convert kilograms to pounds is to multiply by 2.2, and to convert pounds to kilograms, divide by 2.2.
† When meters are known, multiply by 3.28 to get feet, and when feet are known, divide by 3.28 to get meters.

Portion-Controlled Scoop Equivalents

Scoop Number	Customary Fluid Ounces per Scoop	Milliliters per Scoop
4	8	236.6
5	6.4	189.3
6	5.33	157.6
8	4	118.3
10	3.2	94.6
12	2.66	79.0
16	2	59.1
20	1.6	47.3
24	1.33	39.3
30	1.06	31.7
40	0.8	23.7
60	0.53	15.7

Volume-to-Weight Equivalents of Common Food Products...

Ingredient	Customary Measure	Converted to Ounces	Converted to Grams
Almonds, whole unblanched	1 c	5	142
Apples			
peeled, sliced	1 c	4	113
Apricots			
dried, diced	1 c	4.5	128
Asparagus spears	1 c	6	170
Barley, raw	1 c	8	227
Beans			
green, trimmed	1 c	5	142
kidney, dried	1 c	6	170
lima, dried	1 c	6.75	191
navy, dried	1 c	7	198
Bean sprouts	1 c	4	113
Blueberries			
canned	1 c	6.75	191
fresh	1 c	7	198
dried	1 c	5.5	156
Breadcrumbs			
dried, fine ground	1 c	4	113
fresh	1 c	2	57
Broccoli, florets	1 c	2.75	78
Brussels sprouts	1 c	4	113
Cabbage, red or green	1 c	2.5	71
Cantaloupe	1 c	5.75	163
Carrots, raw sliced or diced	1 c	5	142
Carrots, cooked	1 c	5.5	156
Casaba melon	1 c	6	170
Cauliflower, florets	1 c	4.75	135
Celery, diced	1 c	4	113
Cheese			
cubes	1 c	6	170
cottage or cream	1 c	8	227
grated, hard or medium	1 c	4	113
grated, soft (e.g., fresh goat)	1 c	4.75	135
Cherries			
dried	1 c	6	170
fresh, pitted	1 c	5.5	156
Chocolate			
chips	1 c	6	170
grated	1 c	4	113

... Volume-to-Weight Equivalents of Common Food Products...

Ingredient	Customary Measure	Converted to Ounces	Converted to Grams
Cloves, whole	1 c	3	85
Cocoa	1 c	3.75	106
Coconuts			
loose shredded	1 c	2.5	71
packed shredded	1 c	3.25	92
Coconut milk	1 c	8.5	241
Corn flakes	1 c	1	28
Cornmeal	1 c	5	142
Cornstarch	1 c	5.33	151
Cracker crumbs	1 c	3.5	99
Cranberries, raw	1 c	4	113
Cream, whipped	1 c	4	113
Crenshaw melons	1 c	6	170
Cucumbers, diced	1 c	5.5	156
Currants, dried	1 c	5.33	151
Dates, pitted	1 c	6	170
Eggs			
fresh whites (9)	1 c	8	227
fresh yolks (10)	1 c	8	227
raw, shelled (5 eggs)	1 c	8	227
Figs, dried, chopped	1 c	6.5	184
Flour			
all-purpose	1 c	4.5	128
cake or pastry	1 c	4	113
rye	1 c	3.5	99
Garlic	1 c	5	142
Gelatin, granulated	1 c	5	142
Graham cracker crumbs	1 c	4	
Grapefruit	1 c	7.5	
Grapes			
whole	1 c	3.75	106
sliced	1 c	5.75	163
Greens, collard or mustard	1 c	2	57
Half-and-half	1 c	8.5	241
Honey	1 c	12	340
Honeydew melon	1 c	6	170
Horseradish	1 tbsp	0.5	14
Jams	1 c	12	340
Jellies	1 c	10.5	298
Kale	1 c	2.5	71

... Volume-to-Weight Equivalents of Common Food Products...

Ingredient	Customary Measure	Converted to Ounces	Converted to Grams
Kiwis	1 c	7	198
Leeks	1 c	3.25	92
Lemon juice	1 c	8	227
Lettuce	1 c		
butter, green leaf, red leaf	1 c	2	57
iceberg, chopped	1 c	2.25	64
romaine	1 c	2	57
Milk			
condensed	1 c	10.75	305
evaporated	1 c	9	255
liquid, whole	1 c	8	227
nonfat dry	1 c	5	142
Molasses	1 c	12	340
Mustard			
dry, ground	1 c	3.5	99
prepared	1 tbsp	0.5	14
Oats, rolled	1 c	3.5	99
Onions			
yellow, diced	1 c	6	170
green (scallions)	1 c	2	57
Orange juice	1 c	8	227
Parsley, coarsely chopped	1 c	1.25	35
Peaches pitted, diced	1 c	8	227
Peanuts	1 c	5	142
Pears, fresh, cored and diced	1 c	5.25	149
Peas			
dry split	1 c	7	198
frozen	1 c	3.5	99
snow	1 c	3	85
Pecans	1 c	4	113
Peppers, green or red, chopped	1 c	5.25	149
Pimiento, chopped	1 c	6.75	191
Pineapples			
crushed	1 c	8	227
diced	1 c	5	142
Pomegranates	1 c	4.25	120
Poppy seeds	1 c	5	142
Potatoes,			
cooked, diced, or mashed	1 c	7	198
russet, peeled and diced	1 c	5	142

… Volume-to-Weight Equivalents of Common Food Products

Ingredient	Customary Measure	Converted to Ounces	Converted to Grams
Prunes, dried	1 c	6	170
Raisins	1 c	5.33	151
Raspberries, fresh	1 c	5	142
Rice			
uncooked long grain	1 c	6.75	191
uncooked short grain	1 c	7	198
Rutabagas, cubed	1 c	4.75	135
Salt			
granulated	1 tbsp	0.5	14
kosher	1 tbsp	0.33	9
Sesame seeds	1 tbsp	0.33	9
Shallots, diced	1 c	6.4	182
Shortening	1 c	6.75	191
Sour cream	1 c	8.5	241
Spinach, leaf	1 c	0.8	23
Spices, ground	1 tbsp	0.25	7
Squash			
acorn or butternut	1 c	5	142
summer or zucchini	1 c	3.8	108
Strawberries	1 c	5.5	156
Sweet potatoes, diced	1 c	5	142
Sugar			
brown, lightly packed	1 c	5.5	156
brown, solidly packed	1 c	8	227
granulated	1 c	8	227
powdered, sifted	1 c	4.5	128
Tapioca, pearl	1 c	5	142
Tomatoes			
cored and peeled	1 c	6	170
fresh, diced	1 c	6	170
peeled, seeded, and chopped	1 c	6	170
Walnuts, shelled	1 c	4	113
Watermelons	1 c	5.5	156

Approximate Yield Percentages of Fruits and Vegetables

Item Name	Yield %	Item Name	Yield %
Apples, peeled and cored	85	Lime juice (from fresh limes)	45
Asparagus spears, trimmed	60	Mangoes	65
Bananas	65	Onions, large	93
Cantaloupes	56	Orange juice (from fresh oranges)	35
Casaba melons	59	Papayas	69
Cherries, pitted	89	Parsley	75
Crenshaw melons	65	Peaches, pitted	79
Broccoli, spears	75	Pears, cored	78
Broccoli, florets	65	Peas, snow and snap	95
Cabbage (red and green)	80	Peppers, bell	85
Carrots	85	Pineapples	50
Cauliflower, florets	65	Pomegranates	50
Celery	70	Potatoes, russet	80
Cucumbers	94	Scallions (green onions)	85
Figs	97	Shallots	92
Garlic	85	Spinach, leaf	68
Grapefruit	55	Squash, acorn	78
Grapes, stemmed	95	Squash, butternut	85
Green beans, trimmed	90	Squash, spaghetti	70
Greens, collard, mustard, or turnip	70	Squash, summer	95
Honeydew melons	60	Squash, zucchini	95
Kale	70	Strawberries, stemmed	95
Kiwis	87	Sweet potatoes, diced	90
Leeks	50	Tomatoes, cored	98
Lemon juice (from fresh lemons)	45	Tomatoes, cored and diced	93
Lettuce, green leaf, red leaf, and butter	84	Tomatoes, peeled, seeded, and diced	80
Lettuce, iceberg	75	Tomatoes, plum cored	96
Lettuce, romaine	78	Watermelons	50

Common Professional Kitchen Ratios

Biscuits	3 parts flour : 2 parts liquid : 1 part fat (by weight)
Boiled Rice	1 part uncooked rice : 2 parts liquid (by volume)
Cookie Dough	3 parts flour : 2 parts fat : 1 part sugar (by weight)
Mirepoix	2 parts onions : 1 part carrot : 1 part celery
Pie Dough	3 parts flour : 2 parts fat : 1 part water (by weight)
Roux	1 part flour : 1 part fat (by weight)
Simple Syrup	1 part granulated sugar : 1 part water
Slurry	2 parts liquid : 1 part starch (by volume)
Vinaigrette	3 parts oil : 1 part vinegar (by volume)

Pricing Form

Menu Item Name:
Number of Portions:
As-Served (AS) Cost per Portion:
Target Cost %:
Target Price:

Menu Price:
Menu-Item Cost %:

Ingredients	Edible-Portion (EP) Amount	Equivalent Edible-Portion (EP) Amount	As-Purchased (AP) Unit Cost (or recipe cost)	Yield Percentage (YP)	Edible-Portion (EP) Unit Cost	Total Ingredient Cost
					Total Cost:	

Daily Sales Record	
Total Sales	
Total Food Sales	
Total Beverage Sales	
Sales Tax (%)	
Gross Sales (*Total Sales* + *Sales Tax*)	
Cash at End of Day	
Cash at Start of Day	
Total Cash Revenue (*Cash at End of Day* – *Cash at Start of Day*)	
Total Card Revenue	
Credit Cards	
Debit Cards	
Gift Cards	
Total Revenue (*Total Cash Revenue* + *Total Card Revenue*)	
Over (Short) (*Total Revenue* – *Gross Sales*)	

Report completed by: ______________________________ ____________

Signature Date

Glossary

A

angle: A figure consisting of two straight lines that intersect (cross) at a common point.

area: The size of a two-dimensional (flat) surface.

as-purchased (AP) amount: The original amount of a food item as it is ordered and received.

as-purchased (AP) cost: The amount paid for a product in the form it was ordered and received.

as-purchased (AP) unit cost: The unit cost of a food item based on the form in which it is ordered and received.

as-served (AS) cost: The cost of a menu item as it is served to a customer.

average: The sum of a set of numbers divided by how many numbers there are in the set.

B

baker's percentage: The weight of an ingredient expressed as a percentage of the weight of the main ingredient (primary structure provider) in a formula.

baker's scale: See balance scale.

balance scale: A scale with two platforms that uses a counterbalance system to measure weight. Also known as a baker's scale.

break-even point: The minimum amount of revenue a foodservice operation must earn before it can make a profit.

C

cancelling: The process of crossing out and eliminating matching units in the numerators and denominators of fractions in a calculation.

capacity: The volume that can be placed inside an empty three-dimensional object.

capital expense: A cost to an operation for buildings, building improvements, and equipment that is expected to have a useful life longer than one year.

common denominator: A denominator that is the same in two or more fractions.

contribution margin: The amount added to the as-served (AS) cost of a menu item to determine a menu price.

conversion factor: A number used to change one set of measurement units to an equivalent set of measurement units by multiplying or dividing.

converting: The process of changing a measurement with one unit of measure to an equivalent measurement with a different unit of measure.

cooking-loss yield test: A procedure used to determine the yield percentage (YP) of a food item that loses weight during the cooking process.

cost of goods sold: The cost of the food and beverage products purchased that are ultimately sold to customers.

cost percentage: A percentage that indicates how the cost of food or beverages relates to the menu prices and sales of a foodservice operation.

count: A total obtained by counting.

D

data table: A collection of information that is organized into a set of rows and columns.

decimal: A number that represents part of a whole and can be expressed as a fraction with a denominator that is a power of 10 (such as 10, 100, 1000, and so on).

denominator: The number in a fraction at the bottom (or to the right) of a fraction bar that represents the number of parts into which a whole is divided.

density: A measurement of how much a given volume of a substance weighs.

deposit: An amount of money paid by a customer as a down payment or pledge for a special event to be held at a later date.

diameter: The length of a line drawn through the center of a circle to both edges.

digital scale: An electronic scale with a sensor that measures weight and displays the result electronically.

discount: A percentage or fixed amount by which the subtotal is reduced due to a promotion offered by the foodservice operation.

disher: See portion-controlled scoop.

dry measuring cup: A volume measurement tool, shaped like a cup, with a short handle used to measure a specific volume of dry ingredients.

E

edible-portion (EP) amount: The amount of a food item that remains after trimming.

edible-portion (EP) unit cost: The unit cost of a food or beverage item that includes the cost of the unused parts generated by trimming.

estimate: A calculation made using approximate numbers based on research, experience, and best judgment.

F

first-in, first-out (FIFO): The process of dating new items as they are placed into inventory while rotating older items to the front of inventory and new items behind.

fixed expense: An expense that does not vary based on the amount of sales.

fluid ounce: The smallest volume unit of measure in the customary and imperial systems.

fraction: A part of a whole.

G

gratuity: The amount of money left by a customer to show appreciation for the services rendered.

gross pay: The total amount of an employee's pay before any deductions are made.

gross profit: The calculated difference between a foodservice operation's total revenue and the cost of goods sold.

I

improper fraction: A fraction in which the numerator is larger than the denominator.

interest: The fee charged by a bank for providing a loan to the borrower.

inventory: The amount of food and beverage products that have been purchased and are currently being stored for future use.

invoice: A document provided by a supplier that lists the item amounts delivered to a foodservice operation and the prices of those items.

L

ladle: A volume measurement tool that consists of a fixed-size cup attached to a long handle.

liquid measuring cup: A volume measurement tool shaped like a cup or pitcher with graduated markings on the side to indicate the volume of a liquid.

loss: The amount of money lost by an operation when revenue is less than (<) expenses.

loss leader: A menu item priced artificially low in order to attract more customers.

lowest common denominator: The smallest number into which each of the denominators of a group of fractions can divide evenly.

M

measurement: A number with a corresponding unit of measure that indicates an amount or degree of something.

measurement equivalent: An amount in one unit of measure that is equal to another unit of measure.

measuring spoon: A small volume measurement tool, shaped like a spoon, that is used to measure liquid or dry ingredients.

median: The middle value within a set of numbers that are arranged in numerical order.

menu: A document that markets a foodservice operation to customers.

menu-item cost percentage: The as-served (AS) cost of a menu item divided by the menu price and written as a percent.

mixed number: A combination of a whole number and a fraction.

mode: The value that appears most frequently within a set of numbers.

N

net pay: The actual amount on an employee's paycheck and is equal to the gross pay minus payroll deductions.

net profit: The calculated difference between a foodservice operation's gross profit and its operating expenses.

numerator: The number in a fraction at the top (or to the left) of a fraction bar that represents the parts of a whole.

O

operating expense: Any ordinary and necessary cost incurred by an operation as a result of carrying out daily business activities.

ounce: The smallest weight unit of measure in the customary and imperial systems.

overall cost percentage: The total amount of money a foodservice operation spends on food and beverages divided by the total food and beverage sales over a defined period of time and written as a percent.

P

par stock: The amount of a particular product that is to be kept in inventory to ensure that an adequate supply is on hand between deliveries.

payroll expense: The expense of an operation that includes any money paid to an employee who performs work for the operation.

perceived value pricing: The process of adjusting a target price based on how management thinks a customer will perceive the price.

percentage: A number that expresses part of a whole in terms of hundredths.

perishable food: Food that has a short shelf life and is subject to spoilage and decay.

pie chart: A circle that is divided into pieces where each piece represents a percentage of the whole circle (or pie).

point-of-sale (POS) system: A computerized system used to process customer orders, print guest checks, track daily operations, and generate financial reports.

portion control: The process of ensuring that a specific amount of food or beverage is served for a given price.

portion-controlled scoop: A volume measurement tool that consists of a handle with a fixed-size scoop at the end. Also known as a disher.

portion size: The amount of a food or beverage item that is served to an individual person.

pricing form: A tool often used to help calculate the as-served cost of a menu item and establish a menu price.

profit: The amount of money earned by an operation when revenue is greater than (>) expenses.

proper fraction: A fraction in which the numerator is smaller than the denominator.

purchase specification: A written form listing the specific characteristics of a product that is to be purchased from a supplier.

R

radius: The distance from the center of a circle to the edge of the circle and is equal to one-half the diameter of the circle.

ratio: A mathematical way to represent the relationship between two or more numbers or amounts.

raw yield test: A procedure used to determine the yield percentage (YP) of a food item that is trimmed prior to being used in a recipe.

reciprocal: A fraction that is the result of switching the numerator and denominator in the fraction.

revenue: The total amount of money received by a foodservice operation from sales to customers.

rounding: The process of replacing a number with another number of similar value.

S

sales tax: A fee that must be collected from customers based on the requirements of both the federal government and the province where the foodservice operation is located.

scaling: The process of calculating new amounts for each ingredient in a recipe when the total amount of food the recipe makes is changed.

scaling factor: The number that each ingredient amount and the recipe yield are multiplied by in order to increase or decrease a recipe.

shrinkage: The loss of volume and weight of a piece of food as the food cooks.

standard profit-and-loss statement: A form that shows the revenue, expenses, and resulting gross profit and net profit (or loss) over a specific period of time.

standardized recipe: A list of ingredients, ingredient amounts, and procedural steps for preparing a specific quantity of a food item.

statistics: A mathematical system for evaluating sets of numbers.

T

tare: Another term for setting a scale to zero.

target cost percentage: The percentage of food or beverage sales that a foodservice operation plans to spend on purchasing food or beverages.

target price: The price that a foodservice operation needs to charge for a menu item in order to meet its target cost percentage.

U

unit cost: The cost of a product per unit of measure.

unit of measure: A fixed quantity that is widely accepted as a standard of measurement.

V

variable expense: An expense that increases or decreases based on the amount of sales.

volume: A measurement of the physical space a substance occupies.

W

weight: A measurement of the heaviness of a substance.

whole number: A number used for counting, such as 0, 1, 20, or 100.

Y

yield: The total quantity of a food or beverage item that is made from a standardized recipe.

yield percentage (YP): The edible-portion (EP) amount of a food item divided by the as-purchased (AP) amount and is expressed as a percentage.

Index

Page numbers in italic refer to figures.